# Race, Ethnicity and Crime

# Race, Ethnicity and Crime

## Alternate Perspectives

Dianne Williams

Algora Publishing
New York

Library of Congress Cataloging-in-Publication Data —

Williams, Dianne, 1958-
    Race, ethnicity, and crime / Dianne Williams.
      p. cm.
    Includes bibliographical references and index.
      ISBN 978-0-87586-915-5 (soft cover: alk. paper) — ISBN 978-0-87586-916-2 (hard
cover: alk. paper) — ISBN 978-0-87586-917-9 (ebook) 1. Race. 2. Crime and race. 3.
Ethnicity. 4. Mass media and race relations. 5. Justice, Administration of. I. Title.
      HT1521.W535 2012
      305.8—dc23
                              2012002955

Printed in the United States

## Table of Contents

# Preface

Melting pot or tossed salad? The U.S. criminal justice system may prove to be fueling intolerance rather than enabling society to accommodate racial and ethnic differences. This fresh new textbook to balance theory and the real world, addressing topics relating to race, ethnicity, criminality and criminalization, looking at the criminal justice system, the media, the death penalty, as well as two other issues where minorities and public perception play such a big role—terrorism and human trafficking.

In addition to information on crime and incarceration rates, White-collar crime, and the "typical criminal," the discussion of minorities and public perceptions is set within a broader context including related issues such as terrorism and human trafficking.

The manual is designed for junior colleges and four year colleges, including those offering distance-learning courses. It is a thought-provoking combination of facts and questions. The pedagogical focus is on collaborative, problem base-learning, with foundational support for the development of critical thinking and analytical skills as each "Controversy"/"In the News" feature is evaluated.

The author relies, as much as possible, on facts and figures here (deductive logic) rather than on sentiments, presenting a multifaceted argument on each topic. The ultimate goal is to encourage students to analyze and critique the information and formulate their own opinions.

Narrative Case Studies and Vignettes, and Tables and Figures, bring the cold facts to life. The simple, straightforward approach allows instructors to personalize their coverage of the material.

# CHAPTER 1. RACE, ETHNICITY AND CRIMINALITY. IS THERE A RELATIONSHIP?

### OBJECTIVES

- Develop a working definition of "race"
- Develop a working definition of "ethnicity"
- Understand the various theories of "criminality"
- Identify a relationship between race, ethnicity and criminality

### CASE STUDY: THE SUBWAY VIGILANTE

On December 23, 1984, a 37-year-old self-employed electrical engineer named Bernhard Goetz boarded a New York City subway, No. 2 express train. Mr. Goetz, a thin bespectacled White-American, found himself in the same car as four African-American teenagers—James Ramseur, 19, Darrell Cabey, 19, Troy Canty, 19, and Barry Allen, 18.

The story goes that 19-year-old Canty demanded five dollars from Goetz, and in response Goetz stood up, drew a .38 caliber Smith & Wesson revolver from under his blue windbreaker, and began shooting. In the aftermath of the barrage of gunfire, all four teenagers were found wounded, two of them critically. Meanwhile, Goetz had exited the train, rented a car, and driven to Bennington, Vermont, where he proceeded to dispose of the pistol and the windbreaker in the woods. A week later, Goetz turned himself in. By then he was being fondly referred to as the "Subway Vigilante" and had become something of a national celebrity.

Interestingly enough, despite the gravity of Goetz's crime, the vast majority of those who wrote to newspapers, called in to radio talk shows, or participated in man-on-the-street interviews supported his actions. T-shirts identifying Goetz as the "Thug Buster" and demanding his acquittal became a hot sale item on the streets of New York. Surprisingly enough, given the racial undertones of the incident, Goetz also received support from some members of the African-American community. The Congress for Racial Equality offered to raise money to defray the Subway Vigilante's legal fees.

Although New York State law permits citizens to use deadly force in self defense, the prosecution argued that Goetz had gone into the subway that day with murder on his mind. Two of the four youths had been shot in the back while trying to flee; one of them, Darrell Cabey, suffered brain damage and was paralyzed from the waist down. Nonetheless, a grand jury declined to indict Goetz for anything more than the illegal possession of a handgun. Goetz, you see, had no criminal record. His four victims, on the other hand, had nine convictions and ten outstanding bench warrants between them. Cabey was awaiting trial for armed robbery. And, to make matters worse, other passengers came forward to speak on Goetz's behalf. Public sentiment ran three-to-one in favor of Goetz. Notwithstanding the grand jury's decision, the case of the subway vigilante was reopened a few months later when the District Attorney (DA) applied to convene a second grand jury. This time the DA decided to give immunity to two of the victims in exchange for their testimony. Additionally, a subway employee who witnessed the shooting confirmed that Goetz had been looking for trouble that day.

But this was neither the beginning nor the end of this story. Several years earlier, Goetz had been mugged and injured by three youths at a subway station. Although his application for a permit to carry a pistol was denied, he bought the .38 Smith & Wesson anyway. Goetz appeared shy and unassuming and something of a nerd in court, so the prosecutor relied heavily on his confession to police. The prosecution argued, for example, that Goetz had coldly and methodically fired a second round into an already wounded Darrell Cabey.

Despite Goetz' chilling admission that his intention was "to murder them, to hurt them, to make them suffer," after a seven-week trial and four days of deliberation the jury, comprised of ten whites and two blacks, found Goetz not guilty on 17 counts of attempted murder and assault. Public reaction was mixed. When the verdict was announced, the courtroom audience erupted into applause. Others referred to the results as a miscarriage of justice, arguing that if Goetz had been African-American and his victims White-American, the trial result would have been altogether different.

In deciding whether Goetz had acted criminally, the jury was instructed to base its conclusion on what a "reasonable person" would have done under similar circumstances. In the jury's view Goetz had acted reasonably, especially since he had been mugged before. Additionally, one of the victims acted so much like a thug when he took the witness stand that he had to be removed from the courtroom. This no doubt made it easy for the jury to believe that Goetz had felt sufficiently threatened by the four teenagers to perhaps justify his violent reaction. After delivering the verdict, the jurors took turns asking for his autograph. Today, the Subway Vigilante remains hero to many.

### INTRODUCTION

Many people feel that the United States has overcome its history of racism and has become something of a melting pot—accepting of all races and cultures. But contrary to popular belief, the current status of the U.S. criminal justice system may prove that we are more of a tossed salad than a melting pot. The current situation would leave one wondering if this tossed salad is fueling intolerance for racial and ethnic differences, and if it is this intolerance that leads to racism.

In a powerful stab at the American criminal justice system, Reiman (2007) describes racism as,

> ...a distinct, resilient, and powerful form of bias.....[It] has a long, inglorious history in American society, in which massive imprisonment of young black men in the last decade is but the latest in a series of policies controlling and isolating blacks that spans slavery, Jim Crow, and northern 'ghettoization'.

Reiman argues that issues of racism are almost a natural progression because by and large minorities are disproportionately poor and unemployed. In his piece "A Rolling Tide: Changes in the Distribution of Wealth in the U.S., 1989–2001," Arthur Kennickell also makes the following observations:

1. 8.6% of White-Americans and 24.7% of African-Americans were below the poverty level.
2. African-Americans own only 15 to 20% as much wealth as White-American.
3. In 2003, 5% of White Americans were unemployed compared to 10.8% of African-Americans, while 11.2% of White youth

with no college and 24.6% of African-American youth (with no college) were unemployed.

Today, studies suggest that race is the single most important factor in the likelihood of being arrested, convicted and imprisoned, compounded only by employment status.

In other words, being African-American and unemployed increases the chances of arrest, conviction and imprisonment. Moreover, if some of our criminal justice policies are indeed racially and economically biased, then one can reasonably argue that the institutions fundamental to American life—federal and state governments, the judiciary, the social marketplace, and the media—all systematically create and perpetuate racist norms and perhaps even lay the foundation for the very issues the criminal justice system was created to eradicate.

Before we can evaluate whether there is a relationship between race, ethnicity, and criminality we must first establish a clear definition of what race is and what ethnicity is. We must also be willing to acknowledge that there may actually be issues of racism within American society.

## RACE

What is race? We have always been told that we are all members of the human race. Indeed Schwartz (2001) argued that "there is only one race—the human race....there are no alleles that define the black people of North America as a unique population."

But what exactly does that mean? According to the American Journal of Physical Anthropology, all humans beings evolved from and belong to a single species—Homo sapiens. Of course there are many different opinions on how this single species diverged to form new human groups. But the question is, if we are all members of the human race (as opposed to an alien race), where do the other "races" (Black, White, and Asian; or Negroid, Caucasoid, and Mongoloid) fit in?

What is Race? See what PBS.org has to say about the topic at http://www.pbs.org/race/000_About/002_01-godeeper.htm

The earliest documentation of physical differences in human groups can be found in the Bible. For the most part, biblical distinctions were based on religion (Jew or Gentile) and geographic locations (Syrian or Roman) and, although there were clear distinctions based on physical appearance, these groupings in no way gave rise to race as we know it today.

The roots of today's concept of race can perhaps be traced back to the rise of Europe and the discovery of the Americas by the Europeans. According to the history books, as Europeans explored the world, they "discovered" new and strange peoples. People of different skin color, different customs, different beliefs and different values. Christians and Jews alike interpreted the Bible to say that they were God's chosen people; this made it easy to decide that the newly-discovered populations were "not chosen." Moreover, since they were obviously not as advanced, it was convenient to conclude that they must be of inferior status (barbarians). Further, in a "new world" that lacked the manpower to meet its needs, the racially organized exploitation, extermination and enslavement that followed was a natural progression. It can be argued, therefore, that the concept of race was developed and amplified to justify and support both religion and capitalism. This history, influenced by science, government and culture has shaped the concept of race as we know it today.

Another defining factor was the concept of scientific racism. During the Great Depression, scientists such as Charles Davenport, director of the Eugenics Records Office, moved to assert a causal link between race and genetics with characteristics such as criminal behavior, work ethic and intelligence, thereby justifying economic and social inequity.

In other words, Davenport argued that you were likely to be poor, less intelligent, and a criminal because of inferior genes. Indeed, Davenport's "expert" testimony was not only instrumental in Congress's decision to pass the Immigration Act of 1924 but also provided the social framework that would eventually be embraced and abused by Nazi Germany.

As early as the 1900s, mankind was classified into 26 different racial categories (including Hindu and Mexican) which have traditionally been used in a variety or government censuses. In fact, 100 years ago the United States still categorized individuals of Italian, Irish and Jewish descent as belonging to independent racial groups, and during the 19th century, as many as 300 races were identified.

Today, most scientists classify us into nine geographical races: European (e.g., Europeans, North American Whites, Middle Easterners), African (e.g., Africans, Afro-Americans, Haitians, Jamaicans and other Caribbean nationals), East Indian (e.g., Indians, Sri Lankans, Bengals), Asians (e.g., Chinese, Japanese, Koreans, Filipinos), Melanesians (e.g., Fiji, New Guinea), Polynesians (e.g., Hawaiians, Samoans), Micronesians, Australian Aborigines, and American Indians (e.g., Cherokee, Blackfoot, Lumbee, and Eskimos).

Over time, definitions of race have become more ambiguous. While it is clear that race exists from a social standpoint (it must exist for racism to exist), biologically, the definition is not very clear. According to Vivian Ota Wang of the Ethical, Legal and Social Implications Research Program at the Human Genome Research Institute (NHGRI), the concept seems to depend on a collection of physical features used to categorize everyone into groups. Despite this, and a multitude of definitions put forward, we have still not reached either social or even scientific consensus.

Race may be American's single most confusing problem—probably because few people know what it really is. Most of us have had to self identify when we complete college applications, job applications and other important forms. In each case we have been given a list of the racial/ethnic groups, one of which we are told we MUST belong to (see Table 1 for sample).

Some scientists still argue that races are biologically determined either through genetic divisions or as a result of group behaviors. On the other hand, disclaimers made by biologists and geneticists on the subject are now commonplace.

The one point that scientists and sociologists seem to agree on is that the notion that humans can be simply divided by color into White, Black, and Yellow is rather simplistic, and current definitions of race seem to be supported more by social rather than scientific research.

In fact, data compiled by various scientists show that, contrary to popular belief, intra-group differences are greater than inter-group differences (i.e., there are more genetic differences amongst White-Americans, and there are more genetic differences amongst African-Americans, than there are between White-Americans and African-Americans). And, the American Anthropological Association in 1998 argued that the concept of race was invented to assign some groups to a perpetually lower status while other were allowed to access privilege, power and wealth. In essence, most individuals who classify themselves as White-American are not purely white, and most individuals who classify themselves as African-American are not necessarily of African descent—both are a mixture of African, European, Asian, and/or Native American. Similarly, most individuals who identify themselves as European-White are not necessarily White. So, should we all just self identify as "Other," because it seems that's all we really are?

The bottom line seems to be that in this society, race is more of a social construct, based on human interaction rather than human differences. This is important because the construction of race affects other relationships (e.g., gender and class) and has proven to be the determining factor in success versus failure, wealth versus poverty, acceptance versus rejection and even life versus death.

So what is race? "Race" is a word used to describe individuals who look different from White-Americans by virtue of physical characteristics such as skin complexion, hair texture, shape of eye, and other factors such as place of birth and ancestry.

## What is Ethnicity?

Ethnicity is a concept used to divide people into groups based on cultural and traditional origins, cultural characteristics such as language, religious faith and tradition, shared nationality, tribal affiliation and genealogy.

Identifications of ethnicity are usually self-reported.

Interestingly enough, it does not seem to be common knowledge that each racial subdivision is made up of ethnic groups. For example, White-Americans, although not typically considered as ethnic, can be subdivided into Irish, Italians, Poles and Germans, to name a few. African-Americans can be subdivided into West Indians (of Caribbean descent) and Africans (modern-day Africans). Asians can be divided into Vietnamese, Japanese, Sri Lankan, Polynesian and Indians can be subdivided into Pakistanis, and West Indians (as in Indian immigrants to the Caribbean—both Muslim and Hindu). Hispanics can be subdivided into people from Mexico, Dominican Republic, Santo Domingo, Puerto Rico and El Salvador, to name a few.

Each subdivision brings with it a different culture and different customs. Each of the larger racial or ethnic groups is therefore multiethnic, multilingual and even multiracial. One may even venture to say that an individual group (White-American, African-American, etc.) can house multiple ethnicities. Similarly, an individual ethnic group can house multiple races: West Indians may be of African descent (i.e., Afro-Caribbean) and/or East Indian descent (i.e., out of India). This again begs the question of what purpose racial and ethnic categories serve, if not a divisive one.

## Theories of Criminality

Now that we have muddied the water even more with respect to definitions of "race" and "ethnicity", we must attempt to define "criminality" to be able to establish any possible relationship between the three. Whether we are predicting the path of a meteor or estimating the impact of global climate change, scientific predictions are, at best, a combination of many pieces of information. In the social sciences specifically, predictions can only be articulated in terms of statistical guesstimates of the likelihood that a particular event will occur. Predictions cannot and should not be stated in terms of absolute certainty. As such, with respect to violence and degrees of criminality, the best that scientists can do is assess the relative likelihood of criminal behavior based on information collected about the individual or group being evaluated. In situations such as this, the past has indeed proven to be a good indicator of the future.

Research and history have show that by and large, individuals with a history of criminal activity have a higher probability of subsequent criminal activity. Additionally, social and behavioral scientists have identified 3 factors that seem to also be strong indicators of criminality,

1. Demographic factors (e.g., age, gender and ethnicity);
2. Clinical factors (e.g., substance abuse, impulsivity and psychopathic natures), and
3. Contextual factors (e.g., the relative probability of future criminal acts based on the severity of physical correctional constraints).

Not surprisingly, these predictions are constantly challenged. In 1969 for example Dershowitz noted,

> ...for every correct psychiatric prediction of violence there are numerous erroneous predictions. That is, among every group of inmates presently confined on the basis of psychiatric prediction of violence, there are only a few who would, and many more who would not, actually engage in such conduct if released.

Social scientists immediately rose to Dershowitz' challenge and tested the accuracy of their conclusions. Results were consistent—only 33% (one in three) of those identified as being prone to future violent behavior actually engaged in violence. This turn of events led to wide spread criticism of mental health professionals and their ability to predict degrees of criminality.

Today, the attractiveness of such popular television shows as "Law and Order: Criminal Intent", "Law and Order: Special Victims Unit", CSI, CSI Miami, Criminal Minds etc., has resulted in an overabundance of criminal justice students interested in becoming profilers who can not only describe the perpetrator of a crime without personal contact, but who also claim to be able to ascertain degrees of criminality based on extra legal factors such as the method in which the crime was executed, for example.

While criminals are individuals identified as being predisposed to criminal activity, it should be noted that criminals are ordinary people as well—they may go to school, church, the grocery, parties, etc., just like you and me. In fact, it is possible and even probable that if a given set of ordinary, "non criminal" individuals were given similar criminal opportunities (i.e., lots of free time for mischief, living in a neighborhood with unguarded homes, etc.) that some non-criminal individuals might actually find themselves involved in criminal activity.

Even though US society is dominated by a European legacy of crime, criminality here is expected to be concentrated among young men of color, both as victims and as offenders. Moreover, researchers tend to use data from criminal arrests to ascertain offender characteristics and ultimately predict criminality. This method could give misleading results for several reasons.

1. Most crimes are not reported, and so would not feed into the calculations.
2. Most individuals who commit crimes are not caught.
3. Not every individual who is arrested is guilty.
4. Not every individual who is acquitted or whose case is dismissed is innocent.

Where police look for crime and how police look for crime are the determining factors of who gets caught and prosecuted. For example, young people hanging out on a street corner on the "wrong side of town" on a Saturday night will draw more police attention than older executives plotting a crime behind closed doors in the suburbs.

As a society, we may be forced to admit that we are no closer to determining what causes crime than we were 50 years ago. Nonetheless, it is important to at least acknowledge some of the more prominent theories that have been put forth as possible explanations of crime and criminality.

*Durkheim's Anomie Theory*

According to Emile Durkheim, members of certain racial and gender groups are systematically denied the opportunity to accumulate wealth by traditional means based on an unspoken but inherent value system. This theory suggests that (1) minorities are devalued compared to non minorities, and (2) women are devalued compared to men. But the comparison goes deeper than this. In applying Durkheim's ideas to the value system of modern-day American society, the status quo would be as follows:

1. White-American men are valued more than any other human being, including White-American women.

2. White-American women are valued more than African-American men and women, and,

3. African-American women are valued more than African-American men.

Theorists argue that this unspoken hieirachy is is responsible for the inability of those in the lower ranks to access opportunities both socially and financially. These are key factors in the incidence of criminality and deviant behavior, and ultimately, a total loss of social control.

As a result, and, in a bid to regain control, the criminal justice system has "retaliated" by using non legal factors such as race, to control those members of society who dare to step outside of their assigned social and economic place in the hierarchy.

This society has been accused of maintaining a well-oiled economic and social hierarchy. If Durkheim's theory were to be applied, we would find that despite our boast of a laissez-faire, free market environment, economically, only a select few individuals and organizations seem to have access to the production and distribution of goods and services at the highest levels. In other words, the most meaningful economic opportunities—which have traditionally been inaccessible to minorities and women—continue to be so.

## Merton's Social Strain Theory

Merton's Social Strain Theory had its roots in Durkheim's Anomie Theory. It is one of the most influential sociological theories of criminality. It was introduced in the 1950s and is based on Merton's belief that American culture evaluates success based on material wealth yet creates barriers that preclude the average citizen from acquiring wealth by legitimate means. By linking criminality to non-achievement of social and personal goals, Merton is able to identify the source of the conflict that causes the frustrations that result in criminal activity. Merton's theory has been used to explain the lower classes' apparent predisposition to involvement in criminal activity. Critics of this theory argue that it does not explain why certain people commit certain types of crimes, or why all members of the lower class are not predisposed to criminal activity, or even why some members of the upper class commit certain types of crime.

## Differential Association Theory

The Differential Association Theory of crime is one of the most prominent social learning theories of our time. This theory was first put forth by Edwin H. Sutherland in his 1939 text, "Principles of Criminology." Sutherland is best known for his research on intelligence, white-collar crime and professional theft. He was a strong opponent of the notion that crime is a function of hidden feelings of inadequacy and insecurity amongst members of the lower classes. He argued that criminality is a learned process and could affect a person of any gender, race, age, or socioeconomic status. Sutherland's Differential Association Theory of crime is based on nine basic principles:

> **Broken Windows theory**
>
> A criminological theory associated with James Wilson and George Kelling that holds that criminality operates on a continuum that reflects perceptions about the breakdown of the social order. They argue that the prevention of minor crimes (such as vandalism) and the encouragement of physical maintenance of properties and neighborhoods leads to an effective reinforcement ...

1. Criminal behavior is learned.
2. Leaning is a by-product of interaction.
3. Leaning occurs within intimate groups.
4. Criminal techniques are learned.
5. Perceptions of legal code influence motives and drives.
6. A person becomes delinquent because of an excess of definitions favorable to violations of law over definitions unfavorable to violations of law.
7. Differential associations may vary in frequency, duration, priority and intensity.
8. The process of leaning criminal behavior by association is the same as any other learning process.
9. Criminal behavior is an expression of general needs and values.

Critics of this theory have argued that the theory erroneously assumes that criminals have all been socialized into the normative culture. The theory, they argue, also fails to explain why some individuals who are exposed to the same conditions never become involved in criminal activity.

*Social Disorganization Theory*

The Social Disorganization Theory focuses on the physical conditions within a given urban environment that affects crime rate. In areas such as these, the traditional institutions of social control—nuclear family schools and churches no longer have the same impact in the community as they once did. Indicators of Social Disorganization include but are not limited to:

1. higher than average unemployment,
2. higher than average high school dropout rates,
3. deteriorated housing (see Broken Windows theory), and
4. higher than average rates of single parent families.

In situations such as these, residents often feel a sense of hopelessness, helplessness and despair which ultimately breeds antisocial behavior.

## Social Conflict Theory

The Social Conflict theory gained popularity in the 1960s. Official statistics report more crime in "lower-class" neighborhoods, and several influential criminologists began to take interest in this correlation. It would appear to mean one of two things: either

(1) middle-class crime is under or unrecorded, or

(2) members of the "lower class" are more prone to crime.

In 1971, William Chambliss and Robert Seidman wrote "Law, Order, and Power", a piece which documented just how much the justice system was geared toward protecting the interests of the rich and powerful. Chambliss and Seidman argued that control of the political and economic system directly impacted the manner in which the U.S. criminal justice system is administered and that crimes were deliberately defined in a manner guaranteed to benefit those who control the system.

Another noteworthy piece is that of Richard Quinney, who also argued that the law and the definitions of law represent the interests of those who hold power in society.

As such, when conflict occurs between social groups—for example the wealthy and the not so wealthy—the wealthy will create laws that will benefit them and put everyone else at a disadvantage. The major strength of this theory is that it clearly accounts for class differences in crime rates and shows how class conflicts may influence behavior.

## Social Control Theory

Social control theories are based on a belief that there are personality traits and environmental factors that, if supported, can actually prevent individuals from committing crimes. Social control theorists believe that it is the value of an individual's interaction with significant others and with positive social institutions, that determines the individual's ability to resist criminal temptation. These theorists take an unusual approach to crime. Instead of focusing on what causes crime, they focus on such questions as,

1. why law-abiding citizens choose to abide by the law
2. why most individuals choose to follow societal norms and expectations
3. why the average person has a reasonable tolerance for frustration and develops realistic aspirations.

In essence, this theory argues that when social constraints are weak or nonexistent, delinquent behavior will result.

### Labeling Theory

Deviance is not a property inherent in certain forms of behavior; it is a property conferred upon those forms by the audience which directly or indirectly witnesses them.

The Labeling Theory defines crime and criminality as an outward manifestation of name calling—in other words, the perpetrators of the criminal acts may not necessarily be truly criminal. They're just reacting to the fact that this society has labeled them as criminal based on race, geographic factors, socioeconomic status and educational attainment, to name a few. On the other hand, this theory would also argue that a crime is a crime only because we label it as such and not because of the consequences of the "criminal" action (e.g., if chewing gum was labeled as a crime, then those who chew gum are criminals). Labels create a stigma and affect self perception and self confidence. People who are so labeled become social outcasts, and this in many cases has a negative impact on the ability to enjoy social benefits such as higher education and improved standard of living.

This theory has been the subject of many sociological debates. Antagonists claim that very specific conditions must exist for this theory to work and the elements of the theory itself do not make allowances for those conditions. Protagonists argue that stigma and negative labeling are common critical factors in the onset of criminal behavior.

### In the News: The Virginia Tech Saga

On April 16, 2007, Cho Seung-Hui, a 23-year-old English major at Virginia Polytechnic and State University, shot and killed two students in a campus dormitory. Two hours later Mr. Seung-Hui killed 30 more students in a classroom building. Cho, who is of South Korean descent, was raised in suburban Washington, DC, after immigrating to the United States with his parents at the age of nine. He is described as being extremely unfriendly, never making eye contact and rarely speaking to anyone including his suitemates and his instructors. According to Cho's professors, his erratic behavior had been ongoing—scaring his classmates and causing him to be removed from at least one of his classes. The content of his class work was apparently also at issue. Some of his professors described his contributions as filled with anger, intimidating, twisted and filled with macabre episodes of violence. At some point he was even referred

> Institutional discrimination —Most evident when one group is disproportionately absent in the administration of an institution or system, compared to those coming through (being punished by) the system or institution.

to the campus counselor. In the aftermath of what has been described as the worse massacre in recent US history, Cho left an 8-page letter and video tapes in which he made angry references to "rich kids" and religion.

The Virginia Tech incident is one of many that raise questions about how we, as a society, define and determine levels of criminality. Indeed, if criminality is determined by IQ and consequently race as some would have us believe, then Mr. Cho should be African-American. The Virginia Tech Saga is just the latest of a series of such incidents specific to high school and college campuses. This particular trend began to take shape in 1996, and it has taken the lives of 162 with 180 wounded. It is noteworthy that in almost all 49 reported incidents worldwide, the shooters were White-American.

## RACE, ETHNICITY AND POLICY

Despite America's bloody history, or perhaps because of America's bloody history, the main objective of legislation and public policy is to maintain order and social control and to eradicate crime totally. There is no doubt that crime is real, but the depiction of crime is more often than not exaggerated or oversimplified, sensationalized or and deliberately misleading (see Chapter 4). As a result, the American public has certain misperceptions about what crime is and who is a criminal. Ultimately, these misperceptions directly and indirectly influence the direction of legislation and public policy.

For example, by and large the average White-American believes:

a. African-Americans commit most of society's crimes.

b. White-Americans who do commit crimes do not commit the more serious crimes.

c. Street crime is more serious that white-collar crime.

d. African-Americans are innately prone to criminal behavior.

e. The three major components of the American criminal justice system (police, courts, and correction) all operate in an impartial and unbiased manner, particularly with respect to the minorities who pass through the system.

Despite this blind belief, the numbers show that there are disparities concerning people of color in the criminal justice system.[1] In fact, if the numbers are to be believed, the American criminal justice system seems to function in such a way that, at the end of the day, the offender ending up in prison will more than likely belong to one of the lowest social and economic groups in the country. So the following questions can be reasonably asked:

1.   Compared to members of the middle and upper class, are the poor more likely to be arrested?
2.   If arrested, are the poor more likely to be charged?
3.   If charged, are the poor more likely to be convicted?
4.   If convicted, are the poor more likely to be sentenced to prison? and,
5.   If sentenced, are the poor more likely to be given longer prison terms?

Each of us must ask and actively seek to answer whether the disparities are the result of discrimination, (whether institutional or contextual) or whether, as some would argue, minorities are simply more prone to criminal behavior. Regardless of whether the perceived criminality of people of color is real or imagined, the negative stigma associated with minorities in general (but with African-American and Hispanic men in particular) has a long-term social and policy impact.

The conservative approach to crime which evolved in the late 70s early 80s has led to the implementation of stringent crime control measures such as mandatory minimum sentencing, truth in sentencing and three strikes laws, all of which appear to unfairly target minority communities and fuel the growth of the American prison population, fondly referred to as the prison–industrial complex (see Chapter 2). The rapid growth and financial success of the prison–industrial complex in turn influence the direction of other social and financial policies, such as:

a.   changes in sentencing laws (e.g., mandatory minimums),

b.   change of emphasis from rehabilitation to punishment (e.g., reduction in the number of drug treatment, mental health, prisoner re-entry and prisoner education programs),

c.   the elimination of financial aid for prisoners (e.g., Pell grants), and

---

1   Dray, P. (2002). *At the Hands of Persons Unknown: The Lynching of Black America*, New York: Random House.

d.    felony disenfranchisement (temporary and permanent loss of the right to vote).

More importantly, the perception of minorities as criminals only serves to further alienate people of color from mainstream America. Minorities believe that they are more likely to be targeted by law enforcement, more likely to be treated unfairly as they move through the court room process, and are less likely to experience any of the rehabilitative benefits of the correctional system (see Chapter 4 for more discussion). Additionally, there is the impact of the labeling theory of criminality on young African-American men.

Almost every aspect of our lives is based on perception—how we perceive ourselves, how we want society to perceive us but more importantly, how we are portrayed to society (how the media presents us). The importance of perception is quite evident in the media portrayal of minorities (see Chapter 5). Television crime news, whether prime time news reports or reality shows, all tend to feature crime scenes and mug shots that overwhelmingly feature African-American males. The message that this trend sends to society is that minorities in general, but African-American men in particular, are criminals and should be feared. African-American men have begun to question their place and role in this society—if society already believes they are all criminals and expects them to engage in crime, and then perhaps criminal activity is the obvious option.

+++

### What is Race?
by Dr. Joseph L. Graves, Jr.

Race finds itself at the center of controversy in a number of topics found in disciplines from the humanities to the natural sciences. Yet, even as the 21st century begins most people (scholars and laypersons alike) labor under a series of misconceptions which impede their ability to correctly apply this concept to human affairs. This is because race as understood in the context of the Western world is both simultaneously a biological and a social concept. No where is the need to disentangle these different aspects of racial definitions more paramount than in theories of criminal behavior. For example, in 1985, James Q. Wilson and Richard Herrnstein wrote that the differential rates of crime in blacks, may result from genetic differences predisposing this group to criminal behavior[1]. Herrnstein reprised this theme in *The Bell Curve* published in 1994 along with Charles R. Murray[2]. In their version of the story, genes were responsible for differences in general intelligence. They argued that lower intelligence, was related to a variety of social pathologies, including greater rates of criminal behavior. Since more crimes were committed by people with lower IQ, blacks having lower IQ would be expected to commit more crimes. There are a number of flaws in these arguments, but the primary flaw is the idea that one can identify a "black" race, and that such a race would be genetically differentiable from other so-called races.

Biological definitions of race have changed throughout history. For example, Carolus Linneaus in *Systema Naturae* (1735) stressed aspects of physical traits (morphology). Louis Agassiz, in his 1851 *Essay on Classification* relied on the concept of zones of creation which assigned various organisms and their races to particular geographical zones. Finally at the end of the 19th century the race argument began to include the concept of genetic variation. Charles Darwin had already recognized the many weaknesses in race classification in humans by the time he wrote *The Descent of Man* in 1871. The idea that races could be defined by the use of genes weakened as more information on human genetic variation accumulated over the 20th century. It was clear to the community of scientists by the publication of United Nations Educational Scientific and Cultural Organization (UNESCO) statements on race of 1960, that social and biological conceptions of race were not equivalent. Unfortunately, for a variety of reasons, these realizations did not alter either the thinking of the lay public or the majority of scholars in the humanities and social sciences. Modern biological definitions of race rely on genetic variation and how that variation is distributed within and between human populations[3].

One of the reasons that the belief in biological races is so resilient is that in many ways it contradicts "common sense." Physical features do not define racial groups. Yet, observable physical features are what people rely on to justify their belief in the existence of different races. Physical traits such as skin color, hair type, body stature, blood groups, or tendencies to get certain diseases do not alone or in combination, define "racial" groups. It's absolutely true that these physical traits vary among geographical populations. However the *way* that they vary does not allow us to define racial groups. For example, Sri Lankans of the Indian subcontinent, Nigerians, and aboriginal Australians share a dark skin tone, but differ in hair type, facial features, and genetic predisposition for disease. Skin color follows a South-North gradient related to solar intensity. Populations that live in the tropics tend to have more melanic skin, than those who inhabit more northern latitudes. In other words, all major divisions of humanity have groups within them that have dark skin. Conversely, only groups that live at northern latitudes have "fair skin." This excludes groups formerly classified as Negroids, but includes the other two divisions. Either way, skin color cannot be used to assign persons to a racial group. If you try to use any other physical characteristics such as height, body proportions, skull measurements, or hair type to show how human populations are related, your result would not match the measured genetic relatedness and known evolutionary history of our species.

Physical traits fail to define races because local populations produce traits that adapt to climate and other environmental factors wherever those factors occur. This means that, however genetically *or* geographically distant they are, tropical populations will have physical traits that match tropical conditions, such as the sickle cell anemia trait. Sickle cell anemia, and thalessemia, as well as G6PD deficiency, are found wherever malaria transmission is in high frequency. This means that Western Africans, Mediterraneans, Arabians, and East Indians all have varying amounts of these diseases. Groups that live at high altitude also have a unique set of physical features. For example, Kenyans and Peruvians will have greater lung capacities and red blood cell counts. These features are completely independent of their other physical traits. For example, Kenyan populations from high altitudes regions, such as Kalenjin, do not show high frequencies of the sickle cell trait, because the mosquitoes which transmit malaria don't live at that altitude. Thus physical features mix and match with each other around the world, depending upon how natural selection acted upon the genes producing the specific trait. Physical and biological anthropologists call this the **principle of discordance**. This is why no physical feature can be used to demonstrate the existence of biological races within the human species.

There are about 25,000 genes (loci, locations along the chromosome) that code for the features of individual human beings. An allele is an alternative coding that may appear for any specific gene. Human population genetic variation has now been examined for well over fifty years. The following facts are inconsistent with the claim that biological races can be identified within our species:

a. Alleles (genetic variants) are distributed in a cosmopolitan fashion, 86% of all alleles discovered to date are found in every human population, 10% are found over broad continental regions, and only 4% are localized to narrow continental regions.

b. Populations that are located closest to each other are more similar in their distribution of alleles. The relatedness of populations is continuous and not discrete. You can think of this as equivalent to the color spectrum, with red grading into orange, yellow, green, blue, and purple. There are points in the spectrum that are clearly located in a specific color, but there are also points where saying that you are seeing red or orange can't be determined.

c. Sub-Saharan Africans have greater amounts of genetic variation than populations found in other world regions. The amount of genetic linkage between regions of the chromosomes is also smaller in Sub-Saharan Africans than other groups.

Points a, b, c can only be reconciled with one interpretation of human genetic history. Modern humans are a relatively young species which originated and spent most of its time in Sub-Saharan Africa (modern humans evolved around 160,000 YBP and left Africa for the first time between 60,000–70,000 YBP.) This means that across the human genome the amount of genetic variation within populations is greater than that between them[4]. So, if the DNA of any two randomly chosen Northern Europeans or two sub-Saharan Africans were compared, either pair would have a 96% chance of sharing the same gene. This is another way of saying that Northern Europeans are more similar to Northern Europeans, and sub-Saharan Africans are more similar to sub-Saharan Africans. However if a randomly chosen sub-Saharan African and Northern European were compared, they would have an 86% chance of having the same gene. These populations are not dissimilar enough to consider as a biological race, there simply is too much genetic overlap between them to make this distinction viable.

The real question is not whether the human species contains races, but whether the measured genetic distance between human population groups could be contributing to any important physical and behavioral features between groups (however they are defined.) We already understand that human physical variation is discordant. Physical variation results from the interaction of genes, environment, and chance events. This set of causal relationships also governs human behavioral variation, with is also discordant. Thus the idea that biological race plays a causal role in the determination of crime is immediately suspect. The claims of genetic criminality of African-Americans by authors such as Wilson, Herrnstein, and Murray are even more problematic.

Thus the utility of socially defined race in regard to studies of criminal behavior is apparent. However it must be recognized that this concept is not equivalent to biological races, which are not found in modern humans.

### References

1. Wilson, James Q. and Herrnstein, R., Crime and Human Nature, (New York: Simon & Schuster), 1985, 468–472.
2. Herrnstein, R. and Murray, C.R., The Bell Curve: (New York, NY: The Free Press), 1994.
3. Graves, J.L., The Race Myth: Why We Pretend Race Exists in America, soft cover edition with a new preface by the author (New York, NY: Dutton Books), 2005.
4. Marshall, E. (1998) "DNA studies challenge the meaning of race", Science, Genome Issue, v. 282: p. 654-55; Genetics for the Human Race, Nature Genetics Suppl. Vol. 36, no. 11, 2004.
5. Dray, P., At the Hands of Persons Unknown: The Lynching of Black America, (New York: Random House), 2002; Chang, Iris, The Rape of Nanking: The Forgotten Holocaust of World War II, (New York:

Penguin), 1998; Strauss, S. The Order of Genocide: Race, Power, and War in Rwanda (Ithaca, NY: Cornell University Press), 2006.

Dr. Joseph L. Graves, Jr.
Dean, University Studies & Professor of Biological Sciences
North Carolina A&T State University Fellow
American Association for the Advancement of Science, Section G: Biological Sciences

*I received my Ph.D. in Environmental, Evolutionary and Systematic Biology from Wayne State University in 1988. Although I cannot be sure, it is highly likely that I was the first African-American to ever earn a Ph.D. in the field of evolutionary biology. Between 1990—2004, I held appointments at the University of California, Irvine; Arizona State University –West, and as University Core Director at Fairleigh Dickinson University. In 1994, I was elected a Fellow of the Council of the American Association for the Advancement of Science (AAAS) for my pioneering work in establishing the genetic and physiological controls of aging. In 2006, I was asked to participate in "The New Genetics and the Trans-Atlantic Slave Trade" discussion group, sponsored by the W.E.B. Du Bois Institute at Harvard University. Later that year I lectured on racial medicine at the European Social Research Council Genomics Policy and Research Forum, held at the University of Edinburgh, Scotland. My research concerns the evolutionary genetics of postponed aging and biological concepts of race in humans. I have written two books on the biology of race entitled: The Emperor's New Clothes: Biological Theories of Race at the Millennium, Rutgers University Press, 2005 and The Race Myth: Why We Pretend Race Exists in America, Dutton Press, 2005.*

+++

## CONTROVERSIES: THE BLACK RAGE DEFENSE—IS IT A LEGITIMATE DEFENSE IN CRIMINAL PROCEEDINGS?

Not surprisingly, over the past 20 years accusations and perceptions of racism evolved into what is referred to as "the Black Rage defense". A Black Rage defense is a legal strategy used in criminal cases. It asserts that a defendant's crime is the result of social racism and that he or she should not be held criminally liable. It is not a traditional criminal defense. It uses the existence of social and environmental hardships to justify the commission of specific crimes. The strategy is to incorporate racial reality into the traditional doctrine of self-defense (i.e., use deadly force if there is a reasonable belief of imminent harm or serious bodily injury). The Black Rage defense has expanded to include other races and ethnicities as well as other categories of defenses i.e., non-psychiatric defenses. The development of this defense has also been tied to the evolution of the "battered woman" defense as well as a variety of other cultural defenses.

In 1925, for example, Clarence Darrow, one of the most famous criminal lawyers in American history, placed the issue of discrimination squarely in the face of the American criminal justice system. Darrow was defending his client Dr. Ossian Sweet, two of his family members, and seven other African-Americans who were on trial for shooting into a mob of White-Americans who were attempting to force the Sweets out of their home in an all-White neighborhood in Detroit. Although the Sweets' defense was not then described as black rage, the underlying argument made at the time was the same— White-American supremacy, White-American juries, White-American judges and a White-American legal system versus the rage, pride and strength of African-Americans.

In the Sweet case, the defendant fired before the crowd actually attacked, so the defense team needed to prove that the defendants felt a reasonable sense of imminent danger of serious bodily harm. To prove this, the team presented evidence of a history of White mobs beating and killing African-Americans who attempted to move into White neighborhoods. Darrow used what was in effect the Black Rage Defense to argue that in this society, color, class and poverty lines were as clearly drawn at the time he was speaking as they were before the abolition of slavery—in essence, racial oppression still existed. The all-White jury hung in the initial Sweet trial. On retrial the jury acquitted and all charges were dismissed[2]—much like the results of the Subway Vigilante case.

The Black Rage Defense was further developed in the 1970s and continued to challenge the concept of the colorblind courtroom. It should be noted that this concept is not just a defense based solely on issues of racism and discrimination. This defense uses a realistic twist to manipulate such standard legal categories as self defense, insanity, duress and provocation, and diminished capacity.[3] This defense actually uses social reality to create a new concept that is a culmination of all of these defenses. For example, the decision to leave the scene of a crime could be seen as evidence of guilt. An attorney using the Black Rage Defense, however, would argue that an African-American male's decision to leave the scene of a crime could also be the result of fear

---

2  Harris, P. (1997). *Black Rage Confronts the Law*: New York: New York University Press.
3  Ibid.

of police coercion, police brutality, inadequate legal representation or biased jury or judge, all of which are social realities.

Another example of the Black Rage defense is the 1971 case of James Johnson, a Detroit autoworker who shot and killed three co-workers at a Chrysler factory. The defense's argument combined an insanity defense with the poverty and racism Johnson suffered growing up on a Mississippi plantation as well as the discrimination Johnson experienced while working at the Chrysler auto plant. Johnson's attorney for his criminal case exposed the oppressive working conditions at the Chrysler plant. Johnson was acquitted and served 5 years in a mental institution. The criminal defense team, Ken Cockrel and Justin Ravitz, both went on to distinguished legal, judicial and political careers. Johnson's attorney for his workers compensation case also successfully argued that Chrysler had created a "plant culture" and had, in effect "pulled the trigger."[4]

Notwithstanding the powerful and disturbing picture painted by extreme cases of racial discrimination, antagonists argue that a history of racial victimization does not give license to commit crimes.[5] In fact, it may even be reasonable to argue that although there is a causal connection between environment and crime, the countless numbers of African-Americans who have never, and will never commit crimes and who live productive lives, sometimes against seemingly insurmountable odds, proves that poverty and racism do not necessarily cause an individual to resort to crime. Some even go so far as to say that the public is sick and tired of hearing minorities in general and African-Americans in particular, continually blame racism, discrimination and oppression for their plight.[6]

The media has also distorted the concept of a black rage defense with negative portrayals in popular television shows such as "The Practice" (in which a so-called expert on race relations testified that African-American men should not be expected to control their violent urges because of the effects of racism), and "Law and Order" (in which an African-American stockbroker murdered his White-American boss because of mentally oppressive working conditions). It is important note that despite the impact that these shows may have on viewers, they were not intended to reflect reality but focus on only on gaining high ratings.

The Black Rage defense has been described as an anti-racist strategy. It is based on the assumption that people of all races, cultures and

4  Ibid.
5  Dershowitz, A. M. (1994). *The Abuse Excuse and Other Copouts, Sob Stories and Evasion of Responsibility*; Boston: Little, Brown and Company
6  Ibid.

classes can empathize with each other under certain conditions. It refutes the belief that there is a lower class of people who are inherently criminal and who should therefore be ignored by society. The legal strategy rooted in the anger and despair caused by racism and discrimination continues to strengthen and has motivated some in the legal system to rethink their positions.

## CONCLUSION

In a controversial 1975 article entitled "White Racism, Black Crime, and American Justice", criminologist Robert Staples argued that the American criminal justice system is blatantly racist.[7] Staples described the system as one composed of White-American men dedicated to protecting White-American interests and keeping African-Americans down. He claimed that this was evident in the second-rate mostly incompetent legal representation available to indigent African-American defendants, not to mention biased jurors, and racist judges.

A decade later, sociologist William Wilbanks summarily rejected Staples' discrimination theory in his piece "The Myth of a Racist Criminal Justice System." [8] Wilbanks based his argument on a series of studies that revealed definite statistical inequalities in the rate of arrest and imprisonment between White-Americans and African-Americans but nonetheless indicated that the real issue was poverty and the defendant's prior criminal record, and not racial discrimination as Staples had argued.

Today, opinions are still divided on the issue of racism versus poverty as an explanation for overrepresentation of minorities in the criminal justice system. As you move through the remaining chapters, you will be presented with many opportunities to judge for yourself.

## CRITICAL THINKING QUESTIONS

*Subway Vigilante Story*

1. Was Mr. Goetz justified in thinking that the four teenagers were up to anything more than a teenage prank? Was his impression based on their race?
2. According to statistics, a greater percentage of minority populations are involved in criminal activity than of non-minor-

---

7  White, Robert S. (1975) *Racism, Black, Crime and American Justice.* Phylon 1975; 36:14-22
8  Wilbanks, W. (1993). *The Myth of a Racial Criminal Justice System.* California: Brooks/Cole.

ity populations. If this is, in fact, the case, why do you think it is so?

3. If Bernard Goetz had been African-American and the muggers White-American, would there have been a difference in the outcome of the case? What about if both Goetz and the muggers were White-American, or if both Goetz and the muggers were African-American?

## Chapter Resources

*Ready for Review*

Objectives
Case Study: The Subway Vigilante
Introduction
What is Race?
- Biological definition
- Social definition

What is Ethnicity?
- Geography
- Culture
- Religion
- Language
- Genealogy

Theories of Criminality
- Social Strain Theory
- Anomie Theory
- Differential Association Theory
- Social Disorganization theory
- Social Conflict Theory
- Social Control Theory
- Labeling Theory

In the News
- The Virginia Tech Saga

Race Ethnicity and Policy
- Institutional discrimination
- Contextual discrimination
- Prison Industrial complex

Biography
Controversies: Black Rage Defense
Conclusion

*Key Terms*

Anomie Theory
Broken Windows Theory
Contextual discrimination
Criminality
Differential Association Theory
Ethnicity
Indigent
Institutional discrimination
Labeling Theory
Prison Industrial Complex
Profilers
Race
Social Conflict Theory
Social Control Theory
Social Disorganization Theory
Social Strain Theory
Stigma

# Chapter 2. The Criminal Justice System

## Objectives

- To determine whether minorities are overrepresented in the criminal justice system and if so, why?
- To evaluate whether race has any impact on an individual's interaction with the three components of the American criminal justice system.
- To evaluate the impact of the War on Drugs on minority populations.
- To determine if current criminal justice policies unfairly target minorities and the poor.

## Case Study: Policing and the LAPD—The Javier Ovando Saga

Those of us who have watched the XFX original series "The Shield," starring Michael Chiklis, hope and pray that this infamous drama was only an exaggerated view of the life of a police officer and police activity in general. It may come as a shock, therefore, to realize that there are police departments that actually operate in much the same manner as "the barn" and "the strike team". The LAPD, for example, is frequently branded as one of the most corrupt police departments in the country. This is particularly evident when one evaluates the case of Officer Rafael Perez, whose arrest led to one of the most notable police scandals in the history of the country.

The scene was set for the demise of Officer Perez when what appeared to be a routine drug bust ended in the investigation of 70 Los Angeles police officers, the arrest of 4, and the release of 100 prisoners. This was all apparently the result of the actions of one crooked cop—Rafael Perez. Perez was a member of "Crash", an elite anti-gang unit created by the LAPD. He was considered the "star" of the unit and had developed a reputation for having a no-nonsense approach to policing.

The saga began when Javier Francisco Ovando was charged with assaulting Los Angeles police officers Perez and Durden with a semi-automatic weapon as well as seven other felony charges. These charges were based solely on the testimony of Officer Perez. Ovando, who had been shot in the chest and neck, was appointed a public defender, Israeli-born Tamar Toister. Honduran-born Ovando spoke little English; Toister spoke no Spanish.

According to Ovando, who was a member of the notorious 18th Street Gang, he was innocent and the cops were guilty of trying to kill him. No one believed him. No one believed that Perez was a bad cop. On the witness stand, Perez was calm and collected as he gave his version of the events that transpired—Ovando burst into a dark 4th floor room in an abandoned building brandishing a Tec .22 semi-automatic pistol. Officers Perez and Durden fired first and hit Ovando four times, paralyzing him from waist down.

Discrepancies in Perez' testimony made Toister suspicious. Yet at trial, both the prosecutor and the judge seemed to block her attempts to point out police errors.

Toister asked for a continuance and physically examined the crime scene. Three events occurred that brought Perez and the "Crash" unit into the limelight. The first was a seemingly unrelated bank robbery. The teller who was robbed had accepted a delivery of cash from an armored car earlier that day and gave the bank robbers $722,000. Upon investigation, it was determined that the teller had scheduled the delivery. During questioning, she broke down and confessed that the robbery had been orchestrated by her boyfriend David Mack. Mack just happened to be a close friend of Perez and had in fact become his mentor. Investigators soon learned that both Mack and Perez had flown to Las Vegas two days after the robbery. Mack would later be convicted on federal charges of bank robbery and sentenced to 14 years in prison. The stolen money was never recovered nor was the other bank robber or driver of the getaway car ever identified.

The second event occurred three months later when another young gang suspect was detained, choked and beaten until he was vomiting blood. When the gang member was eventually released, he checked himself into a hospital and reported the incident. The incident was investigated and administrative charges were brought against the officers involved. One of the officers was fired.

The third event occurred a month later when the LAPD property division discovered that Officer Raphael Perez had signed out six pounds of cocaine for a court appearance and had never returned it. Since the case had already been adjudicated, internal affairs launched a secret investigation. The investigation revealed that Officer Perez had also checked out cocaine for other cases, including cases in which he was not involved. Internal affairs intensified its investigation tracking Perez' every move and gathering evidence.

Finally, two years after the Javier Ovando incident, members of his own department arrested Raphael Perez at his home. Perez was charged with possession of cocaine for sale, grand theft and forgery. At trial the jury deadlocked and Perez was retried. While he was awaiting retrial, investigators examined his financial records and found unexplained deposits. To protect his wife and child, Perez cut a deal and negotiated an agreement to expose misconduct with his unit in exchange for a five-year sentence (16 months with time off for good behavior).

According to Perez' confession, he began dealing drugs when he and his partner arrested a suspect and confiscated a pound of powder cocaine. They kept the drugs as well as the dealer's pager, and began taking orders which eventually led to the evidence locker. Perez also admitted to having set up gang members on drug and weapons charges but argued that this tactic had been approved by his commanding officer, David Mack.

Perez was also very explicit about how Javier Ovando had been framed several years earlier. The judge who had presided over the case and had prevented Perez' cross examination apologized to Ovando's public defender. The paralyzed Ovando, who had already served 3 years of his 23-year sentence, was released.[9]

## INTRODUCTION

In Chapter 1 we discussed the evolution of "race" and "racial categories" as a precursor to our discussion of the impact of racial definitions on the various segments of the criminal justice system. In Chapter 2, we will analyze the impact of race and ethnicity on each of the three parts of the criminal justice system: Part 1 – Police, Part II – Courts and Part III – Corrections.

---

9   Cannon, Lou. (2000). "One bad cop." *The New York Times Magazine*, October 1, 2000

Let us begin by taking a general look at the numbers. There are just over 7 million people under the control of the U.S. criminal justice system—either incarcerated, on probation or under parole supervision.[10] This is more than 3% of the adult U.S. population. There are varying estimates of what percentage of the prison and correctional population is minority but the general consensus seems to be about 60%.[11] The U.S. Census Bureau breaks it down as follows: about 46% of the adult correctional population is White-American, approximately 41% is African-American, and approximately 19% is Hispanic.[12]

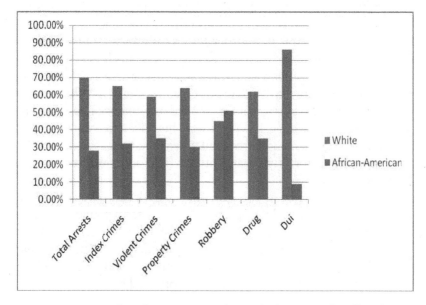

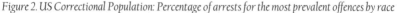

*Figure 2. US Correctional Population: Percentage of arrests for the most prevalent offences by race*

Although there is general agreement that minorities in general, and African-Americans in particular, are overrepresented in the American criminal justice system, where there is disagreement is what causes this overrepresentation. On the one hand, it can be argued that minorities simply commit more crime than non-minorities. On the other hand, it is possible that the criminal involvement of minorities is proportionate to their percentage of the population but that they are targeted for apprehension, arrested and prosecuted at disproportionately higher rates. To determine which is the case, this chapter will eval-

10  Department of Justice, Bureau of Justice Statistics (BJC) (2000). Sourcebook of criminology Justice Statistics online 2005. See http://www. albany. edu/soursebook/pd/t612005. pdf (Sept 30, 2008)

11  U.S. Census Bureau, Statistical Abstract of the United States 2003–5, 124th ed. (Washington, DC: U.S. Government Printing Office) p. 372, Table 571

12  Ibid.

uate the involvement of minorities through the entire criminal justice system, from their interaction with police (Part I) through their involvement with the courtroom players (Part II). Finally, we will evaluate the passage of minority offenders through the American correctional system (Part III).

## DISCRIMINATION AND THE CRIMINAL JUSTICE SYSTEM

Racial bias has a horrendous impact at all stages of the criminal justice process. The most visible impact of racism is the gross imbalance between the number of White-Americans and the number of minorities in U.S. prisons. One in 3 African-American males between the ages of 20–29 are somewhere in the American criminal justice system.[13] There are three specific areas in which racial bias has been identified in the treatment of suspects, defendants, and prisoners:

1. The use of racial and ethnic profiling in determining whom to stop and search;
2. The impact of harsher crack cocaine sentences on minorities compared to power cocaine sentencing on White-Americans, and
3. The application of the death penalty at both state and federal levels, by prosecutors, judges and juries.[14]

As far back as the 1930s, a number of studies argued that there was clear and consistent bias against non-Whites in sentencing.[15] African-Americans represented 43% of arrests, 54% of convictions, and 59% of prison admissions for violent crimes in 1994[16] indicating that arrested African-Americans were more likely to be imprisoned compared with White-Americans. Additionally, between 1930 and 1973, Southern jurisdictions also put to death 398 black men and 43 white men for the crime of rape.[17] This early research focused on the social prejudice against minorities and even pointed fingers at the Ameri-

---

13  Decker Scott (1981) "Citizen Attitudes Towards the police: A view of past findings and suggestions for future Policy": *Journal of Police Science and Administration* 9:80-7; Flanagan, timothy J. and Michael S. Vaughn (1996). "Public Opinion about Police Abuse of Force, pp113-28 in *Police Violence*, Edited by W. Geller and H Toch New Haven CT: Yale University Press

14  Feagin, Joe R. & Melvin P Sikes (1994) *Living with racism: the black middle-class experience.* Boston, MA: Beacon Press.

15  Wilson, W. J (1987). *The truly disadvantaged.* Chicago, IL: University of Chicago Press

16  Ostrom, Elinor & Gordon Whitaker (1974). "Community control and Governmental Responsiveness the case of police in black neighborhoods". Pp303-34 in *Improving the Quality of the Urban Environment*, edited by D. Rogers and W. Hawley hills CA Sage.

17  Smith, Douglas, Nanette Graham and Bonnie Adams (1991). "Minorities and the police: attitudinal and Behavioral Questions." Pp 22-5 in *Race, Crime and Punishment in America*, New York: Oxford University Press.

---

can judiciary.[18] These researchers concluded that "equality before the law is a social fiction.[19] Moreover, researchers were able to find pointed examples of racism to support their argument such as in the following case.

Judge Chargin of Santa Clara, California, made a statement in 1969, during juvenile court proceedings against a Chicano boy:

> We ought to send you back to Mexico. You belong in prison for the rest of your life for doing things of this kind. You ought to commit suicide. That's what I think of people of this kind. You are lower than animals and haven't the right to live in organized society—just miserable, lousy, rotten people.....Maybe Hitler was right.[20]

While Judge Chargin was censured by his colleagues and forced to retract this statement and publicly apologize, he was re-elected in 1972, receiving twice as many votes as his closest opponent.[21]

Following in the wake of the Civil Rights Movement, increased fears of urban street crime and high rates of unemployment caused by an economic recession turned attention away from eliminating the sources and consequences of discrimination and repression and toward more extensive social control.[22] Although any obvious manifestations of discrimination were no longer socially acceptable (at least in public forums), researchers began to argue that perhaps minorities were overrepresented in the criminal justice system and prisons because of their greater proportional involvement in crime and not because of any bias in the system.[23] Later on, other researchers exam-

---

18  Alpert Geoffrey & Roger Dunham (1988). *Multi-Ethnic neighborhoods.* New York: Greenwood Press

19  Harris D. (1999) "The stories the Statistics and the law: Why Driving while black" *Matters Minnesota Law Review* 84(2): 265-326; Huston Chronicle News Service 1999.

20  Hernandez, c. A., M. J. Haug, and n. N. Wagner (1976) "Chicanos: Social and psychological perspectives." St. Louis: C. V. Mosby; Kennedy, Sheila. (1997). "Making Traffic stop Based on Race" *Indianopolis Star*, January 29; Donohue, Brian and Barrett, Kathy (2000) "Motorist city disagree Over Civil rights lawsuit." *La Cruces Sun-News*, June 8, 1; *Washington Post* (1996). Driving while Black on 195. November 16; Dr Elmo Randolph, an African-American dentist from Bergen county New Jersey was stopped by state troopers 50 times between 1991 and 2000. Dr Randolph who drove a gold BMW, was never issued a ticket but on each occasion his license and registration was requested and he was asked if he carried drugs or weapons in the vehicle; Alvin Penn, deputy president of the Connecticut State Senate was stopped as he drove through town of Trumbull. Penn, an African—American was asked if he knew which town he was since Bridgeport which is & 5% African American/Latino bordered Trumbull which is 98% White-American. Penn asked why he needed to know which town he was in to which the officer replied that he did not need to give a reason for the stop and that he would cited Penn for speeding if he made an issue of it.

21  Newport, Frank. (1999). *Racial profiling is seen as widespread particularly among Young Black men.* Princeton. NJ: Gallop News Service 1999

22  Birzer, M L, & Harris Birzer G (2000). "Race matters: A Critical profiling, it's a matter for the courts": *Journal of Criminal Justice*, vol. 34, issue 6, pp. 643-651

23  Report of Dr. John Lambert. Plaintiff's Expert. "Revised statistics of incidence of Police Stop and Arrest for black Drivers/ travelers on the New Jersey Turnpike between Exits or

ined data drawn from several points in time, and concluded that although sentencing was discriminatory in the late 1960s, changes in the composition and bureaucratization of the judiciary did away with this bias in the 1970s.[24] And that, supposedly, was the end of that. Or was it?

Let us take a look at the relationship between law enforcement and how certain policies and procedures may impact minorities and minority communities. Research indicates that minorities are more inclined to view police officers unfavorably than White-Americans.[25] It is reasonable to argue that that African-Americans in particular, and a growing number of Hispanics (as opposed to non minorities), have such negative interactions with social institutions that the issue must be race—i.e., lower-class Americans are more likely to experience police abuse than their middle-class counterparts, regardless of race.[26] On the other hand, there are those who argue that race is becoming less significant, and the real issue is class divisions.[27] This argument is particularly important in policing because the decision to arrest is the step that sets the criminal justice process in motion. For many, it becomes a point of no return regardless of guilt or innocence. In other words, an innocent person who is wrongfully arrested may never be able to repair the damage done. Let's walk through the process.

When criminal activity is reported, police officers are the first point of contact for anyone involved in the commission of a crime. As such police officers have a tremendous amount of discretion as to whether to divert the suspect from the criminal justice system or to pursue an arrest. If there is indeed negative interaction between the police and minorities, it is necessary to identify and evaluate the impact of this interaction on decisions to arrest or divert.

Interchanges 1 and 3 from the year 1988 through 1991. State v Pedro Soto." 734 A. 2d 350(NJ. Super. Ct. Law Div. 1996)

24  Brazil Jeff & Steve Berry (1999). "Color of Driver is key to stop in I-95 Videos." *Orlando Sentinel*, August 23, 1992, p. A1

25  Harrell, Erika. (2007). "Black Victims of Violent Crime": U.S. Department of Justice, Office of Justice Program; Washington DC

26  Cole, D. (1999). *No equal justice: Race and class in the American Criminal Justice System*. New York Press.

27  Harris, D. A. (2002) *Profiles in injustice: why racial profile cannot work*: New York : New Press; Ramirez, D McDevitt, J & Fellel, A (200). *A resource guide on racial profiling data collection system: Promising practices and lessons learned*. Washington, DC. U.S. Department of Justice; Lafree. G (1995) "Race and crime trends in the United States, 1946-1990." InD. F. Hawkins (Ed.), *Ethnicity, race and crime: Perspectives across time and place*(pp. 169-193). Albany State University of New York Press; Gross, S. R. & Barnes Y. (2000). "Read Work: Racial Profiling and Drug Interdiction on the Highway." *Michigan Law Review*, Vol. 101, No. 3 (Dec., 2002),pp. 651-754; Bureau of Justice Statistics (2000). "Characteristics of Drivers stopped by Police 2006": Washington D. C: Available at http://www. ojp. usdoj. gov/bjs/abstract/cdsp02. htm

In analyzing decisions to arrest or divert, we must consider the argument that middle-class Americans, regardless of race, are more likely to live in "low-crime" neighborhoods where policing tends to be less intrusive and less aggressive than in inner-city neighborhoods. As you evaluate this statement, be aware that since "low-crime" neighborhoods attract less police attention, it follows that fewer arrests will be made. This may not necessarily mean that the incidence of crime is any less in "low-crime" neighborhoods compared to "high-crime" neighborhoods, but this is the general perception. Similarly, it is logical that those who live in "high crime" neighborhoods are more likely to be targeted by police (regardless of their involvement in criminal activity). As such more arrests will be made regardless of race.

Nonetheless, while some have found that middle-class African-Americans who live in "low-crime" neighborhoods tend to view the police as negatively as do lower-class African-Americans living in high-crime areas[28], others have found that the opposite to be true[29] and yet others have found no significant difference in class or perception.[30] In essence, "high crime" neighborhoods may not necessarily be neighborhoods with "high crime" rates but could be neighborhoods with high arrest rates. High arrest rates would necessarily result from high police presence. High police presence would result from perceived or real "high crime" incidence and the cycle perpetuates itself. But is this perception justified or is this a case of media propaganda? Is this a case of the chicken and the egg—which comes first, high crime or high police presence?

## THE WAR ON DRUGS

This country has not been fully successful in addressing the issues of racial and ethnic incorporation, simply framed as Black–White issues. While the circumstances of African-Americans and the nature of Black–White relationships at the end of the 20th century appear to be better than they were under slavery, Reconstruction, Jim Crow, and the pre-Civil Rights era, this may be just that—an appearance. The reality of the situation may be that there may be a subtle resurgence of pro-slavery tactics.

The 1980s ushered in a period of increased violent crime that stirred such fear in citizens that policy makers were quick to imple-

---

28  Mehta, Seema (200). "Anaheim to settle profiling lawsuit." *Los Angeles Times*, 25 December 2002, 4(B) available at http:/www. latimes. com/news/local/la-me-profile25dec25. story

29  Cannon, Lou (1999). *Official Negligence: how Rodney King and the Riots changed Los Angeles and the LAPD*. Boulder, CO Westview Press

30  Hann M. S. (1997). *Apocalypse In Oklahoma: Waco and Rubyridge Revenged*, Boston, Ma : Northeastern University Press

ment stiffer punishment. Media coverage seemed to focus on street crime, so this became the target of the criminal justice system. Researchers argued that the media and politicians exploited the perceived dangers of street crime to sell news and to further political careers.[31] The problem with this approach was that most street criminals were being portrayed as young, male, and minority.[32]

At the same time the phenomenon that was the "War on Drugs" created policies designed to "reduce the supply, distribution, and use of illicit narcotics."[33] In implementing these policies, the burden fell on young minority males who suddenly became the preoccupation of law enforcement. In fact, at the height of this war on drugs, the arrest rate of African-Americans was 5 times that of White-Americans, despite evidence of similar rates of drug use.[34] Additionally, according to Bureau of Justice Statistics (BJS) numbers,

1. A disproportionate number of African-Americans were convicted of drug trafficking compared to White-Americans—57% versus 42%.

2. A disproportionate number of African-Americans were convicted of all drug offenses compared to White-Americans: 53% versus 46%.[35]

3. The African-American prison population grew by 27% as the result of drug arrests, compared to only 14% growth in White-American prison population.[36]

Additionally, thanks to the media, Hispanic men began to be stereotyped as drug couriers or traffickers, and African-American men began to be profiled as drug addicts and gun toting murderers (see Chapter 4 for more on the media). Indeed, new and ongoing research shows that Hispanic defendants will be treated more harshly than African-American defendants, who in turn are treated more harshly than White-American defendants because of the picture that the current "war" on drugs paints of African-American and Hispanic men.[37]

31  Dershowitz, Alan (1997). *Reasonable Doubts: The Criminal Justice System and O. J. Simpson case.* Touchstone: N. Y

32  Terry Don (1995). Philadelphia Shaken by Criminal Police Officers. The New York Times, available at http://www. nytimes. com/1995/08/28/us/philadelphia-shaken-by-criminal-police-officers. html

33  Human Rights Watch (2001). "Letter to U.S. Attorney General Ashcroft on Human rights Agenda": March 20th, 2001

34  New York City Complaint Review Board (2004). "Status Report: January-December 2003", See http://www. nyc. gov/html/ccrb/pdf/ccrbann2003. pdf

35  Ibid.

36  Ibid.

37  Joan Petersilia (1983). *Racial Disparities in the Criminal Justice System*: Rand Corp, Santa Monica, California

Some research argues that the disparity that has resulted from the "war on drugs" should have been anticipated by policy makers for a number of reasons:

1. Activities such as retail drug dealing occur on the streets and alleys in poor neighborhoods, making it easier to implement undercover activity, target and arrest offenders.
2. In working-class and middle-class neighborhoods, activities such as drug dealing are more likely to occur indoors.
3. Police departments find it easier to focus on disadvantaged minority urban neighborhoods than on suburban white neighborhoods.
4. It is easier to make arrests in socially disorganized neighborhoods compared to urban blue-collar and urban or suburban white-collar neighborhoods.[38]

There is no argument that these changes in social policy have had a profound effect on income distribution, employment opportunities, community development, and family structure in every segment of society, but especially in African-American communities. In fact, the U.S. government has been accused of spending more money housing African-American male prisoners than preparing them for higher education and the job market, and there have even been arguments that the growth of the criminal justice system in the past twenty years has a direct correlation to economics and changes in social policies.[39] The BJS Sourcebook of Criminal Justice Statistics 2009, has already pointed out that,

1. 81% of full-time sworn personnel in local police departments are White-American as compared to 11% African-American.
2. 68% of correctional officers in state adult correctional systems are White-American compared to 23% African-American.[40]

These statistics support other societal factors that play additional roles in the over- and under-representation of minorities in the criminal justice system. These factors include employment opportunities and other economic conditions, educational opportunities, minority role models, and the portrayal of minorities in the media.

The war on drugs of the 1980s and 1990s has been the single most significant indicator that minorities are more likely than non-minorities to violate drug laws. In 1986, for example, the Drug Enforcement Agency (DEA) instituted a program entitled "Operation Pipe-

---

38 Cassia Spohn, John Gruhl and Susan Welsh (1987). "The Impact of the Ethnicity and Gender of Defendants on the Decision to Reject or Dismiss Felony Charges": *Criminology* 25: 175-91

39 Richey Mann, Coramae (1993) *Unequal Justice: A question of Color.* Bloomington Indiana University Press

40 Gilbert, David (2001) "Capitalism and Crisis: Creating a Jailhouse Nation"; *Monthly Review,* Vol. 52, No. 10

line". Under this program some 27,000 police officers across the country were trained to use "pre-textual" stops as a way to control drug trafficking.[41] The DEA also created a "Drug Courier Profile as part of the effort to control drug trafficking on a bigger scale. As the use of drug courier profiling spread, minorities began to feel a disproportionate impact. More and more African-Americans were stopped by DEA agents based on the profiling criteria. Needless to say, more and more allegations of racial profiling were brought to court. In one incident, for example an African-American Harvard Law School graduate and public defender for the District of Columbia was a passenger in a car that was pulled over by a Maryland police officer. The officer asked for permission to search the car, the driver refused, the officer ordered the occupants out of the car, had a drug dog sniff the car and issued a traffic ticket when the search yielded nothing. A lawsuit was filed, and as the case proceeded to court, it was discovered that a week prior to the incident, the Maryland State Police had issued a memo to its officers to be on the lookout for drug couriers who were "predominantly black males and black females."[42] The officer in this case was only doing his job.

It should be noted that as a result of this case, the Maryland police were required to keep statistics on the number of African-Americans stopped and searched. The results showed that although African-Americans constituted a small fraction of the driving population, they accounted for as much as 73% of all drivers stopped. Also of interest in this particular case is the fact that 37% of the officers involved as well as the commanding officer were African-Americans themselves. Notwithstanding the negative overtones of racial profiling, New Jersey Governor Christine Todd Whitman has admitted quite openly that the practice occurs in her state. [43]

In other relevant incidents, a New Jersey state trooper filed suit because he was required to implement a racial profile validated by his governor's admission.[44] In Reynoldsburg, Ohio, an African-American resident was awarded a settlement after he was arrested by a group of officers who called themselves the "Special Nigger Arrest Team".[45]

41  LaFree, Gray D. (1980). "The Effect of Sexual Stratification by Race on Official Reactions to Rape", *American Sociological Review*, Vol. 45: 842-854

42  Radelet, Michael (1981) "Racial Characteristics and the Imposition of the Death Penalty". *American Sociological Review* Vol. 46:918-27

43  Riley, K. J. Rodriguez, N, Ridgeway, G et al (2005) "Just Cause or Just Because? Prosecution and Arizona." Prepared for the Robert Woods Johnson Foundation SAPRP: Rand Corp. Santa Monica, CA:

44  Schmitt, Christopher (1991). "Plea Bargaining Favors Whites, as Blacks Hispanics Pay Price": *The San Jose Mercury News*, Dec. 8, 1991, at 1A ("Mercury News Report").

45  Patterson, E Britt &Michael J. Lynch (1991). "Biases in Formulized Bail Procedure" in Michael J Lynch and E. Britt Peterson(Eds.) *Race and Criminal Justice* (pp. 36-53) Albany,

There have also been incidents of "celebrity" traffic stops that have hit the news. LeVar Burton, Johnnie Chochran, Christopher Darden, Michael Eric Dyson, Will Smith, and Wesley Snipes have all complained about arbitrary stops based on the color of their skin.[46]

With respect to air travel, the "profile" in question is actually a laundry list of personal and situational characteristics that are sometimes contradictory but nonetheless have been highlighted as helpful in identifying potential drug smugglers. This "profile" includes but is not limited to being:

1. first off the plane,
2. last off the plane,
3. using a one-way ticket,
4. traveling alone,
5. acting too nervous,
6. acting too calm.[47]

Despite criticisms, profiling has had its share of success and the Supreme Court has even given its approval of profiling in general.[48] Bringing a law suit alleging profiling, racial or otherwise, is rarely successful. Not only are the legal requirements for success difficult to meet, but courts have held that police may in fact legally use race as part of the decision to detain a suspect[49] despite the fact that the generally-accepted principle is that only legal factors should determine police action and reaction in any given situation. One wonders, however, if it is possible that extralegal factors such as environmental and personal characteristics play a more important role, for example,

1. the officer's perception of social class (judged by dress, speech and general demeanor),
2. race, age, gender, physical size, and
3. whether the general demeanor of the detainee (verbal and non verbal) is aggressive, rude, or disrespectful.

These factors may determine how dangerous an officer believes the situation to be. With the exception perhaps of race, individually, each

New York: Harrow and Heston

46 Farnsworth, Margaret & Patrick Horan (1980) "Separate Justice: an Analysis of Race Differences in Court Processes": *Social Sciences Research* Vol. 9(4): 381-399

47 Albonetti, Celesta A., Robert M. Hauser, John Hagan, Ilene H. Nagel (1989). "Criminal Justice Decision Making as a Stratification Process: The Role of Race and Stratification Resources in Pretrial Release": *Journal of Quantitative Criminology* 5: 57-82

48 Albonetti, Celesta A (1989) "Bail and Judicial Discretion in the District of Columbia": *Sociology and Social Research* 74 (1): 40-45; C. E. Frazier, E. W. Bock and J. C, Herretta (1980) "Pretrial Release and Bail Decision": *Criminology* 18(2):162-81; John S. Goldkamp and Michael Gottfredson (1979): "Bail Decision Making and Pretrial Detention Surfacing Judicial Policy": *Law & Human Behavior* 3(4): 227-49; Ilene H. Nagel (1983) "The Legal/Extra-Legal Controversy: Judicial Decision in Pretrial release": *Law & Society Review* 17: 481-515

49 Syuker, R, Nagel and John Hagan(1983) "Methodology Issues and Court Research: Pretrial Release Decision for Federal Defendants": *Sociological Methods and Research* 11:469-500

of these factors may have little or no effect on an officer's decision-making process. However, any combination of these factors could influence the decision on how a given situation should be handled.

It is also important to understand that officers are human and their life experiences will undoubtedly have some impact (conscious or unconscious) on their decisions to take formal legal action. Research conducted about 40 years ago suggests that the manner in which an officer evaluates the degree of danger posed by any given situation is initially based on his personality (more aggressive versus less aggressive)[50], but more importantly, it is based on his experience (which by necessity will include his biases or prejudices).[51] More recent research indicates that younger officers tend to be more aggressive than older, more experienced officers.[52] When you combine these more aggressive, younger officers with younger, perhaps more disrespectful, suspects, you have all the ingredients for a very volatile interaction.

Nonetheless, race has been described as the most important individual factor in police citizen interactions.[53] It has been accused of being used as justification for perceptions of increased risk of danger and criminality.[54] For example, a young African-American male who avoids direct eye contact with an officer may be perceived as having something to hide. A young African-American male who stares unwaveringly at the office with distaste and aggression will be perceived as threatening. Both will attract negative responses albeit for different reasons. Over time, this type of response can even develop into an informal and sometimes formal stereotype.

Another issue of concern is the impact of drug enforcement policies on minorities and minority communities. Researchers argue that drug enforcement arrests are disproportionately concentrated in urban areas with large minority populations and, as such, the "War on Drugs" is really a war on minorities.[55] But why is this so? Are African-Americans and Hispanics simply more likely to use and traffic

50  Clarke, S. H & G. G. Koch (1976). "The Influence of income and Other factors on whether Criminal Defendants go to prison": *Law & Society Review* 11:57-92; Ronald A. Farrel and Victoria L. Swigert, (1978). "Prior Offense Record as a self-Fulfilling Prophecy", *Law & Review* 12:437-453

51  Marcus, R. (1994). "Racism in our courts: The Underfunding of Public Defenders and its Disproportionate Impact upon Racial Minorities", *Hastings Constitutional Law Quarterly*, 22 ; 219-268.

52  Unnever, J. D. (1994) "Direct and Organizational Discrimination in the Sentencing of Sentencing of Drugs Offenders", *Social Problems* 30; 212-25

53  Ah Sin v Whittman 198 U.S. 500 (1905).

54  Butler v Cooper, No. 75-49-N, 8 (E. D. Va. Aug. 13. 1975)

55  United States v Clary 846 F. Supp. 768, 786 n62(E. D. Mo) *rev'd*, 34 F.3d 709 (8th Cir. 1994)

drugs?[56] Or do more subtle reasons exist? Based on the numbers, there is no doubt that there is disparate handling of minorities compared to White-Americans throughout the process of arrest to incarceration. So one wonders if legislative policies that were implemented to control crime support instead economic, geographic and cultural biases. If these actions are deliberately geared to target one segment of the population, how do we restore a sense of legitimacy to our criminal justice system? All fingers point to the implementation of legislative policy as follows:

1. The use of double standards must itself become a punishable crime.
2. Police departments must become more representative of the communities they serve, and diversity training must become the norm.
3. Society must proactively seek alternative methods of dealing with crime, since incarceration does not seem to be the answer.
4. Policies must be put in place to get and keep the media from enflaming unreasonable and unfair perceptions of minorities. The media breathes fear into the population and this fear fuels sometimes unreasonable reaction in power hungry politicians.

In the final analysis, you must ask yourselves:

a. Is it the fear of crime rather than crime itself that shapes criminal justice policies (lobbying, media sensationalism)?

b. Do politicians capitalize on society's fears about crime (caused by the media) and use this fear to feed campaign strategy?

As a society we must also reevaluate our rationale for incarceration-punishment or rehabilitation. This would mean addressing the issue of private profiteering. The Prison–Industrial complex, for example, has become a lucrative business. As long as private corporations are allowed to profit from prison labor any effort to support an impartial criminal justice system will always be suspect. (See Part III– Corrections: Controversies.)

### RACIAL PROFILING

One of the issues of growing concern to policy makers is the increasing number of charges of racial and ethnic profiling that have

---

56 14th Amendment of the U.S. Constitution is available at U.S. Constitution online http:/ www. usconstitution. net/xconst_Am14. html

been brought against law enforcement. Racial profiling is defined as the behavior that results when legal authorities make decisions based on race.[57] This practice can occur in any and all areas of the criminal justice system, but has been applied most often to the behavior of law enforcement officers. In fact, there is anecdotal as well as legislative records to support a theory that racial profiling occurs across both social class and gender.[58]

According to a 1999 Gallop survey, for example, 59% of all adults polled felt that some law enforcement officers stopped motorists of certain races or ethnicities because the officers believed that members of these races and ethnicities were more likely than members of other races or ethnicities to commit certain types of crime.[59]

In essence, law enforcement officers have been accused of disproportionately and indiscriminately stopping and detaining individuals who they perceive as being more likely to be involved in criminal activity. Traffic stop statistics bills were even initiated by African-American legislators in North Carolina who claimed to have been victims of the practice themselves. This raises an important question. How can a police officer tell that someone has a greater likelihood of being involved in criminal activity simply by looking at them? There is, of course, the impact of the media. The media has been accused of perpetuating negative stereotypes of minorities with respect to their involvement in criminal activity. On the other hand, there are those who would argue that a negative perception in inevitable, given prior interaction between minorities and law enforcement.

Indeed, in accusations of profiling, research shows that the decision to stop and detain is usually based on non-legal factors such as:

1.   Driving in the wrong type of car.
2.   Driving in the wrong neighborhood.
3.   The race or ethnicity of the driver.[60]

But who determines what is the "wrong" car? Who decides what is the "wrong" neighborhood? Who decided that certain people should or should not drive certain types of cars or be found in certain neighborhoods? Following are examples of Traffic Stops studies that provide hard evidence that law enforcement officers target motorists based on race. The most notable of these studies were conducted in New Jersey and Florida.

---

57   Gideon v Wainwright (373 U.S. 335 (1963)

58   Ibid.

59   Worden, Alissa Pollitz (1993). "Counsel for the poor: An Evaluation of Contracting for Indigent Criminal Defense", *Justice Quarterly* 10(4):613-637

60   Johnson, S. L. (1998). "Responsibility, Race Neutrality and Truth Reviewed work(s):Race, Crime and the Law by Randall Kennedy": *The Yale Law Journal*, Vol. 107, No. 8( Jun., 1998), pp2619-2659

## TRAFFIC STOPS

### New Jersey

The New Jersey study fondly referred to as "the Turnpike violation census" was in effect a statistical analysis of the racial distribution of traffic stops. Its purpose was to evaluate the rate at which African-Americans were stopped compared to the rate at which White-Americans were stopped on the same stretch of road. Teams of observers in cars merged into the traffic with cruise control set at 5 miles above the speed limit. The teams observed the frequency of violations by race and compared it to the race of the violators pulled over. They observed the following:

1. There was no difference in the rate of violations between races.
2. 13.5% of the cars on the road had an African-American driver or passenger.
3. 73.2% of the drivers stopped and arrested were African-American or had an African-American passenger.[61]

### Florida

In 1992, the Orlando Sentinel conducted a study of a drug interdiction program along a stretch of the Interstate 95 corridor in Florida. Video cameras were attached to the vehicles of some of the law enforcement officers involved in traffic-related stops. The information gathered from the video cameras was as follows:

1. Of the 1084 vehicles targeted, 5% of the drivers were African-American.
2. Almost 70% of the drivers actually stopped were African-American.[62]

It is noteworthy that this particular study was later challenged based on the argument that the results actually showed that stops based on racial profiling were actually less likely to occur than stops based on valid traffic violations, e.g., of 1,084 vehicles targeted, only 155, or approximately 15%, were actually for speeding. Most of the stops were for a variety of other offenses such as following too closely (237, or approximately 22%); swerving (253, or approximately 23%); burned-out license tag illumination bulbs (71, or approximately 7%); improper license tags (46, or approximately 4%); failure to signal lane change or unsafe lane change (67, or approximately 6%); and miscel-

---

61 Batson v Kentucky, 476 US 79, 89, 106 S. Ct. 1712, 1719, 90 L. Ed. 2d 69(1986).
62 Moore, Charles and Miethe, Terence (1986) "Regulated and non-regulated sentencing practices under the Minnesota felony sentencing guidelines." *Law and Society Review* 20: 253-65

laneous other traffic violations (255, or 23%). In other words, most of the stops were within the officer's reasonable discretion and speeding stops were less than 1/7 of all of the stops.[63]

Even so, the implications were so startling that Connecticut, Missouri, Texas and North Carolina all implemented programs which required law enforcement agencies to collect racial data during traffic stops. These programs required officers to complete fact sheets for any officer-initiated motor vehicle or pedestrian stops regardless of the outcome of the stop. In the case of Houston, fewer citations were written.[64]

If these numbers do, indeed, present a true picture, then it raises the question of whether minority drivers are indeed targeted because of a perception among law enforcement officers that minority drivers, specifically young African-American and Hispanic males, are more likely to be transporting drugs and carrying unregistered weapons, and if they are targeted, then why? (See Media discussion in Chapter 3).

Additionally, if law enforcement personnel are more likely to stop, question, search and arrest young minority males, wouldn't it stand to reason that official crime statistics such as the Uniform Crime Report and National Incident-Based Reporting System, both of which are based on arrest data, would show a disproportionate representation of minorities? According to the National Crime Victims Survey (NCVS), for example, African-American males are significantly more likely to be arrested for drug offenses and violent crimes.[65]

But what if these perceptions are wrong? What if the perception drives the number of arrests, which drives the perception and ultimate actions of law enforcement? One survey indicated that of 1,263,141 drivers stopped and searched, 16.6% of the White-American drivers, 9.4% of Hispanic drivers and 7.1% of African-American drivers were reported to have some contraband item.[66]

What these numbers indicate is that White-Americans are more likely to transport contraband items than minorities but are less likely to be stopped by the police. Yet law enforcement continues to disproportionately target minorities.

63  Mustard, David (2001). "Racial Ethnic and gender disparities in sentencing: Evidence from the U.S. Federal courts." *Journal of Law and Economics* 44:285-314

64  Bridges, George S. and Steen Sara, (1998) "Racial disparities in official assessment of Juvenile offenders: Attributional stereotypes as mediating mechanisms." *American Sociological Review* 63(4):554-571

65  Steffensmeier, Darrell, Jeffery T. Ulmer, and John Kramer (1998). "The interaction of race, gender and age in sentencing : The Punishment cost of being young, black and male": *Criminology* 36(4):763-798

66  Ibid.

Another survey revealed the following:

1. 11.2% of African-Americans compared to 8.9% of White-Americans are more likely to be pulled over while driving.[67]
2. 80% of Hispanic drivers, 76% of African-American drivers, and 66.6% of White-Americans stopped for speeding were likely to be ticketed.[68]
3. 16% of African-American male drivers, 12.2% of Hispanic male drivers and 7.9% of White-American male drivers were likely to have their vehicles searched in a traffic stop.[69]

To their credit, some states are implementing corrective policies in response to these apparent negative and unethical trends. California, for example, has approved legislation requiring all officers to participate in mandatory cultural diversity training. In keeping with this new approach, in December 2000 the city of Anaheim, California agreed to pay $50,000 to a Korean-American citizen who claimed to have been racially profiled by officers. According to Young Ho Choi, he was taken into custody at gun point after he was identified by eye-witnesses as the individual who had been detained by an officer who was subsequently gunned down.[70] Although he was eventually released, Choi was wrongfully detained for two days on suspicion of killing a California highway patrol officer.

On a more general level, the behavior of law enforcement personnel has also come under a growing amount of scrutiny within recent years. From the cases of Rodney King in Los Angeles[71] to Randy Weaver at Ruby Ridge and the Branch Davidians at Waco, Texas[72], to Mark Fuhrman's tainted testimony in the O.J. Simpson trial,[73] and the planting of evidence in Philadelphia,[74] mistrust of law enforcement has hit record levels. Unfortunately, each new headline affects the police/community relationship and ultimately affects the reputation of the many ethical, hardworking law enforcement professionals.

---

67  Johnson, E. H (1957). "Selective Factors in Capital Punishment", *Social Forces* 58: 168-69

68  Lemert, E. M. and J. Rosberg, (1948). "The Administration of Justice to Minority Groups in L. A. County", University of California Publications in *Culture and Society*:1-27; Thorsten Sellin (1935). "Race Prejudice in the Administration of Justice"; *American Journal of Sociology* 41:212-17

69  Kramer, John, H. & Jeffrey T. Ulmer(2000) "Report prepared for the Pennsylvania Supreme Court Committee on Race and Gender Bias"; Appendix Vol. 1

70  Halliday, S. (2000). "Institutional Racism in Bureaucratic Decision-Making : A Case Study in the Administration of Homelessness Law." *Journal of Law and Society*, Vol. 27, No. 3. (Sept., 2000), pp 449-471

71  Ibid.

72  Ibid.

73  Petersilia, Joan (1983) *Racial Disparities in the Criminal Justice System*. Santa Monica Calif. : Rand

74  Klein, Stephen, Joan, Petersilia & Susan, Turner (1990). "Race and Imprisonment Decision in California", *Science* 247: 812-16

Notwithstanding the thousands of law-abiding law enforcement professionals that do exist, thousands of allegations of police abuse and police brutality continue surface every year. According to the Human Rights Watch, over 12,000 civil rights complaints against police officers were filed with the U.S. Department of Justice in 1999 alone.[75] Despite these numbers, only 31 officers have been convicted of crimes under civil rights statutes and there is no real evidence of accountability (perhaps because no local or federal prosecutor wants to challenge law enforcement) but the issue does not end here.[76] In 2003, approximately 75% of all substantiated allegations of police misconduct in New York City were made by people of color.[77] African-Americans (who constitute 24.5% of the New York City population) accounted for 52.6% of the substantiated allegations of police misconduct and 64.9% of the suspected officers were White-American.[78] Unfortunately, policy changes are limited because many states view the implementation of these policies as an admission of guilt with respect to agency support of practices such as racial profiling. The argument could be made that as long as the officer operates within certain parameters, the system seems to give the officer the benefit of the doubt which, in effect, can be perceived as a sign of encouragement.

But these are just numbers. It is possible that these numbers are just coincidental and are not necessarily an indication of contextual discrimination. On the other hand, it is also possible that this is exactly what the problem is. You decide.

### Minority Victims

The American criminal justice system has also been accused of focusing on minority offenders to the almost total exclusion of minority victims. Homicide victimization rates for African-Americans, for example, have been at least five times those of White-Americans for the last 50 years, sometimes reaching more than ten times the rate of White-Americans.[79] In 2009, non-Hispanic whites and Asians had the lowest homicide victimization rates (3.5 and 4.6 per 100,000 resident population), followed by American Indians (9.8), Hispanics (12.4), and Blacks (29.8). Males are almost four times more likely than females to be victims of homicide. Males aged 15 to 24 (not shown in

---

75  Zatz, Marjorie S. (1984) "Race, Ethnicity and Determinates Sentences: A new Dimension to an old Controversy"; *Criminology* 22: 147-71

76  Albonetti, Celesta (1991). "An integration of theories to explain judicial discretion." *Social Problems* 38(2):247-266

77  Supra at 78

78  Ibid.

79  Ibid.

chart) have the highest homicide victimization rate, and the differences across racial and ethnic groups are even larger for this group: Blacks have by far the highest rate (123.1 per 100,000 population), followed by Hispanics (48.9), American Indians (26.6), Asians (15.6), and non-Hispanic whites (6.4).

It is important to note that the likelihood of victimization varies by neighborhood and lifestyle, for example, the routine activities of residents in these neighborhoods, the severity of social disorganization within these neighborhoods and the degree to which negative subcultures are entrenched within these neighborhoods. Additionally, minorities disproportionately reside in higher crime areas due to residential segregation which increase their risk of victimization as well as their rates of involvement in serious crimes.[80] More importantly, there is the phenomenon of victim-offender overlap in which most offenders are often victims themselves. [81]

+++

MENTAL ILLNESS, RACE AND CRIMINAL JUSTICE: A TALE OF TWO STANDARDS

by Dr. Carlene Smith

In a recent (2007) high profile celebrity case, hotel heiress Paris Hilton was sentenced to serve 45 days in a county prison for violating the terms her probation. She had been originally sentenced in an alcohol related reckless driving case. After serving a few days in jail Ms. Hilton was released and sent to serve the remainder of her reduced 25 day sentence at home under house arrest. The Los Angeles County sheriff indicated that the release was prompted in part because of concern regarding Ms Hilton's emotional deterioration over a three day period (Cohen, 2007). Hilton was then ordered back to jail after a judge overruled a sheriff's decision to place her under house arrest.

Contrast the Hilton case with another high profile case from Georgia reported by the Associated Press. At 17, Genarlow Wilson was convicted of having consensual sex with a 15-year-old. He received a 10 year prison sentence. Although he was ordered to be released from jail in June 2007, after serving 24 months, the state Attorney General plans to appeal the decision. He is to be kept in jail until the matter is resolved.

Blacks are seven times more likely to serve time in prison than Caucasians (Beck AJ, Gillard DK, 1995). According to Myer, L. (2006), the Bureau of Justice Statistics reports that at least 16 percent of adult U.S. prisoners are "mentally ill". Also at least 20 percent of children

---

80  Cassia, Sophn, John Gruhl and Susan Welch (1981-82). "The Effects of Race on Sentencing : A re-examination of an Unsettled Question", *Law & Society* 16:71-88
81  Ibid.

within the juvenile justice system have serious mental health problems". In Stephanie Hartwell's (2001) review of the literature she reported that although the Black population is 12 percent of the national total, they make up 50 percent of the incarcerated population. Thus it would intuitively seem that a large proportion of the incarcerated Black population would be suffering from emotional distress.

Hartwell's study from a pool of 169 inmates of diverse ethnic backgrounds found that the Caucasian participants were more likely to have affective disorders and to report a history of substance use problems. Black and Hispanic participants were more likely to have thought disorders. According to Hartwell, people of color are overrepresented in the correctional system, yet the offender population identified as mentally ill is disproportionately Caucasian." Some effort should be made to explore whether mental illness in persons from minority groups is underidentified in prison and whether the referral process for mental health services is culturally biased (Hartwell S., Orr K., 1999). Given that Blacks do not have a greater disposition to mental illness in the general community, the trends found in Hartwell's study are troubling.

However in the context of healthcare disparities Hartwell's findings are not surprising. A June 2007 study published in the Journal of American Medical Association found that Black patients were less likely to receive specialized life extending procedures such as angioplasty and open heart surgery than their white counterparts. This was a large study in which 1.2 million Medicare recipients who were at least 68 years old were tracked after being treated for a heart attack. Patient data came from 4,627 hospitals. Best practices for patient care following a heart attack are well known and not subjective, yet "the study found large differences in the way heart attacks are treated in black patients compared with white patients."

In jails across the country individuals suffering from mental illness languish in prison. Incarceration is difficult for the emotionally healthy. It is meant to be difficult. However punishment and the redemptive aspects of rehabilitation may be lost on the mentally ill depending on their individual condition. Unbiased detection and mental health treatment needs to be insured for all prisoners.

## References

1. Cohen, W. (2007): Paris Hilton Back in L.A. Women's Jail, June 14, 2007 for Associated Press, http://hosted.ap.org/dynamic/stories/P/ PARIS_HILTON

2. Tonry M: Malign Neglect: Race, Crime, and Punishment in America. New York, Oxford University Press, 1995

3. Beck AJ, Gillard DK (eds): Prisoners in 1994. Washington, DC, Bulletin of the Bureau of Justice Statistics, 1995

4. Kessler RC, McGonagle KA, Zhoa S, et al: "Lifetime and 12-month prevalence of DSM-III-R psychiatric disorders in the United States." Archives of General Psychiatry 51:8-19, 1994

5. Hartwell, S.: "Psychiatric Services" 52: 234-236, February 2001, American Psychiatric Association.

6. Hartwell SW, Orr K: "Models of care: Massachusetts' forensic transition program." *Psychiatric Services* 50:1220-1222, 1999

7. McCaffrey, S. (2007) for Associated Press: Judge Voids Sentence in Teen Sex Case Georgia Youth Convicted After Consensual Oral Sex.

8. Myer, L. (2006) in APA Monitor, vol. 37, $ 5 Million Will Fund Offender Treatment http://www.apa.org/monitor/feb06/treatment.html

Carlene Romans Smith, Ph.D. is a clinical psychologist and consultant. She has designed and taught numerous seminars and workshops over the past t-wenty years. Topics have included Officer Involved Shooting, Communication Skills, Stress Management, and Conflict Resolution. In clinical practice she has worked with victims and perpetrators of crime.

Dr. Smith has been interviewed by the media on issues such as sexual harassment, professional ethics (a television newscast interview regarding the O. J. Simpson trial) and family teamwork. In its February, 1996 issue *Essence* magazine published an article featuring Dr. Smith's views about family teamwork.

Dr. Smith is a clinical psychologist who graduated from Cornell University (B.A.), Roosevelt University (M.A.) and City University of New York (Ph.D.). Dr. Smith interned at Columbia-Presbyterian Medical Center in New York. She is a former associate professor of psychology at Livingstone College in NC. She has also taught courses at the graduate and undergraduate level at City University of New York, San Diego State University, National University, and California State University, San Marcos. Dr. Smith Is currently a supervising psychologist in the internship program at California State University, San Marcos.

+++

ECONOMIC INEQUALITY

As we evaluate the many variables that could impact the likelihood of criminal involvement, we cannot ignore the importance of economics (i.e., the haves vs. the have nots). In 2009, for example more than half of all state prisoners reported an annual income of less than $10,000 prior to their arrest.[82] In 2009, while roughly 75% of all U.S. men of working age were employed full-time, only 55% of state prison inmates were working full-time at the time of their arrest.[83] Not only can those who can afford bail aid in their own investigation and present a stronger case but, more importantly, those with higher incomes can also afford better attorneys, expert witnesses and private detectives and are therefore less likely to be found guilty especially if they are innocent and be wrongfully accused.[84]

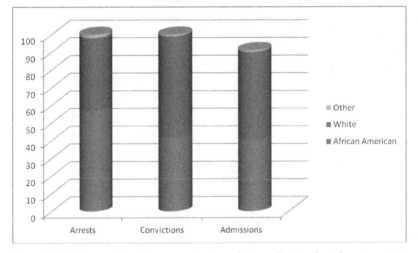

*Figure 2.1 Racial Composition of arrests, convictions and prison admission for violent crimes, 2009*
*Source: Bureau of Justice Statistics available at http://bjs.ojp.usdoj.gov/content/pub/pdf/p05.pdf*

This is particularly apparent in figure 2-1 which presents an overview of the racial composition of arrests, convictions, and prison admissions for violent crimes in 1994, including murder, rape, robbery, and aggravated assault (African-Americans: 43% % of arrests, 54% of convictions, and 59% of prison admissions compared with White-Americans). According to these numbers, African-American are more likely than White-Americans, to be convicted if arrested and are more likely to be imprisoned if convicted. The question continues to be

82  Kramer, John H. and Ulmer, Jeffery T. (1996) "Sentencing disparity and departure from guidelines." *Justice Quarterly* 13:401-425

83  Ibid.

84  U.S. Department of Justice (DOJ), Federal Bureau of investigation. Crime in the U.S. (2004) Washington DC: Government Printing office, 2003, pp252-9

raised as to whether this phenomenon is the result of discriminatory behavior on the part of law enforcement or whether minorities simply commit more crime.

In 1998, the Higher Education Act was amended to deny federal financial aid for post-secondary education to anyone with a drug conviction (i.e., not only drug traffickers but also drug addicts).[85] As such, a student who has been convicted of any offense under any federal or state law involving the possession or sale of a controlled substance is not eligible to receive any grant, loan or work assistance if the money will be used to attend college. To date approximately 100,000 students have been denied access to financial aid because of this provision.[86] It is important to note that individuals convicted of non-drug related offenses, such as murder or rape, retain eligibility under this law.[87]

Not only are individuals convicted of drug related offenses denied Federal Aid but the negative stigma of a criminal conviction often makes it impossible for ex-offenders to obtain jobs—criminal records are easily available to potential employers, landlords, and other community members.[88] Additionally, federal and state statutes prohibit ex-offenders from being employed in certain fields and from obtaining licenses for several occupations. In some states, for example, former prisoners are barred from the auto body repair, nursing, and real estate fields whether or not their prior conviction was related to these occupations.[89] In essence the penalty of imprisonment extends far beyond the prison walls.

Another important consideration is housing. Individuals convicted of a felony drug charge or individuals who are in a drug treatment program and are found using illegal drugs can be denied public housing admission.[90] Entire families can be evicted under the terms of the federal "One-Strike" eviction policy if only one family member engages in illegal conduct. The federal "One-Strike" policy also allows

85  U.S. Department of Justice (DOJ), Federal Bureau of investigation. Crime in the U.S. (2002) Washington DC: Government Printing office, 2003, pp252-9

86  U.S. Department of Justice (No Date). Homicide Trends in the U.S. Washington DC: Authur. Available at www. ojp. usdoj. gov/bjs/homicide/tables/totalstab. htm. Accessed on May 23, 2010

87  U.S. Census Bureau, Population Division. U.S. and World Population Clocks-POP Clocks available at http:/www. census. gov/main/www/popclock. html

88  Beckett, Katherine & Theodore Sasson (2004) *The Politics of Injustice: Crime and Punishment in America*. Thousand Oaks, California: Sage Publications.

89  Bureau of Justice Statistics, Sourcebook Criminal Justice Statistics (2005)(Pub NCJ) 215091) Washington DC: BJS, 2005 Table 6. 1 Available at www. albany. edu/sourcebook.

90  Federal Bureau of Investigation, "Uniform Crime Reports: Crime in the United States, 2003" (Washington, D. C: US. Government Printing Office, 2004)

public housing agencies or Section 8 landlords to evict a tenant, any guest or "other person under the tenant's control" who is involved in "drug-related criminal activity" on or off public housing premises.[91] Additionally, in some states a criminal record is used as leverage to deny parental rights. Prior convictions may also be used to deny former prisoners from becoming foster or adoptive parents, regardless of whether or not the crime is relevant to parenting abilities.

When prisoners are released, they are expected to rejoin society. However, prisoners and their families face sometimes insurmountable economic and social obstacles after leaving prison. These barriers seek to extend the punishment by limiting or denying ex-offenders access to social services and by making their transition back to life on the outside far from easy. This has become increasingly important because of legislative action— welfare reform and the War on Drugs—which seem to be particularly harmful to people who are convicted of drug felonies or who have histories of drug use. Not surprisingly, these policies disproportionately affect poor people of color. These "collateral consequences" seem to be more detrimental than imprisonment itself.

+++

## THE PSYCHOLOGY OF RACISM AND THE CRIMINAL JUSTICE SYSTEM
Dr. DeReef F. Jamison

The concept of racism should not be confused with prejudice. While both concepts are related, there are differences in how they are conceptualized and manifested in social reality. Jones (1997) defines prejudice as "a positive or negative attitude, judgment, or feeling about a person that is generalized from attitudes or beliefs held about the group to which the person belongs (p. 10). This definition includes the sub-concepts of stereotypes and discrimination. To some extent there is a kernel of truth in every stereotype, however, the overgeneralization of these beliefs and the behaviors associated with these beliefs culminate in racism. The three types of racism are identified as: (1) individual racism which can be defined as a prejudice or a preconceived belief in the superiority of one's own race/group; (2) institutional racism, which is the institutional extension of individual racist beliefs that are used to maintain a racist advantage over others as well as the restriction of choices, rights, mobility, and access of groups of individuals and (3) cultural racism which can be defined as the individual and institutional expression of the superiority of one race's cultural heritage over that of another race (Jones, 1997, pp. 13-14).

The psychology of racism and oppression with a primary empha-

---

91  Ibid.

sis on institutional racism addresses several practical implications of psychological research relative to people of African descent. The implementation of theories that address racism and oppression requires an understanding that there are economic counterparts to the maladjustments in the Africana personality. Which is to say that African-American cultural perceptions of self identity not only influence abstract notions of self-esteem, but indirectly impact the economic decisions that determine their quality of life, and ultimately their life chances. Hence, a critique of racism without an analysis of the political economy of racism is null and void. Harrell (1999) argues that stress accumulated from racism, prejudice and oppression contribute to a unique understanding of problems associated with African-American experiences that might not be considered by Euro-American psychology. The research on the psychology of oppression by Sears (1995) supported the notion that the psychology of racism and oppression and its practices, while not limited to people of African descent, had manifestations that were of particular significance to people of African descent in the area of social policy. Crucial in these findings were: (1) that opposition to social policies that support African-Americans can be better explained by anti-black sentiment than by adherence to other politically relevant beliefs; (2) that anti-black symbolic scores for whites are correlated with whites' degree of support of the idea that policeman make streets safe, the support of the death penalty and, support to oppose welfare spending and of assistance to the poor and (3) anti-black symbolic racism predicted whites' opposition to group based quotas. Thus, it is imperative to consider how the political psychology of racism, prejudice and oppression impacts the quality of life experienced by people of African descent. Anti-black sentiments are not new phenomena; in fact, white resentment of African-American success can be traced to Reconstruction and Jim Crow era politics.

Historical Background

It is impossible to fully understand the intricate and intimate relationship between racism and the justice system, unless we situate the relationship within an historical context. In Who Needs the Negro (1993), Sydney Wilhelm raises a poignant and pertinent question, "Why were Negroes brought to this country?" The answer is simple yet profound and complex. A cursory glance at historical records pertaining to the transatlantic dispersion of Africans confirms that people of African descent were brought to the "New World" to serve as a cheap labor force. Thus, the simple answer is that Africans were brought to the Americas to work. During slavery, Africans functioned in this enslaved capacity for over two hundred years and served as the foundation for a burgeoning free-market society and capitalist accumulation of wealth. In making a distinction between slavery in the ancient world and slavery in the Americas, Du Bois argued that although there have been many examples of humans' inhumanity against humans through slavery, only the African has been considered chattel/property. The distinguishing characteristic of humans as property during slavery in the Western hemisphere is inextricably linked to the profit-oriented aspect of slavery in the Americas. The economic need and want to gain profit from a product that is produced from what is considered to be property has its origin and essence in the economic system of chattel slavery. When viewed within a historical perspective, it can be argued that the contemporary prison industrial complex is a continuation of a slave system that fulfilled the psychological and economic imperatives of a profit-oriented society.

As long as the legal institution of slavery was in full effect, the racial and social hierarchy that supported and reinforced the cultural logic of white supremacy remained in tact. However, once dejure slavery came to an end, the situation changed drastically. This cataclysmic change was an assault on the psyche of those people who had bought into the concept of white privilege since it challenged the psychological and economic underpinnings of the master/slave dialectic. The master/slave relationship was based on Manichean thinking that emphasized White superiority and Black inferiority. Without the psychological and economic safety net of slavery, new mechanisms and means of maintaining and perpetuating the prevailing racial and social hierarchy would have to be implemented. Lynching, Black codes, and the convict lease system are all examples of a collective consciousness amongst the majority population that sought to protect and preserve the status quo.

The lynching of African-Americans was a primary means of social and economic control. Between the years 1889-1932, 3,745 people were lynched. A large proportion of these victims were males of African decent accused of raping white women when in reality they were not actually involved in the crime. Why do we find more documented acts of violence committed against African-Americans after slavery was officially over than during enslavement? Is not slavery the quintessential manifestation of humans dehumanizing humans? Perhaps, it is because there was more empirical data being collected during this time period since African-Americans were now legally free. Another argument is that that there was more violence directed toward African-Americans because the violence was an attempt to protect the economic, political and psychological vulnerabilities of particular classes of white males who felt that their investment in white privilege was threatened by the possibilities and potential of the newly emancipated African-Americans.

Segregated Justice

If the answer to Wilhelm's original question is that African-Americans were brought to the Americas to work during slavery, then the question now becomes are African-Americans still needed after slavery? Within a capitalist system that thrives on production and consumption, the answer is emphatically yes! As long as a significant segment of the African-American population remains an easily accessible workforce that can be co-modified and as long their labor is needed for profit, then the African-American is needed. The role and function of African-Americans who fulfilled this role was not only needed but desired.

Several parallel historical trends surface when comparing and contrasting the segregated justice of the Reconstruction and Jim Crow eras and the dynamics of the contemporary prison industrial complex. Black Codes attempted to circumnavigate the new emancipatory laws and create a late 19th century new world order that incorporated the rules and regulations of the old slavery regime. The Black codes were essentially a sophisticated form of slavery. Black codes consisted of: (1) requiring that people of African descent carry passes, (2) forbidding interracial marriages, (3) forbidding contracts and licences, (4) forbidding vagrancy/loitering and (5) requiring literacy tests. Sharecropping mandated that newly emancipated Africans work the land in exchange for food, clothing, and shelter. These labor contracts constituted another form of slavery that essentially cheated these newly emancipated Africans out of vital means of acquiring financial means and advancing in society.

Even when the horrors of Black codes and sharecropping are taken into consideration, it is the conflict lease system that exemplifies the degree of exploitation that took place during this time. Darlene Clarke–Hines identifies the following as major characteristics of the convict lease system:

1. Black prisoners——many incarcerated for vagrancy, theft, disorderly conduct, and other misdemeanors ——spent many months and years in oppressive conditions and were subjected to the unrelenting abuse of white authorities.

2. Convicts were released from the state to build railroads, clear swamps, cut timber, tend cotton, and work mines without pay. Some states found this so remunerative that law enforcement officials were encouraged to charge even more black men with assorted crimes so they could contribute to this lucrative enterprise.

3. They sustained terrible injuries on the job and at the hands of guards; diseases proliferated in the camps. Hundreds died, meaning they had, in effect been sentenced to death for their petty crimes.

4. Businessmen and planters found such cheap labor almost irresistible...It was worse than slavery because these black lives had no value to either the government or the businesses involved in the sordid system.

Hines states that, "Black people received longer sentences and larger fines than white people. In Georgia, black convicts served much longer sentences for the same offense—five times as long as for larceny....Three days for stealing and eighty-seven days for being colored (Hines, 2000, p. 329)

The contemporary prison industrial complex almost mirrors what occurred during the reconstruction and Jim Crow eras. There are many similarities between the convict lease system and the prison industrial complex. According to Palaez (2005), there are several factors that increase the profit potential for those who invest in the prisons. These factors include: (1) jailing persons convicted of non-violent crimes, (2) long prison sentences for possession of microscopic quantities of illegal drugs, (3) the passage of laws that require minimum sentencing without regard for circumstances, (4) a large expansion of work by prisoners creating profits that motivates the incarceration of more people for longer periods of time, and (5) more punishment of prisoners that lengthens their sentences.

The similarities between the old and contemporary systems of containment and incarceration are striking. From slavery to freedom, the historical record suggests that there has been very little change in how Black bodies have been perceived and valued. The disproportionate number of African-Americans in the criminal justice system is a prime example of how institutional racism continues to permeate the institutions that control our society. During slavery, it was clear that the value of the Black body was in its ability to work and produce a product. However, after slavery people of African descent envisioned themselves as citizens as opposed to an unpaid labor force. As citizens, African-Americans thought they were entitled to a better quality of life. The second class-citizenship that greeted them proved to the contrary.

Slavery was replaced with Black Codes, sharecropping and a convict lease system that maintained and perpetuated the same Manichean structure that took place during enslavement. The unfair sentences for petty crimes, the profit made from the labor of Black prisoners, and being worked and/or sentenced to death for being Black continued. The Black labor that resulted in white wealth without benefiting the worker relationship that was established during slavery was not abolished but only reinforced by more sophisticated systems of exploitation that continued to benefit the ruling class. Thus, what we witness in the contemporary prison industrial complex is not entirely new phenomena, but a continuation and reconstruction of racial, ethnic and class dynamics with origins that are deeply embedded in the peculiar institution of slavery.

## REFERENCES

1. Harrell, J. (1999). *Manichean psychology*. Washington D.C.: Howard University Press.

2. Hine, D.C., Hine, W.C., & Harrold, S.C. (2000). *The African-American Odyssey*. Vol. 2. New Jersey: Prentice Hall.

3. Jones, J. M. (1997). *Prejudice and racism*. 2nd Edition. New York: McGraw-Hill.

4. Palaez, V. (2005). The US Prison Industry: Big business or slavery. *Infowars.com* [On-line serial].

5. Sears. D. O. (1988). "Symbolic Racism." In P.A. Katz and D.A. Taylor (Eds.), *Eliminating Racism: Profiles in controversy* (pp. 53-84). New York: Plenum

Wilhelm, S. (1993). *Who Needs the Negro*. Chicago: Third World Press.

**Dr. DeReef F. Jamison**
Assistant Professor and Coordinator of Africana Studies
Savannah State University

I received my Ph.D. in African-American Studies from Temple University. During my teaching career, I have taught classes such as: (1) Introduction to African-American History and Culture (2) Africa, African-Americans and Pan Africanism, (3) The Psychology of the African-American Experience (4) The Psychology of Prejudice and Racism in the African Diaspora and (5) African-American Health Perspectives. My research interests are African-American cultural and gender identity, community activism among Black psychologists, the psychological aspects of oppression and liberation, and the intellectual history and diasporic connections of Africana Psychology. In conducting my research, I have followed the theme of investigating the cultural and psychological experiences of people of African descent throughout the diaspora as it relates to issues of identity, gender and popular culture. My articles have been published in *The Journal of African-American Studies, The Griot, The Journal of Pan African Studies* and the *Journal of Social and Behavioral Science*. I am a firm believer in the Du Boisian adage that education is not just about obtaining a job, but about facilitating the process of creating complete human beings. Thus, in the spirit of those pioneering scholars at HBCUs such as Sterling Brown, E. Franklin Frazier, Rayford A. Logan and Alain Locke, I seek to contribute to the intergenerational transmission of knowledge and wisdom.

+++

## DISPROPORTIONATE MINORITY OVERREPRESENTATION (DMO)

There is no disagreement that minorities are overrepresented in the criminal justice system. The differences of opinion arise in the determination of why minorities are overrepresented in the Criminal Justice system. A frequent explanation of the overrepresentation of racial minorities is that minorities commit more offenses and/or more serious offenses than the majority and thus their representation in the criminal justice system reflects this differential offending pattern.[92]

While there may be social, economic, and environmental factors that impact the rates at which minorities interact with some aspect of the American Criminal Justice System, it is clear from many of the DMO studies conducted that when the seriousness of offense and length of the previous record are controlled, minorities are more likely to be detained prior to a hearing and more likely to be placed in a State correctional institution at disposition than non minorities.[93]

Another explanation is that the policies, procedures, and practices within the criminal justice system are created especially to lead to differential treatment of minority versus majority offenders. The sources of this disparity are varied and focus on law enforcement's emphasis on certain communities, legislative policies and the decision-making practices of criminal justice practitioners who are able to exercise broad discretion in the justice process.[94]

Whether or not minorities actually commit more crime, is it arguable that they are still victims of social, economic and environmental policies? Is the racial disparity in drug possession arrests the result of law enforcement's focus on crack users as opposed to powder cocaine, meth and designer drug users? And is this focus in any way related to the racial and ethnic composition of those who use the specific drugs? Is this the direct cause of the overrepresentation of minorities in the CJ system? Let's see what the numbers show.

There is a considerable range in the rates of incarceration among the various U.S. states.

1.  Minnesota has the lowest rate, 121 prisoners per 100,000 residents
2.  Louisiana the highest, with a rate of 763 per 100,000

---

92  Prison Activist Resource Centre (No date). Racism Fact Sheets : "Latinos and the Criminal injustice system" Available at http://www. prisonactivist. org/archive/factsheets/racism. pdf

93  Blumstein, Alfred (1993) Racial Disproportionally of U.S. Prison Revisited University of Colorado Law Review, 64, pp. 743-760.

94  The Sentencing Project (2008). "Fact about prisons and Prisoners." Washington DC: Bureau of Justice Statistic available at www. sentencingproject. org/publicationDetails. aspx?publicationID=425

3.  The District of Columbia, an entirely urban jurisdiction, has a rate of 1,600 per 100,000.[95]

Almost every state has a prison incarceration rate that greatly exceeds those of other Western democracies, in which between 35 and 145 residents per 100,000 are behind bars on any given day.[96] In 1923, for example, White-Americans constituted 90% of the population and 67% of those incarcerated in prisons and jails.[97] African-Americans constituted 9% of the population and 31% of the correctional population.[98] Today, African-Americans are incarcerated at over 6 times the rate of White-Americans.[99] White-Americans are incarcerated at a rate of 289 per 100,000 and African-Americans are incarcerated at the rate of 1,860 per 100,000.[100] Just about half of the state and federal prison population is African-American in contrast to their 13% share of the national population.[101]

Native Americans are also disproportionately imprisoned compared to their population size. In Montana, for example, 16% of prisoners are Native Americans even though they constitute just 6% of the state's population. In North Dakota, Native Americans are 5% of the state's total population, but are 19% of the prison population.[102] In 1953 Congress passed Public Law (P.L.) 280, which offered states the opportunity to assume jurisdiction over reservations within the state borders. P.L 280 was passed without any tribal consent. In P.L. 280 law enforcement for Native reservations is typically handled by state policy and county or state courts.[103] Public Law 280 has denied Native Americans the right to control their own law enforcement processes and this has resulted in what appears to be discriminatory sentencing.

In 1923, only 17% of those committed for prohibition violations were African-American, compared to 55% White-Americans and 23% foreign-born whites.[104] More importantly, only 20% of those convicted for drug law violations were African-American, compared to 55% White-

---

95  Ibid.

96  Ibid.

97  U.S. Department of Justice. Office of Programs, Bureau of Justice Statistics (2003) Prison Statistics: Summary findings. Available at http:/www. ojp. usdoj. gov/bjs/prisons. htm

98  U.S. Bureau of Justice Statistics (1987b). "Jail Inmates 1986." Bureau of Justice Statistics Bulletin No. NCJ-107123. Washington, DC. U.S. Government Printing Office.

99  Welch Ronald & Carlos Angulo (2000) *Justice on Trial: Racial Disparities in the American Criminal Justice System.* Washington DC: Leadership Conference on Civil Rights

100  Ibid.

101  Toward Freedom online Magazine (2001). Behind Bard; Native Incarceration rates increase. Available at http://www. towardfreedom. com/2001/aug01/nativeprison. htm

102  Ibid.

103  Political Research Associates (2005) How is the Criminal Justice System Racist?. http:// www.defendingjustice.org/pdfs/factsheets/10-Fact%20Sheet%20-%20System%20as%20 Racist.pdf

104  Ibid.

Americans and 14% foreign-born whites.[105] Not only did African-Americans play a relatively small role in drug and Prohibition incarcerations, but the incarcerations had a relatively small impact on African-American communities. Just 2% of African-Americans prisoners were imprisoned for drug violation.[106] Since the advent of the War on Drugs, however, the rate of increase in the number of African-Americans imprisoned for drug offenses is twice the rate for White-Americans.[107]

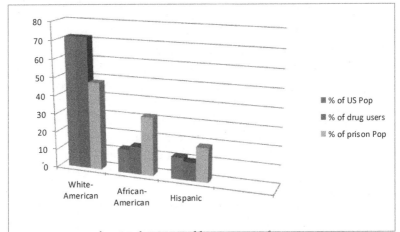

*Figure 2.2 Percentage of US Population vs. % of drug users vs. % of arrests*

| Race | % of US Pop | % of drug users | % of prison pop |
|---|---|---|---|
| White-American | 72% | 72% | 48% |
| African-American | 12.85% | 15% | 32% |
| Hispanic | 12% | 10% | 18.6% (22.5% convicted of drug use). |

Official crime data indicate that minorities are involved in a disproportionate share of criminal activity.[108] This is to say that although people of color make up small numbers within the American population (African-Americans: 12.85% and Hispanics 13%). Have minorities suddenly become more criminal? Or has law enforcement's preoccupation with minority communities manifested itself in increased minority numbers? Here is what the numbers say.

---

105  Final Report of the California Judicial Council Advisory Committee on Racial and Ethnic Bias in the Courts (1997). p. 174. Available at http://www. courtinfo. ca. gov/reference/documents/rebias. pdf

106  Ibid.

107  New Jersey Supreme Court Task on Minority Concerns, Final Report (1992), pp. 110, available at http://www. judiciary. state. nj. us/reports2002/minconpart1. pdf

108  Report of Michigan Supreme Court Task Force on Racial/ Ethnic Issues in the courts (1997) p. 9. Available at http//courts. michigan. gov/mji/webcast/alimony/execsummary. pdf

1. Minorities are involved in close to 65% of all reported crimes.[109]
2. African-Americans make up 12.85% of the national population, yet African-American males are incarcerated 9.6 times the rate of White-American males.[110]
3. African-Americans comprise 13% of monthly drug users yet are 39% of drug arrests.
4. Between 1986 and 1991, the number of African-American drug offenders in state prisons more than quintupled from 14,000 to 80,000.[111]
5. In 1993, African-Americans made up 45.7% of all arrests for violent crime—which means that White-Americans made up approximately 50%. Yet African-Americans are convicted and incarcerated at rates of 55% and 74% respectively.[112]
6. For drug related crimes in particular, African-Americans comprise 62.7 % and White-Americans 36.7 % of all drug offenders admitted to state prison, even though federal surveys and other data clearly show that this racial disparity is alarmingly disproportionate to the racial differences in drug use and even drug arrests.[113]

There are, for example, five times more White-American drug users than African-American yet African-American men are admitted to state prison on drug charges at a rate that is 13.4 times greater than that of White-American men.[114]

It would appear, therefore that the racial disparities in incarceration for drug offenses, have a significant impact on the overall rate of incarceration of African-American males compared to White-American males. African-American males, for example, are incarcerated for all offenses at 8.2 times the rate of White-Americans.[115] One in every 20 African-American men over the age of 18 in the United States is in state or federal prison, compared to one in 180 White-American men.[116] As shocking as these national statistics are, they mask even worse disparities in individual states. In seven states, for example,

1. African-Americans constitute between 80 and 90% of all drug offenders sent to prison.

---

109  Schlosser, Eric (1998) "The Prison Industry Complex." *Atlantic Monthly*, December pp. 51-77
110  Ibid.
111  Ibid.
112  Ibid.
113  Pelaez, V. (2008). "The Prison industry in the United States: Big Business or New form of Slavery?" Global Research available at www. globalresearch. ca/index. php?context=va&aid=8289
114  Ibid.
115  Ibid.
116  Ibid.

2. In at least fifteen states, African-American men are admitted to prison on drug charges at rates that are from 20 to 57 times greater than those of White-American men (these racial disparities in drug offenders admitted to prison also skew the racial balance of state prison populations.)[117]

3. In two states, one in every 13 African-American men is in prison and in seven states African-Americans are incarcerated at more than 13 times the rate of White-Americans.[118]

The imprisonment of African-Americans for drug offenses is part of a larger crisis of over incarceration in the United States. Prison was intended to be used as a last resort to protect society from violent or dangerous individuals. Today, more people are sent to prison in the United States for nonviolent drug offenses rather than for crimes of violence.

1. Throughout the 1990s, more than 100,000 drug offenders were sent to prison annually.

2. More than 1.5 million prison admissions on drug charges have occurred since 1980 and the rate at which drug offenders are incarcerated has increased nine fold

3. At the end of 2010, there were 7.1 million persons under the supervision of adult correctional authorities.[119]

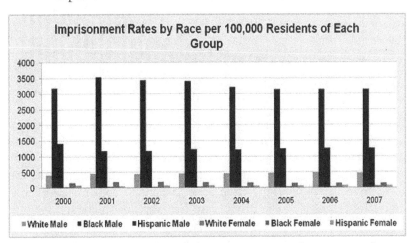

*Figure 2.3 Imprisonment Rates by Race Source: U.S. Department of Justice, Bureau of Justice Statistics*

---

117  Ibid.

118  Davis, Angela, Y. (1998) "Masked Racism: Reflections of the Prison Industrial Complex." Available at www. corpwatch. org/article. php/id=849

119  Bureau of Justice Statistices. Office of Justice Programmes. *Correctional Populations in the United States, 2010* Available at http://bjs.ojp.usdoj.gov/index.cfm?ty=pbdetail&iid=2237

Drug policies constitute the single most significant factor contributing to the rise in prison populations in recent years with the number of incarcerated drug offenders rising 510% from 1989 to 1994—in eleven states the rate of incarceration of African-American males is 12 to 26 times that of White-American males and in D.C. the rate is 49 times. In fact, according to Zatz (2000:525), "In the 5-year period from 1986 to 1991, the number of African-Americans incarcerated in State prisons for drug offenses increased by 465 percent." By 1994, African-Americans and Latinos constituted 90% of all drug offenders in State prisons."[120]

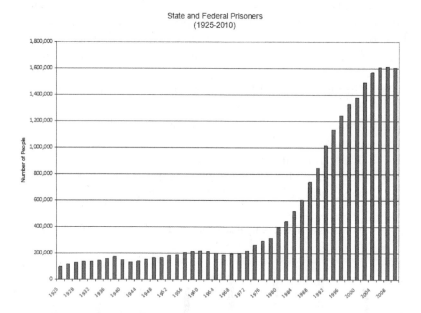

*Figure 2.4 Trends in U.S. Corrections . Source: The Sentencing Project available at http://www.*
*sentencingproject.org/template/page.cfm?id=107*

Nationally, incarceration rates amongst African-American males have grown exponentially from 39% in 1979 to 53% in 1990 (new convictions only).[121] The arrest rate for African-Americans for violent crime is 45%. Although grossly disproportionate this rate has not changed significantly for the past two decades. For drug offenses, however, the African-American proportion of arrests increased from 24% in 1980 to 39% in 1993, well above the African-American propor-

---

120  Zatz, Marjorie S. (2000). The Convergence of Race, Ethnicity, Gender, and Class in Court Decisionmaking: Looking Toward the 21st Century. In J. Horney (Ed.), *Criminal Justice 2000, Vol. 3, Policies, Processes, and Decisions of the Criminal Justice System* (pp. 503-552). Washington, DC: U.S. Department of Justice.

121  Ibid.

tion of drug users nationally.[122] Drug arrests have almost tripled since 1980, rising from 471,000 in 1980 to 1,351,000 by 1994, and the African-American proportion of drug arrests has increased during this time as well, rising from 24% in 1980 to 38% in 1994. The chances of imprisonment after being arrested for a drug offense have increased dramatically, rising by more than 400% from 1980 to 1992.[123] The past three decades have witnessed dramatic growth in the United States prison population. The U.S. rate of incarceration is 730 per 100,000, and has increased by over 22% since 1989. In 1975 there were 250,000 persons incarcerated in state and Federal prisons, as compared to the nearly 1.3 million as of mid-1999 and just over 2.2 million as of March 2012 – a 500% increase over the last 30 years.[124]

The United States boasts the largest prison population in the world amongst industrialized nations. This rate is 5 to 8 times the rate of almost all other industrialized nations, and sadly enough, of the almost 2.3 million Americans behind bars 583,000 or almost 50% are African-American. This is cause for concern, since only 537,000 African-American males are enrolled in higher education.[125]

**RATE OF INCARCERATION PER 100,000, BY GENDER AND RACE, 2010**

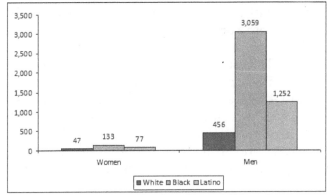

Source: Guerino, P., Harrison, P. M., & Sabol, W. (2011). *Prisoners in 2010.* Washington, DC: Bureau of Justice Statistics.

*Figure 2.5 Rate of Imcarceration by Race, 2010*

122  International Center for Prison Studies. *World Prison Brief.* Available at http://www.prison-studies.org/info/worldbrief/wpb_country.php?country=190

123  Ibid.

124  Bureau of Justice Statistics (1999). *Criminal offenders' statistics.* Washington, DC: U.S. Department of Justice;

Pattillo, M., Weiman, D. & Western, B. (2006) Imprisoning America: The Social Effects of Mass Incarceration.

125  Ibid.

This exponential growth has been attributed to the increasingly severe sentencing practices for drug offenses. In fact, the risk of receiving a prison sentence for a drug offense increased by 447% between 1980 and 1992 and the percentage of state prisoners incarcerated for a drug offense nearly quadrupled from 6% in 1980 to 23% in 1996.[126] Similarly, the percentage of federal prisoners serving time for a drug offense increased from 25% in 1980 to 60% in 1996. In fact, the increase in drug offenders accounted for nearly three-quarters of the total increase in federal inmates and one-third of the total increase in state inmates during this 16-year period.[127]

These statistics reflect a crime control policy based on a theory of deterrence. The assumption is that subjecting drug offenders to long prison sentences will deter current and prospective offenders and will eventually lead to an overall reduction in drug abuse and drug-related crime. However, this theory rests on the unsupported assumption that more severe criminal penalties will alter behavior. This has not happened. What *has* happened is the following

1. The lifetime chance of an African-American male going to prison is 16.2%. For a White-American, it is 2.5%.[128]
2. African-Americans compose almost 75% of defendants charged with robbery or weapons offenses and 62 % of those charged with a drug offense.[129]
3. Federal reporting agency numbers show that African-Americans and Hispanics constitute almost 90% of offenders sentenced to state prison for drug-related crimes.[130]
4. At least 45% of all African-American males in the U.S. age 20 to 29 have been either in prison, jail, on probation, or on parole. In contrast, White-American males of the same age had an incarceration/parole rate of 6.7% for the same period.

It may be argued that these numbers are related to the fact that, at the time of arrest,

1. Some 63% of African-American males were unemployed,[131]
2. At least 41% had less than a 12th grade education[132] and, generally,

---

126  Ibid.

127  Ibid.

128  West, H. C. & Sabol, W. J., (2008), *Prisoners in 2007*. Bureau of Justice Statistics Bulletin, http://www. ojp. usdoj. gov/bjs/pub/pdf/p07. pdf Last accessed 11. 2. 11.

129  Ibid.

130  Ibid.

131  U.S. Census Bureau Current Population Survey, Annual Social and Economic Supplement, 2005. Accessed

July 6, 2006. URL: http://www. census. gov/hhes/www/cpstc/cps_table_creator. html

132  Ibid.

3. The average annual income of African-Americans is $4,000 below the federally-mandated poverty level?[133]

FBI crime data for 1997 show that African-Americans are seven times more likely than White-Americans to be homicide victims and eight times more likely than White-Americans to commit homicides.[134] This phenomenon was actually predicted in 1987 when researchers warned that structural changes in the society, relative to the labor market and hiring practices, would fuel the societal stress evident in the inner-city African-American male youth population as it relates to violence.[135] No one listened. The results speak for themselves.

## CONCLUSION

Despite the fact that most self-report surveys, specifically with juveniles, show that the racial differences in reported involvement in crime are not very different, arrests and convictions of minorities, particular minority juveniles, continue to be disproportionately high. Additionally, disparate minority treatment by courts, parole and probation officials may also exist and perhaps should be addressed in a genuine effort to eliminate racially biased drug laws and law enforcement strategies. More stringent evaluation standards for law enforcement personnel should be put in place and minorities should be assured more and better-quality access to the court system and adequate legal representation. Until this society is willing to acknowledge its shortcomings and make genuine efforts to correct injustices, minority issues will continue to spread within the U.S. criminal justice system.

## CRITICAL THINKING QUESTIONS

1. What are the disparities between African-American, White-American and Hispanic defendants in each of the following key decision points?

---

133 FBI, Crime in the United States, 2002 (USGPO, 2003), pp. 68-76. Census Bureau, 2002 American
Community Survey, "Percent of People Below Poverty Level in the Past 12 Months (State Level)" (Census Bureau), http:// www. census. gov/acs/www/Products/Ranking/2002/ R01T040. htm. Accessed July 9, 2005. US, Dept. of Labor, Bureau of Labor Statistics, "Regional and State Employment and Unemployment: December 2002" (Washington, DC: US, Dept. of Labor, Bureau of Labor Statistics 2003), http:// www. bls. gov/news. release/archives/ laus_01282003. pdf. Accessed July 11, 2011. Census Bureau, 2010 American Community Survey, "Percent of People 25 Years and Over Who Have Completed High School (State Level)" (Census Bureau) http://www. census. gov/acs/www/Products/Ranking/2002/ R01T040. htm. Accessed July 9, 2010
134 Ibid.
135 Ibid.

      a. Arrest
      b. Plea bargaining
      c. Jury verdicts
      d. Sentencing

2. What do you think accounts for these disparities? Explain.
3. According to Andrew Hacker, author of *Two Nations, Black and White, Separate, Hostile, Unequal*, there is a belief that an African-American man who rapes/robs a White-American has inflicted more harm than a White-American who rapes/robs an African-American. Do you agree with this statement? Why or why not?

# CHAPTER 3. RACE, ETHNICITY AND THE MEDIA

## OBJECTIVES

- To determine whether society's view of crime and criminality is distorted by the various forms of media
- To determine whether media construction of crime and criminals lead to excessively punitive criminal justice policies
- To determine whether the media paints a negative picture of minorities and their involvement in criminal activity
- To determine whether media have any influence on public perception of crime

### CASE STUDY: O.J. SIMPSON—MEDIA MESS

O.J. Simpson has been a figure in the news for over thirty years. He was hailed as a sports superstar during the seventies and part of the eighties. From the nineties until today, however, he is being called a criminal.

The facts of the case are as follows: On June 12th, 1994, Nicole Brown Simpson, ex wife of O. J. Simpson, and her friend Ron Goldman were murdered. O.J. Simpson was notified of the murders on June 13th, while in Chicago on a business trip. According to the narrative that unfolded during the trial, the course of events in this case was played out as dramatically as in a Hollywood movie.

On the night of June 12th, a limousine picked O.J. up from his house around 10:25pm and took him to the airport where he boarded a plane to Chicago for a previously-planned business trip. The lapse of time between O.J.'s limousine departure and the time of the murders came into question during the trial. On June 13th, O.J. returned home and was taken in for questioning. On June 17th O.J., about to be arrested for murder, tried to slip away in his white Ford Bronco, driven by his good friend A.C. Cowlings. Police located O.J. on a Los Angeles expressway and a forty-minute police chase ensued. When Simpson finally returned to his home, he was taken into custody. Upon his arrest, O.J. pleaded "absolutely not guilty" to all charges, and the trial events were set in motion.

Due to the high profile of this case, the jury was sequestered for the full length of the nine month trial. During the trial a lot of DNA evidence was brought forth, particularly those items which were allegedly found and/or planted (in the words of the Defense) in O.J.'s Bronco SUV and home. However, according to the Defense, much of the evidence submitted by the prosecution was "tainted". The Defense also argued that the lead investigator, along with other members of the Los Angeles Police Department (LAPD), conducted a sloppy and irresponsible investigation. Their process of collecting evidence was questionable and there was also evidence that certain members of the LAPD assigned to the case were racist and had planted certain items on O.J.'s property. Mark Fuhrman was the lead investigator with the LAPD and, in an effort to support the accusations of racism, the Defense team pulled his personnel records.

The Prosecution, on the other hand, argued that a bloody black leather glove similar to the glove found at the murder scene was found at O.J.'s house and blood stains were found in the Ford Bronco. Much was said about the "infamous" glove; the glove did not fit O.J.'s hand, so according to the defense, the jury had no choice but to acquit. Further, both the forensic expert and the coroner testified that both victims were killed with sharp blunt objects, the use of which would not account for the glove being soaked in blood the way it was found. The Defense reiterated, "If it doesn't fit, you must acquit!" The Defense also raised the argument that there must have been two perpetrators as opposed to just one. Could O.J. kill two persons with such force in such a small amount of time? The evidence presented seemed to leave a reasonable doubt.

Mark Fuhrman, LAPD detective, was alleged to have been the main character in the Defense Counsel's conspiracy to convict O.J. Because of his prior behavior and language about African-Americans, his actions raised questions as to the impartiality of the LAPD's investigation. The Defense challenged the veracity of the prosecution's DNA evidence in part based on Fuhrman's documented prejudice against African-Americans but also based on the LAPD's history of reckless and irresponsible handling of crime scene evidence. The trial continued until October 3, 1995, when a majority African-American jury found O.J. Simpson "not guilty" on two counts of murder.

Despite the "not guilty" verdict, two questions remained. Did O.J. commit the crimes of which he was accused? And, is O.J. Simpson still on trial in the media for the murder of his wife?" No doubt, the fact that O.J. was African-American and his wife was White-American only served to add fuel to the fire. Indeed, this case received so much divisive media attention that the country seemed to be transported back to an era when it was against the law for an African-American man to look at, much less marry, a White-American woman. At times, it seemed as if O.J. Simpson was actually on trial firstly for marrying a White-American woman, and then for possibly killing her.[136]

### Introduction: Where Americans get their News

Before we evaluate the impact of the media on minorities and minority communicates, we must first understand the power of the media. The term "media" refers to the variety of methods used to disseminate information to the public (media is plural and refers to a combination of television, radio, newspaper and more recently the internet). More than 75% of all Americans consider television and newspapers their most important sources of news.[137] Perhaps it is because the television has become the greatest source of news that the public is becoming increasingly dissatisfied with the quality of television programming. From concerns about too much explicit sex and violence to the botched predictions of the 2000 presidential elections, the grumblings are growing.[138]

Although public perception of crime is influenced by many sources, the media arguably has the greatest impact on common perceptions and myths about what constitutes a criminal activity, who the criminals are, and whether crime control policies are fair or unfair.

---

136  Dershowitz, A. M. (1997). *Reasonable doubts: The criminal justice system and O. J. Simpson case.* New York: Touchstone.

137  Federal Commissions Commission (2003). "Consumer Survey on Media Usage", prepared by Neilsen Media Ressearch; Cooper, M. (2003) in *Consumer Federation of America, Promoting the public interest through Media Ownership Limits*

138  For background, see brain Hansen: "Combating Plagiarism," *The QC Researcher*, Sept. 19, 2003. pp. 773-796 and Kathy Koch, "Journalism under Fire." *The QC Researcher*, Dec. 25, 1998, pp1121-1144.

Crime first appeared in the media in the mid-1600s.[139] Initially crime was publicized solely as entertainment. However, the frequency and degree to which it is dramatized has been increasing at alarming rates. The degree to which crime has taken over the media has raised two important questions:

1. How much influence do the media really have on public perception of crime?
2. How realistic is the picture of crime that the media paint?

Let us first address these questions from a historical perspective.

In the early 1950s, studies were conducted to determine whether there was any correlation between the frequency with which crime was reported by the media, and actual official crime statistics. These studies revealed disturbing results.

1. There was no relationship between official crime statistics and crime as reported in the media.
2. Public perception of crime depended almost exclusively on what was read in the newspaper.[140]

Even back then, the impact that the media had on public perception was undeniable. This was, of course, with respect to print media only, prior to the widespread popularity of the television.

Since the introduction of television as the more popular source of information, crime has been identified as the single most popular "news event" in history. Commercial television with crime-related shows account for one fourth to one third of all prime time shows.[141] As early as 1935, it was argued that "crime waves are now and probably always have been products of newspaper headlines."[142] Even then, many believed that the media presented a distorted crime picture. According to one study, the decision to select crime news was based on four very specific criteria:

1. the seriousness of the offense,
2. whimsical or unusual elements,
3. sentimental or dramatic aspects and
4. the involvement of famous or high-status persons.[143]

Today, it is no secret that the average citizen depends on the media in all its forms for news. This is particularly true for local televi-

---

139  Surrette, R. (1998). *Media, crime and criminal justice: images and realities.* 2nd ed. Belmont, CA: Wadsworth Publishing Co.

140  David, F. J. (1952). "Crime News in Colorado Newspapers": *America Journal of Sociology,* 57, 325-330.

141  The State of New Media 2004: An annual Report on America Journalism Available at http://www. stateofthemedia. org/2004/narrative_radio_ownership. asp?cat=5&media=8

142  Fishman, M. (1976). "Crime Waves as Ideology." *Social Problems,* 25, pp. 531-543.

143  Roshier, B. (1973). "The Selection of Crime News by the Press." In S. Cohen and J. Young (eds). *The Manufacture of News. Beverly Hills:* Sage Publication :28-39; Graber, D. A. (1980). "Crime, Crime News and Crime Views." *Public Opinion Quarterly,* 45:492-506.

sion news, from which most citizens form their opinions about crime and crime control policies.

Not surprisingly therefore, the media have been accused of perpet-uating three major assumptions about crime:

1.  Crime is on the rise and society should be afraid of the "su-per predator".
2.  This "super predator" is minority and male between the ages of 17 and 25.
3.  African-Americans are considerable more likely than White-Americans to commit crime.[144]
4.  Are these assumptions true? If they are true, then controlling crime should be simple:
5.  Focus policing strategies on minority communities.
6.  Revamp criminal justice policies to institute more punitive measures.
7.  Incarcerate as many of the "super predators" as possible and build more prisons to house them.
8.  Support the media in its continued attempt to educate the general public about crime through entertainment.

In reality, all of these strategies are part of the current status quo. On the other hand, if these assumptions are NOT true, then three questions immediately come to mind:

1.  What could possibly be the media's rationale for continuing to perpetuate these myths?
2.  What is the rationale for encouraging and supporting media manipulation of the American citizenry?
3.  How much damage has the belief in these assumptions had on public perception and race relations?

To answer these questions, let's take a look at a few of the stud-ies done on the subject of media portrayal of minorities. A 1996 study of network news by Gilens found that African-Americans were over-whelmingly associated with poverty.[145] Other work by Gilens (1999) concluded that it is perhaps this portrayal of African-American on

---

144   Dorfman, L., and V. Schiraldi (2001). "Off balance: Youth, Race and Crime in the news." Washington, DC: Justice Policy Institute; Gross, K., and S, Aday. 2003. "The Scary word in your living room and neighborhood: using local broadcast news, neighbor crime rates, and personal experience to test agenda setting and cultivation": *Journal of Communication*, 53:411-426

145   Gilens, M. (1996a). "Race and poverty in America: Public misperceptions and the American news media." *Public Opinion Quarterly*, 60,515-541.

---

network news that has contributed to the belief that as a race they are lazy and undeserving of welfare assistance.[146]

Other studies, most notable by Entman (1990, 1994; Entman & Rojecki, 2000) found that African-Americans were, more often than not, portrayed as perpetrators or victims of crime, and that African-Americans were more likely than White-Americans to be portrayed on network news as perpetrators in drug related or violent crime stories.[147] Yet other studies have also suggested that the media may perceive and therefore portray African-Americans with a number of stereotypes including being aggressive, hostile, and poor.[148] Dixon and Linz (2000a) for example, also found that African-Americans were overrepresented as criminals on local television news stations in Los Angeles. African-Americans were portrayed as perpetrators of crime 37% of the time when official crime reports indicated that they comprised only 21% of those arrested.[149] Additional studies of local news programming in Chicago, Philadelphia, and Los Angeles found similar disparities.[150]

It is important to note that concurrent studies also found that White-Americans featured on both local and network news programs were typically portrayed in more positive roles in crime stories, such as the role of victim.[151] There is also evidence that the media tends to promote cases of interracial victimization of White-Americans. A study done by Dixon and Linz (2000b), for example, suggests that almost 50% of the White-American victims, and 70% of the African-American and Latinos victims in Los Angeles were victimized by

146   Gilens, M. (1999) *Why Americans have welfare: race, media and the politics of antipoverty policy.* Chicago: University of Chicago Press.

147   Entman, R. M. (1990). "Modern racism and the images of Blacks in local television news." *Critical Studies in Media Communication,* 7(4), 332-345; Entman, R. (1994) "Representation and Reality in the Portrayal of Blacks on Network News", *Journalism Quarterly* 71(3): 509-20; Entman, R. and A. Rojecki (2001) *The Black image in the white Mind: Media and Race America.* Chicago, IL: University of Chicago Press.

148   Dixon, T. L. (2006a). "Psychological reactions to crime news portrays of Blacks criminals: Understanding the moderating roles of prior news viewing and stereotype endorsement." *Communication Monographs,* 73 (2), 162-187; Dixon, T. l. (2006b) ""Race coding" and white opposition to welfare." *American Political Science Review,* 90 (3), 593-604

149   Dixon, T. L. and D. G Linz (2006a). "Overrepresentation and Underrepresentation of African Americans and Latinos as Lawbreakers on Television News": *Journal of Communication* 50(2): 131-54

150   Entman, R. (1992) "Blacks in the News: Television, Modern Racism and cultural change", *Journalism Quarterly* 69(2): 341-61; Also see Supra at 12

151   Gilliam, F. D., S. Iyengar, A Simon and O, Wright. (1996) "Crime in the Black and White: The Violent, Scary World of Local News": *Harvard International Journal of Press/Politics* 1(3):6-23; Romer, D., Jamieson, K. H., & De Coteau, N. J. (1998). "The treatment of persons of color in television news: ethnic blame discourse or realistic group conflict?" *Communication Research,* 25, 268-305.

African-Americans or Latinos.[152] In addition, a study by Romer et al. (1998) concluded that portrayals of White-Americans as victims on television news in Philadelphia overrepresented African-Americans as the offenders.[153] In this study, White-Americans victimized by African-Americans represented 42% of all victims presented on television news, but, according to official crime reports, White-Americans were only 10% of all reported victim.

Finally, Dixon and Linz (2002) found that African-American defendants were twice as likely as White-American defendants to have negative pretrial publicity aired about them on news programs when their victims were White-Americans.[154] These studies, as well as a number of others all argue that African-Americans are portrayed as perpetrators of crime while White-Americans are portrayed as victims of crimes in crime news.[155]

## MEDIA IMPACT ON SOCIETY

The media are agents of social control. Each of the multiple components may pursue different goals but their collective impact on society may be nothing short of brainwashing. Moreover, although the different parts of the criminal justice system (Policing, Courts and Corrections) may be impacted in different ways ultimately the collective impact can only lead to direct or indirect modes of social control.

The news, for example, has been accused of reporting crime in such a sensationalistic manner that the process has a significant impact on how individuals perceive crime.[156] As citizens and taxpayers, it is every citizen's right to expect—no, to demand—that the media provide the general public with an accurate and unbiased picture of

---

152   Dixon, T. L. and D. G. Linz (2000b) "Race and the Misrepresentative of Victimization on Local Television News", *Communication Research* 27(5):547-73; Dixon, T. L. C. Azocar and M. Casas (2003) "The Portrayal of Race and Crime on Television Network News", *Journal of Broadcasting & Electronic Media* 47(4): 498-523; Sorenson, S. B. J. G. Manz and R. A. Berk (1998) "News Media Coverage and Epidemiology of Homicide": *American Journal of Public Health* 88(10): 1510-14

153   Romer, D., Jamieson, K. H. ,DeCoteau, N. J. (1998) "The treatment of persons of color in local television news: Ethnic blame discourse or realist group conflict?" *Communication Research.* 25 (3) ppp. 286-305

154   Dixon, T. L. and D. G. Linz (2002) "Television News, Pretrial Publicity and the Depiction of Race", *Journal of Broadcasting and Electronic Media* 46(1):112-36; Dixon T. L and K. B. Maddox (2005) "Skin Tone, Crime News and Social Reality Judgements: Priming the Stereotype of the Dark and Dangerous Black Criminal", *Journal of Applied Social Psychology* 38(8):1555-70

155   Oliver, M. B. (1994) "Portrayals of Crime, Race and Aggression in "Reality-based" Police Shows: A Content Analysis", *Journal of Broadcasting & Electric Media* 38(2): 179-92; see also Supra at 12, 15, 17

156   Teece, M. & T. Makkai (2000). "Print Media Reporting on Drugs and Crime 1995-1998" in *Trend and Issues in Crime and Criminal Justice* No. 158; Australian Institute of Criminology, Canberra.

the nature of crime. But does the average citizen care enough to take a stand?

Given the decreasing crime rates of the last decade, should we not expect the media to present an improving picture of the crime situation in the United States? Instead, more crime and violence is being depicted on television and the print media also seem to focus on the more disturbing reports of crime. It is arguable that this trend actually distorts the problem, and possibly even contributes to the problem because most viewers, rightly or wrongly, perceive media presentations as actual reflections of society.

Can and should the average citizen bear the responsibility of differentiating between information and entertainment and even infotainment? Do some people go out into society and mimic what they have viewed (i.e., copycat crimes)? And, if they do, is it the media's fault that the average citizen may not be savvy enough to differentiate reality from entertainment? Perhaps society has lost sight of the fact that the ultimate goal of the media is to attract an audience for the sole purpose of earning larger profits. Indeed, do we have realistic expectations of the entertainment industry in a country that values free speech and personal expression so highly?

There is a growing body of evidence to suggest that violent media can and has impacted the direction of crime rates.[157] According to researchers, the introduction of home video players, DVDs, cable TV, personal computer and video games like "Grand Theft Auto" has exponentially increased the availability of media with violent content.[158] This trend, researchers say, is directly reflected in the sharp increase in teen violence rates.[159] Indeed, researchers have always argued that watching violence on TV is correlated to aggressive behaviors, particularly in individuals with a preexisting tendency toward crime and violence.[160]

---

157 Marsh, J. (1991). "A Comparative Analysis of Crime Coverage in Newspapers in the United States and other Countries from 1960 to 1989: A Review of the Literature" : *Journal of Criminal Justice*, 19:67-79.

158 Miles, Jack (1991). "Imagining Mayhem: Fictional Violence vs. 'True Crime'." *North American Review* Dec. 1991:57-64

159 Bushman, B. J,. & C. A. Andrew (2001). "Media Violence and the American public: Scientific facts versus media misinformation." *American Psychologist*, 56 (6-7): 477-489.

160 The Grand Theft Auto videogame series focus on different protagonists who attempt to rise through the criminal underworld, although their motives for doing so vary in each game. The antagonist in each game is commonly a character who has betrayed them or organization or someone who has the most impact impeding their progress; See also Ward, Michael R. (2009). Video Games, Crime and Violence. Net Institute Working paper no. 07-18

## Impact on the Criminal Justice System

There was a time when the television market could be depended on to bring the viewing public either news or entertainment. Over time, the distinction between news and entertainment has become blurred. This blurring perhaps began with the 1952 CBS airing of the first police drama called "Police Story". It was a live, 30-minute program that dramatized actual criminal activity taken from the files of law enforcement agencies around the nation. The show aired until 1977. Ten years later, four made-for-television movies based on the original script of "Police Story" aired on ABC. They were created by Los Angeles police officer and writer Joseph Wambaugh. This police drama laid the groundwork for future reality-based police programs such as "Law and Order", "Cops", and "CSI".

1. Today, despite the plethora of research that recognizes the growing influence of the media on public opinion and society's understanding of criminal justice issues,[161] this type of news entertainment programming is allowed to proliferate. In fact, some researchers would even argue that,

2. Increased coverage of crime—both in print and on air—has a significant effect on the size of police agencies and policy making.

3. Crime-drama viewers are more likely to "favor eased restrictions on carrying concealed guns" and "are more likely to think that being armed is advantageous."[162]

In addition to the steady diet of fictionalized TV violence and crime, there has been an increase in the graphic display of crime on many TV news programs. Crimes reported on TV news are also more frequently violent than real crimes are.[163] An article in The Washingtonian says that the word around two prominent local TV news stations is, "If it bleeds, it leads."[164]

161  Johnson, J. G., Cohen P., Smailes, E. M., Kasen, Brook, J. S. (2002). "Television Viewing and Aggressive Behavior During Adolescence and adulthood." *Science Magazine* 29, Vol, 295. No. 5564,pp. 2468-2471

162  Fox, Richard L. and Robert W. Van Sickel (2007). *Tabloid Justice: Criminal Justice in an Age of Media Frenzy*; Lynne Rienner Publishers, 1800 30th Street, Ste. 314 Boulder, USA; Feinberg, Seth L. (2002). "Media Effects: The Influence of Local Newspaper coverage on Municipal Police Size." *American Journal of Criminal Justice* 26(2):249-68; Dowler, K (2002). "Media influence on attitudes guns and gun control." *American Journal of Criminal Justice.* 26(2), 235-247

163  This answers Graeme Newman, who observes that most criminals on TV are white and wonders what the "ruling class" or conservatives "have to gain by denying the criminality of Blacks". Graeme R. Newman. (1990). "Popular Culture and Criminal Justice: A preliminary Analysis". *Journal of Criminal Justice*, Vol. 18(3), pp. 261-274

164  Matusow, Barbara (1988). If It Bleed, It Leads: Washingtonian, January 1988, p. 102.

Additionally, the Center for Media and Public Affairs reports a dramatic increase in homicide coverage on evening news programs starting in 1993, just as homicide rates were beginning to fall significantly.[165] Other researchers found that news programs were highly selective in the homicides they reported. The murders that were chosen for coverage tended to be committed by strangers in neighborhoods where average household incomes were over $25,000 a year.[166] This is misleading, because most murders occur between people who know to each other and typically take place in low-income neighborhoods. The effect seems to be a magnification of the risk of lower-class crime to middle-class individuals. Is it any wonder that fear of crime has persisted even as crime rates have gone down sharply? What's more, a new breed of non-fictional "tabloid" TV shows has begun to appear in which viewers are shown films of actual violent crimes—blood, screams, and all—or reenactments of actual violent crimes, sometimes using the actual victims to play themselves! Among these are COPS and America's Most Wanted.

The Wall Street Journal has taken notice of this phenomenon and has the following to say about it: "Television has gone tabloid. The seamy underside of life is being bared in a new rash of true-crime series and contrived-confrontation...talk shows."[167] Even on so called Tabloid TV, the focus is on violent one-on-one crimes rather than crimes which present a threat to a greater number of people, like deadly industrial pollution, or white collar crime, for example (see Chapter 7 for more discussion).

The media has often been accused of only focusing on crimes that affect viewers in a visceral fashion such as crimes that inflict harm one on one. Larger crimes seem not to have the same dramatic impact. Further, someone who deliberately creates unsafe conditions which result in a mine disaster in which hundreds of miners die is not considered a mass murderer. A good example of this was seen in the newspaper coverage of a food-processing plant fire in which 25 workers were killed and criminal charges were brought. A study concluded that "the newspapers showed little consciousness that corporate violence might be seen as a crime."[168] This, the study argued, was due to society's fixation on the model of the "typical crime".

---

165  Supra at 207
166  Ibid.
167  The Wall Street Journal (1988): "Titillating Channels: TV Is Going Tabloid as Shows Seek Sleaze and Find Profits, Too": *The Wall Street Journal*, May 18, 1988, pp 1-15
168  Wright, John P., Francis T. Cullen and Michael B. Blankenship (1995). "The social Construction of Corporate Violence: Media Coverage of the Imperial Food Products Fire": *Crime & Delinquency*, Vol. 41(1), 20-36

What keeps a mine disaster from being a mass murder in our eyes is that it is not a case of one-on-one harm. What is important in one-on-one harm is not the numbers but the desire of one person or set of persons to harm another person or set of persons. An attack by a gang on one or more identifiable person or an attack by one identifiable person on several people fit the model of one-on-one harm. In other words, for each person harmed, there existed at least one identifiable person who wanted to execute the act to cause the harm. The argument is that once the victim is selected, the rapist, the mugger, or murderer, for example, wants the person they have selected to suffer.

The CEO of a mining company, on the other hand, does not want his employees to be harmed—he just wants to increase profits. In fact, he would prefer that there be no accidents and no injured or dead miners. However, if what the CEO wants is maximum profits at minimum costs, he may sometimes feel pressured to cut corners to save money, one could say that he is just doing his job. If a hundred men happen to die because he cut corners on safety, we may think him greedy and heartless, but we may not call him a murderer. The harm he causes is seen as indirect (as opposed to one-on-one harm which is perceived as more direct).

Because those who have economic power own the newspapers, endow the universities, finance the publication of books and journals, and control the television and radio industries, have a prevailing say in what is heard, thought, and believed by the millions who get their ideas—their picture of reality—from these sources, these sources become the picture of reality that the masses will adopt. This does not necessarily mean that those in control consciously deceive or manipulate those who receive their message.

Recognizing this involves no disrespect for the so-called common person. It is simply a matter of facing reality. The average man or woman is almost wholly occupied with the personal tasks of earning a living, feeding a family, and surviving in this society. He or she lacks the time (and usually the training) necessary to seek out and evaluate alternative sources of information. Most people are lucky when they have the time to catch a bit of news on television or in the papers. Moreover, except when there is division of opinion among those who control the media, the average person is so surrounded by unbroken "consensus" that he or she takes it for granted that that is the way things are, with no reason to even consider the possibility that there are other sides of the issue to be considered, much less to seek these out.

For example, how often do you see the officers on the TV show "COPS" investigate consumer fraud or failure to remove occupational hazards? When "Law & Order" detectives Green and Fontana happen to track down a criminal, it is almost always for a violent or street crime such as murder. A study of TV crime published by the Media Institute in Washington, D.C, indicates that while the fictional criminals portrayed on television are on average both older and wealthier than the real criminals who factor into FBI Uniform Crime Reports, crimes featured on TV are almost 12 times more likely to be violent crime compared to the types of crimes committed in the real world. [169]

Several studies have also confirmed that violent crimes are overrepresented on TV news and fictional crimes shows, and that young people, African-American people, and people of low socioeconomic status are overrepresented as offenders and underrepresented as victims in television programs in general.[170] But in the real world:

1.  Nonviolent property crimes far outnumber violent crimes, and
2.  The young, poor, and African-American do not necessarily comprise the majority of criminals, even though they are disproportionately present in relation to their ratio of the general population), and
3.  Victims are predominately young, poor, and/or of minority status.[171]

There is another interesting perspective worthy of mention. Although TV crime shows focus on the crimes typically committed by the poor, they do not present criminal activity as being unique to the poor. In other words, TV crime shows present a double-edged message indicating that the wealthy commit the same one-on-one crimes committed by the poor; therefore, this type of crime is not a result of poverty. In this approach, TV shows make the criminal justice system appear to pursue rich and poor alike, in essence arguing that if the criminal justice system happens to mainly target the poor in real life, it is not because of any class bias. In other words, what is most important about the televised portrayals of crime is the kinds of crimes that are shown and not who is typically portrayed as the criminal. Therefore, by over representing violent one-on-one crimes, television confirms the view that these one-on-one street crimes are a greater threat to us than, say... white collar crimes, for example. Since, in the real world, those one-on-one crimes are disproportionately committed by

169   Freeman, Jonathan L. (2007). "Television Violence and aggression: Setting the record straight": *The Media Institute/Policy Review.*

170   Voigt, Lydia, William E. Thorthon, Jr., Leo Barrile, and Jerro M. Seamon (1994). *Criminology and Justice*: New York: McGraw-Hill, Inc.

171   Dominick, J. R. (1994). "Crime and Law Enforcement on Prime-time Television": *Public Opinion Quarterly*, 37:241-250

poor people,[172] this is enough to create the view that it is the poor who pose the greatest threat to law-abiding Americans.

With this in mind, we should be concerned that entertainment media present a particularly distorted picture of crime, criminals, and crime control policies, especially since crime-related television is said to account for about one third of all television entertainment shows.[173] Information that the public receives from these shows may be misleading. In fact, studies have indicated that:

1. The least-committed crimes, such as murder and assault, appear more frequently than those crimes committed more often, such as burglary and larceny;
2. Violent crimes are portrayed as being caused by greed or attempts to avoid detection rather than by passion accompanying arguments which is more typical;
3. The necessary use of violence in police work is exaggerated;
4. The use of illegal police tactics is seemingly sanctioned;
5. Police officers appear to be above the law; and
6. The police nearly always capture the "bad guys," usually in violent confrontations. [174]

Another emerging and perhaps more dangerous form of media is the Internet. The advent of the World Wide Web (www) has had a profound and irreversible effect on modern day society. The web has been accused of posing a real danger to society by supporting subtle forms of social control as well as criminal activity,[175] yet its impact is downplayed. For example, the problem of sex offenders recruiting young people for illicit sexual purposes, online stalkers, and the proliferation of all types of pornography has been well documented and lamented by the media.[176] Yet despite the rapid growth, the perception of Internet crimes being serious crimes is still understated. It is important to note that the media has already begun to capitalize on this type of crime by offering such shows as "Apartment X,"[177] the con-

---

172 Gitlin, T. (1979) "Prime Time Ideology: The Hegemonic Process in Television Entertainment". *Social Problems*, 26:251-266

173 "Apartment X" was an undercover sting operation of the Guilford Country, North Carolina Sheriff's Office which result in the arrest of many local internet Sexual Predators. The TV story made it possible through a partnership with the Guilford county Sheriff's Office Computer Forensic Investigators and Vice Division.

174 CNN (2004). Stewart convicted on all charges. Available at CNNmoney. com

175 Linder, D. (2003). The McMartin Preschool Abuse Trial: a commentary. At http://www. law. umkc. edu/faculty/projects/ftrials/mcmartin/mcmartinaccount. html

176 Butterfield, F. (1990). "Dispute Emerges In Boston Murder." *The New York Times*. Available at http://query. nytimes. com/gst/fullpage,html?res=9C0CE6DC133BF936A35757C0A9695 8260&sec=&spon=

177 Supra at 182

tent of which, for some strange reason, is seen as entertainment and not real crime.

All would agree that the Internet has empowered us with access to unlimited sources of information. None would disagree that the Internet also has empowered a wide range of criminals (from sexual deviants to international terrorists).

## MEDIA PORTRAYALS OF CRIME AND CRIMINALS

Media portrayal of crime and criminals typically follow a set pattern. The ideal criminal,

a.　is a clever and heartless predator
b.　is usually a minority,
c.　preys on weak, defenseless victims
d.　is an outsider, stranger, foreigner, alien, and intruder who lacks essential human qualities.[178]

The ideal victim is

a.　usually portrayed as women, children and the elderly
b.　innocent, naïve, trusting, obviously in need of protection
i.　Children are the typical innocent victims and are key symbols in the media's portrayal of crime.[179]

The ideal crime fighter

a.　is a solid, dependable hero
b.　usually portrayed as middle-class White-American, and male
c.　displays admirable human qualities of selflessness, natural intelligence and strength.[180]

Unfortunately, the real world is not black and white. Social problems are not always distinctly good or bad, right or wrong. Some problems come bundled together, others overlap. For example, crime is typically found with:

a.　poverty
b.　unemployment,
c.　poor health,
d.　poor schools,
e.　high divorce rates,
f.　high out-of-wedlock pregnancy rates,
g.　community decay and deterioration,
h.　drug use,
i.　illiteracy,

---

178　Stix, N. (2005). "Howard Beach II: More White Male Monsters." *Men's News Daily*

179　Icard . L. D. (1998) "Racial Minority Status and Distress Among children and Adolescents." *Journal of Social Service Research* Volume:25 Issue1/2

180　Bennet, L. D. (2006). Media Put Accuser on Trial in Duke Rape. National Organization for woman. Available at http://www. now. org/issues/media/061506duke. html

j.    high school dropout rates.[181]

That does not mean that the wealthy, gainfully employed and well educated people do not commit crime (see the Martha Stewart story).[182] Yet the media would have you believe that crime is an isolated phenomenon not at all related to historical, social, or structural conditions. In the same vein, media focus seems to support retribution and deterrence as opposed to rehabilitation and social reform.

So, what types of criminal behavior and criminal offenders do the media focus on? Comparisons can be made with actual crime statistics to discover whether certain types of criminals or crimes are underrepresented or overrepresented by the various forms of media. For example, are minorities and ethnic groups singled out by the media as criminals at a rate higher or lower than their actual participation in crime? Are "hate crimes" against minority groups given far more exposure than warranted or not enough exposure? Are serious crimes such as murder and rape given exposure at a rate that is so out of proportion with their actual occurrence that the public is unnecessarily alarmed? Has the media in fact created crime panics in such areas as child abductions and child sexual abuse? Has media coverage of such high profile news stories as the Bernard Goetz subway shootings (see Chapter 1 Case Study), the McMartin preschool and other ritual abuse cases[183], the Stuart murder in Boston[184], the OJ Simpson case (with a special emphasis on Internet coverage of the trial)[185], and several white on black murders in New York City (Howard Beach and Bensonhurst)[186], been used to sell panic and fear?

The question is no longer whether the media have any impact on public perception of crime and criminality but how and how severely their impact will be felt. There is no argument, for example, that the media in all its forms have increasingly blurred the lines between news and entertainment, and between fact and fiction. In the process, crime stories have become the springboard for hybrid infotainment programs which only serve to create an even more dramatic disparity between media-constructed reality of crime and the actual social reality of crime. Media seem fixated on a single image of crime. Often an image of uncontrolled criminality unchecked by traditional criminal justice methods—images such as the traffic stop and beating of Rodney King and the World Trade Center attacks, not to men-

---

181   Ibid.

182   Reuters. (2004) "Stewart Sentenced to five months in prison." Published in *The Sydney Morning Herald*. July 17, 2004

183   Ibid.

184   On MSNBC's The Situation with Tucker Carlson aired on April 12, 2006

185 . Ibid.

186   On MSNBC's The Situation With Tucker Carson aired on June 15, 2006

tion the new breed of crime and justice reality shows created just for the media.

How long will society continue to allow the corporations that own, produce and distribute media depictions of violence to argue that they are simply "giving the public what it wants"? And, how do the media know what the public wants? On the one hand although Americans are fiercely protective of free speech, they still want to be informed about the levels of violent or sexual content in television programs, computer games, music, and movies to which their children could be exposed. On the other hand, the media can only continue to supply the public with what it believes the public wants if the public allows them to do so.

So how does the portrayal of the average criminal impact perceptions of race and ethnicity? Let's evaluate a real life example. In 1998 an intriguing study was conducted on U.S. drug policies. Twelve hundred adolescents aged 12–17 were interviewed by a child advocacy group. The adolescents were evenly divided into the four largest racial groups and their opinions were sought regarding television programming. The results were disturbing. Across the board the adolescents associated positive characteristics with White-American characters and negative characteristics with minority characters.[187] That is the power of the media on perceptions of crime and criminality as presented through the major mass media. In particular, crime movies, television crime dramas, television news and newspaper crime coverage are the major sources of data for uncovering how the media portray society's struggle with the crime problem. More importantly, we must acknowledge the fundamental role the media play in defining what constitutes deviance and criminality in American society.

## In the News

On March 14, 2006, members of the Duke University men's lacrosse team hired two exotic dancers for a private party. The two dancers—both women—who had never met, claim to have been subjected to racial and misogynist slurs. One of the women also reported being attacked in a bathroom during a period when (according to both women) the dancers were separated from each another. This young woman accused three men of raping and assaulting her. The three men, all members of the prestigious Duke University lacrosse team, were indicted on charges of rape, sexual offense and kidnapping.

Both of the dancers were African-American and all three of the defendants were White-American. This fact, combined with the re-

---

187  On MSNBC's The Situation With Tucker Carson aired on April 19, 2006

ports of racial slurs being hurled at the women on the night of the incident, added a racial element to the case which, unfortunately, the media found irresistible. It is important to note that the accuser was a mother, a university student, and a former member of the U.S. military—yet the media conveniently neglected to focus on these important facts and chose instead to refer to the accuser simply as a "stripper". Moreover, one of the accused men had been arrested on assault charges just months before the Duke incident, yet his prior acts did not seem to attach any stigma or implications as to his character or possible guilt.

At the same time, the Durham police said that the accuser changed her mind several times, and lawyers for the accused argued that the accuser had been intoxicated and possibly on drugs. Additionally, the prosecutor was accused of pursuing the case despite the absence of physical evidence, the accuser's lack of credibility, improper actions by the police to undermine the investigation and, more importantly, despite the fact that DNA testing failed to connect any of the 46 members of the team to the alleged sexual assault.

Perhaps even more disturbing is how this case was turned into a media circus. For example, on an episode of CNN's "Showbiz Tonight", guest Lida Rodriguez-Taseff said of the case, "It's a little bit of CSI: Miami meets Wild On meets Martin Luther King Jr.'s 'I have a Dream' speech playing in the background."[188] By discussing the case in such a way, the accuser becomes nothing more than one of the characters in a badly-written a story. The heinousness of a potential rape is stripped away, and it loses its impact as the story becomes fictional. Another guest on the same show, Howard Kurtz, said, "Television loves a melodrama, and this is shaping up to be a first class one."[189] This comment effectively turned a potential rape case into a story—relegating the reality of rape, and the threat it poses to all women, to nothing more than entertainment.

The attitude of the television media toward the accuser has also perpetuated stereotypes about exotic dancers. On Fox's "Hannity & Colmes," this unsympathetic attitude was evident when Sean Hannity summarized guest Ann Coulter's article entitled, "Lie Down with Strippers, Wake Up with Pleas." Hannity said; "If you're a woman who undresses before strangers, you're saying in this piece: Expect trouble in your life."[190] This attitude places the blame on the woman, implying that since it was her decision to pursue this particular

---

188  On MSNBC's The Abrams Report aired on May 18, 2006
189  Finckenauer, J. O., and Gavin P., Hovland A. & Storvoll E. (1999). *Scared straight: The panacea phenomenon revisited.* Prospect Heights Ill. USA: Waveland Press
190  Supra at 228

career, then she should be prepared to deal with potentially violent consequences. This seems to say that the guilt or innocence of the accused is not the issue (the lacrosse players may have raped her, but in her line of work that's to be expected.)

Another guest on this same show, criminal defense attorney Mercedes Colwin, said that potential jurors would think, "She's an exotic dancer. She was scantily clad. They're going to do it. It's something that's going to happen, and that's certainly going to impact on her credibility."[191]

Certain television media, particularly cable news programs, perpetuated blatantly negative portrayals of the accuser and unashamedly treated the case as entertainment—in some cases treating the crime as something to be joked about. Rape survivors were further belittled on an episode of MSNBC's "The Situation" with Tucker Carlson. While discussing the NAACP's involvement in the case, Carlson said, "That doesn't make the accuser Rosa Parks."[192] Carlson came back to this idea on a later episode of the show when he said to North Carolina NAACP President Barber, "You are making the accuser in this case some sort of modern day civil rights hero, and I just can't imagine why."[193] Whether intentionally or not, Carlson sets the bar impossibly high for any woman who reports a rape and hopes to be taken seriously.

In the same vein, on another episode of "The Situation with Tucker Carlson", Carlson seems to support a perspective that media respond harshly and with knee jerk sensationalism, even before facts are are presented. As such, it becomes more and more difficult to evaluate the situation with some measure of impartiality.[194] Ultimately, the goal is to give the facts more power than any preconceived notions.

On another episode of MSNBC's "The Abrams Report", Dan Abrams responded to guest Georgia Goslee in a similar manner. Abrams told Goslee, who was defending the accuser, "That's called pulling the gender card."[195] Abrams and Carlson appear to agree that the feminist theory is "fluff," and that rape should not be seen through a gender lens.

191  Chiricos, T. (2004). *The Media, Moral panics and the politics of crime control. In the Criminal Justice System: Politics and Politics*, 9th ed. Eds. G. F. Cole, M. C. Gertz and A. Bunger. Elmont, CA;Wadsworth.

192  Kappeler, V. E. (2004). *Inventing criminal justice with social construction. In theorizing criminal justice: Eight essential orientations*, ed. P. Kraska. Long Grove, IL: Waveland Press

193  Christie, N. (2000). *Crime control as industry: Towards GULAGS, Western style*: Routledge, 11 New Fetler Lane, London

194  R. G. and B. B. Brown (2000). "The crime control industry and the management of the surplus population." *Critical Criminology* 9(1-2):39-62

195  Cordes, C. (1984) "Media found able to "prime" votes": *APA Monitor*, June, p. 31.

Surely viewers in general, and women in particular, were appalled to see the subject of rape bantered about in such an offhand manner. The treatment of this case should be disheartening to those who have worked for so long to stop violence against women. At times, it was only feminists who would even talk about rape and domestic violence, but in the world of cable news this works against them. The Duke University rape case has consumed much media ink and airtime, and the manner in which the accuser and the accused were portrayed at times should be reason to take a different view of the media.

In the final analysis, despite sometimes racially divisive coverage by the media, those accused of this crime were not only found not guilty but were actually proclaimed innocent by the North Carolina Attorney General's office. Moreover, the prosecuting attorney was himself brought up on ethics charges and subsequently disbarred. It is important to note that the issue at hand here is not the guilt or innocence of the accusers but the quality of media coverage and the impact of media coverage on the case, the community and society's perception of both the victim and the accused.

RACE, ETHNICITY AND POLICY: THE MEDIA, POLITICS AND CRIME

It is no secret that one of the greatest concerns of the general public is that of rising crime. Politicians capitalize on this fear and perhaps even encourage it. Advocating a "get tough" approach to crime may help win elections; however, the sad truth is that the focus on the punishment, as opposed to the rehabilitation of offenders, almost automatically overshadows any positive results that good treatment programs may have. In fact, some policy makers admit that they tend to reject social science research that favor rehabilitation because of

a.   Skepticism about the research itself, and

b.   Their personal beliefs that punishment is simply more efficient. [196]

They claim, "It is easier for legislators to continue such programs and avoid angering constituents than it is to stop them".[197]

Notwithstanding, the importance of negative political implications, there are even greater social implications that need consider-

---

[196]   Shanyang, Zhao (2006) "Humanoid social robots as a medium of communication": *New Media & Society*, Vol. 8, No. 3, 401-419

[197]   Hallin, Daniel C. (1984). "The Media, the War in Vietnam and Politics Support: A Critique of the Thesis of an Oppositional Media": *Journal of Politics*, 46: 2–24 (February 1984) 19; for a more extensive treatment, see Daniel C. Hallin, The *Uncensored War* (New York: Oxford Univ. Press, 1986);Clarence R. Wyatt, "At the Connon's Mouth: The American Press and the Vietnam War", *Journalism History*, 13 (Autumn-Winter 1986), 104-13; For a more in depth treatment, see Clarence R. Wyatt, *Paper Solders*: The American Press and *The Vietnam War* (Chicago: Univ. of Chicago Press, 1995).

ation. By and large, all the proposed solutions to crime seem to place the responsibility for each crime on the immoral choices of the individual criminal. With the help of the media, this trend has been successful in diverting public attention from the social and economic conditions that may be the actual underlying causes of violent crime. There is continuous discussion that the ultimate goal is to create a crime-free society. However, sometimes the interest of the wealthy and the powerful seem to be better served by advocating punishment as a solution instead of addressing the very real social and economic problems that contribute to crime. Instead of clamoring for more severe punishment, perhaps the public should be demanding that the media focus on enlightening the public on the social and economic problems that actually cause crime:

a. Poverty
b. Income inequality
c. substandard inner-city schools
d. unemployment, and
e. urban decline[198]

Of more concern is the growing number of accusations that governmental interests are becoming intertwined with the interests of the media. The media and the government have a complex and far reaching relationship which seems to feed off of current portrayal of crime and criminals. Some even argue that the media and the government are the only real beneficiaries of this preoccupation with crime and the super predator.[199]

In fact, analyses of recent trends toward increasingly punitive penal policies have revealed that "the emotional force of ubiquitous mass media coverage of such events as the crimes of Willie Horton, the murders of Megan Kanka and Plooy Klaas, and the cocaine-overdose death of Len Bias produced moral panics...and lead to increased calls for punitive penal policies".[200] Not surprisingly therefore, an examination of the growth of the "criminal justice industrial complex" clearly indicates a developing relationship between criminal justice, media, and corporate entities.[201]

As we evaluate the effects of the media on criminal justice policies, we must remember that the degree to which the media impact criminal justice policy will ultimately translate into how limited tax

---

198  Ibid.

199  Darley, W. (2005). "War Policy Support and the Media." *Parameters*, Summer 2004, pp. 121-34. Available at https://www. carlisle. army. mil/USAWC/Parameters/05summer/darley. pdf

200  Von Clausewitz, Carl (1942). *Principles of War*. Translated and edited by Hans W. Gatzke. The Military Service Publishing Company

201  Ibid.

monies are spent and what actually happens to offenders and victims. Some research results even argue that the media can directly affect what actors in the criminal justice system are able to do, without having to first change the public's attitudes or agenda.[202] Indeed, there are some indications that among criminal justice officials, even more than among the public, the media significantly influence both policy development and support. Still, are we expected to believe that the policy changes can occur simply because of intense coverage of an external event?

Of course, we understand that the media is not a public service. These are profit-driven corporations, and it is not their principal mission to construct a crime-and-justice policy. Nonetheless, their influence cannot be ignored. In addition, in response to the question of whether media coverage of crime is, in and of itself, a cause of criminal behavior, there is also the issue of copycat criminals. Copycat criminals view portrayals of heinous crimes or new crime techniques in the media and then decide to repeat them. This of course begs the question of whether the constant emphasis on criminal violence in the media has the potential to produce an even more violent society.

In the final analysis, we must ask the question, "Do the media truly have the power to influence the processing and disposition of cases?" And if they do, "Is it any wonder that the average citizen believes that minorities are more dangerous than non minorities?"

+++

NOOSES, THE MEDIA, AND THE RISE OF HATE CRIMES IN THE UNITED STATES

Tanya Y. Price, Assistant Professor, Cultural Anthropology

According to the FBI, the incidence of hate crimes rose nearly 8% in 2006. More than half of these incidents were racially motivated. Across the nation, police reported 7,722 criminal incidents targeting victims or property on the basis of bias against a particular race, religion, sexual orientation, ethnic or national origin, physical or mental disability. Although this number was up 7.8 percent from 2005, it is difficult to compare the statistics year-to year due to the non-comprehensive nature of federal hate crime reporting. In fact, out of more than 17,000 local, county state and federal police agencies in the country, only 12,600 participated in the hate crime reporting program for 2006. (Sniffen, 2006) With a different mix of agencies reporting each year, hate crimes are difficult to track with accuracy. From 2006-2007 for example, the small town of Jena, located in La Salle Parish, Louisiana, riveted the nation's attention on the poignancy of the hangman's

---

202  Ibid.

noose as a symbol of racial hatred, as well as the unequal treatment of Black and White students at the hands of the criminal justice system. Neither Jena, nor LaSalle Parish reported a single federal hate crime in 2006. (Sniffen, 2006)

Although anthropology and biology both confirm that "race" should be considered a social construct rather than a biological fact, (Graves, 2004) the United States remains a country divided along racial lines with constant political struggles centered on the content and import of racial categories. (Omni &Winant, 1989, pp. 66-69). The role of the media is unclear in this equation—does media reporting merely educate the public, thus lessening the ignorance that gives rise to hate crime—or does relentless reporting on certain incidents exacerbate hate crime? The increasing significance of the "noose" as a signal of racial hate, is an interesting case study to examine the role of the media in the committing of racially motivated hate crimes.

Both the Southern Poverty Law Center, a non-profit legal organization that traces the activity of hate groups, and Diversity, Inc, an online and print journal dedicated to promoting diversity in the workplace, reported that copycat noose incidents were on the rise during the weeks and months following the "Jena Six" incidents. *Diversity, Inc* reported 78 noose incidents nationwide as of *December* 12, 2007. According to the web site, most of the sightings took place on schoolyards and in the workplace. (DiversityInc, 2007)

According to hate crimes expert Mark Potok, "the Southern Poverty Law Center normally hears about fewer than about a dozen cases each year." (Potok 2007) The organization's *Intelligence Report* took note of "white supremacists burning up the Internet with furious denunciations, bloody predictions, promises of apocalyptic violence, and calls for lynching," even before the September 20th rally. "We're seeing a lot of generalized white resentment," Potok said. "The conversation among many white people, particularly in the South, amounts to the idea that Jena was a black-on-white hate crime that is being widely misconstrued as a case of racial oppression of blacks." (2007)

The rising noose incidents prompted CNN to air a news special entitled, *Nooses, an American Nightmare.* Due to news coverage of a massive brush fire in California, the report was pre-empted for several days; however, when the report finally aired, it commented on the circumstances under which more than 4,700 Americans, more than two-thirds of them African-American, were lynched between the end of the Civil War and 1981.(Phillips, K. 2007) Although these particularly tortuous executions were most prevalent in the "deep south" of the United States, they also occurred in all areas of the nation. The special, featuring interviews with experts, agonizing pictures with specific historical details regarding individual lynching cases over the last one hundred years, left no doubt that the noose was a symbol of racial hatred. (Phillips, 2007)

Recently, there is no doubt that the media has taken note of the noose trend, which appears to have both increased the incidence of nooses and called attention to their use as a symbol of racial intimidation. The use of the "noose" as a symbol of racial hatred –perhaps as a silent symbolic plea for the strangulation of the Black body, and with it, Black cultural influence, appeared for a time to be on the rise.

Although the events surrounding the Jena 6 case may have prompted a white racist backlash, even "introducing some racists to the noose," (Pottok, 2007). It is my contention that the "noose" has never disappeared. Since the last documented lynching by neck, of an African-American by a Klansman, occurred in 1985, the noose has been utilized as a symbol of white supremacy and the desire on behalf of its user for the annihilation of the Black body.

A case in point occurred in a rash of noose sightings in and around Nashville and Clarksville, Tennessee, roughly between 2001 and 2006. The noose sightings appeared to parallel the Civil-Rights struggles of African-American police and college professors seeking redress from the courts for racial discrimination on the job. In 2001, an African-American police detective found a noose near his desk. He also charged that black officers had been "subjected to racial slurs and a cartoon featuring derogatory comments about African-Americans that were hung in a prominent location." According to the National Action Network, a civil rights organization presided over by the Reverend Al Shaprton, two years after the incident; local FBI agents still had not interviewed African-American officers at the department, (Edwards, 2004). Similarly, a group of African-American women professors at Austin Peay State University, Clarkesville charged that then-President Sherry Hoppe had badly mistreated the school's black black students, faculty and staff by forcing out "as many as 17 faculty members through termination or not renewing contracts." They also charged her with violating the 2001 state settlement of a long-running higher education desegregation lawsuit." (Groups Demand Resignation, 2004) In both cases the employees sought redress from the courts.

As part of their grievance, professors cited campus noose sightings that were not adequately investigated. A university administrator sighted a noose hanging in a tree outside the Austin Peay State University Bookstore on October 21st, 2004 and reported it to campus authorities. Pieces of a second apparent noose were also observed lying on the ground below the tree. Initially, officials resisted investigating the incident until a college professor applied public pressure for an investigation to ensue. Following this application of pressure, campus police reluctantly conducted an investigation in order "to determine if any evidence existed that the noose was a form of purposeful civil rights intimidation... (That) Injures or threatens to injure or coerces another...from the free exercise or enjoyment of any right or privilege...secured by the Constitution or the laws of the state of Tennessee." Such an act would "be reportable to the state, and ultimately the FBI under the 1990 Hate Crime Statistics Act." Officers also investigated a rumor that a student who observed the noose being hung days before had been chased into a nearby dorm by a short white male and threatened with death on Halloween. Members of a fraternity were questioned, however no one was found guilty of the act. Officers concluded that the noose had 8 loops wrapped around its slip-knot, whereas "the symbology associated with lynching or hanging, appears to be the wrapping of exactly 13 loops around the slip-knot. Further, although it is capable of creating asphyxiation, the noose recovered doesn't have the tensile strength to drop or suspend the weight of an adult human being." After some mention of nooses associated "with medieval or Dungeons and Dragons-type culture," the report concludes that "No evidence has yet been received or developed to constitute probable cause that a crime has been committed in this incident."(Memorandum, 2003)

Although the Austin Peay campus was eventually forced to report the noose incidents, this case illustrates the potential for hate crime under-reporting and minimization, either in an attempt to cover up the frequency of such racist incidents; or to protect embarrassed institutions fearing bad publicity, lawsuits and other negative repercussions resulting in the loss of revenue and public confidence in institutions such as police departments, public schools, colleges and universities. Most hangmen's noose incidents are unlikely to rise to the level of media scrutiny on the local or national levels. The Jena incidents, which seemed to precipitate a "spike" of such incidents, came to light because of a persistent publicity campaign by a well-oiled and funded advocacy group. In my estimation, the heightened media attention to Jena, Louisiana precipitated a temporary spike in interest around the significance of nooses due to the extreme nature of incidents in Jena and the blatant inequalities in the punishments that were netted out, not unlike the media attention riveted on the Civil Rights struggles of the 1960's. The "Jena" cases, as well as the Clarkesville incidents are unlikely to spark structural change. Hate crimes will continue to occur under the media radar and hate incidents will continue to be under-reported. Despite the present success of presidential candidate Barack Obama, the United States has far to go before it is truly a "colorblind" society.

## References

1. Davis, Ida. (2008, February). "The Noose and American Terrorism is a Part of Black History in America." *The Greensboro Times*, pp. 1-2.

2. DiversityInc Noose Watch (2007). Accessed on *diversityinc.com*, December 21, 2007.

3. Edwards, Holly (2004) "African-American detective found noose near desk in 2001." *The Tennessean.*

4. Graves, Joseph L. (2004). *The race myth*: why we pretend race exists in America, New York: Dutton.

5. Groups demand resignation of APSU president. (2004, December 21). *Associated Press*.

6. Jena Update—the Campaign Continues. (2007, August 11) *Colorofchange.org*. Accessed 5/26/08.

7. Omi, Michael and Winant, Howard, (1986/1989). *Racial Formation in the United States: From the 1960s to the 1980s*. NY: Routledge.

8. Phillips, K. (2007). K Phillips Reports, Nooses, an American Nightmare, Accessed via CNN Video website, Accessed March 2, 2008.

9. Potok, Mark, Editor. (2007, winter) Behind the Noose, *Intelligence Report*, Southern Poverty Law Center. Accessed 3/28/08, Southern Poverty Law Center web site.

10. Provost, Eric. L., Director/Chief of Public Safety, APSU Campus Police (2003, November 11). Memorandum—Formal Inquiry, "Noose" found on Campus.

11. Sniffen, Michael. (2006). Hate Crimes Rose 8% in 2006. *Associated Press*, Retrieved November 19, 2007, Yahoo! News web page.

Tanya Y. Price, Assistant Professor, Cultural Anthropology

+++

## Controversies: Media Impact on the Wars

For years, there has been ongoing argument about the phenomena of media rampage on public opinion. How much do the media really influence the American people? Many believe that the media have an uncanny psychological impact on society.[203] Others, like Daniel Hallin and Clarence Wyatt, say no, the media have no impact on the deci-

---

203 Johnson, K. A. (1987b). *Media images of Boston's black community*. Boston: William Monroe Trotter Institute, University of Massachusetts–Boston; Hacker, A. (1997). "Are the Media really "White"?" In E. E. Dennis & E. C. Pease (Eds.), *The media in black and white* (pp. 71-76). New Brunswick & London: Transaction. Changes and Illusion 141; Sorenson, S. B., J. G. Manz and R. A. Berk (1998). "News media coverage and the epidemiology of homicide." *American Journal of Public Health*. 1510-1514; Wimmer, R. D. and J. R. Dominick (2005). *Mass Media research: An introduction* (8th ed. ). Belmont, CA: Wadsworth

sion making process of the American public.[204] For example, the idea that "so called negative images of war shown to the American people would stain their moral judgment to engage in war" was found to be untrue. As a matter of fact, Hallin and Wyatt found no evidence to support any causal relationship between the editorial tone and bias in the media with loss of public support for the war.[205] So how, then, do the media affect the American public?

There is ongoing discussion about whether the various forms of media have a psychological and emotional impact on the lives of the American people. Many of the issues that are discussed today are explained and brought to life by the media, whether it be print media, television (tell-a-vision, someone's vision), radio, Internet, etc. The media state that they simply report what they see. Well, this may be true, but everyone knows that each person has his or her own view of what they see to tell. So we get many different views from each storyteller. The story tellers in this case are the varied forms of media, which are growing daily. Each has its own version depending on its audience and ownership, which we will discuss a in a few moments.

Ohio State University professor John Mueller, whose study on media and public opinion is widely used, conducted a comparative analysis of the Korean and Vietnam wars. He said, "The support for the wars on the general public followed a pattern of decline that was very similar, even though the media were neither as pervasive nor as critical during the Korean conflict as they were during the Vietnam War."[206] According to Mueller, during the Korean War, television was in its infancy, but the ways in which the American public supported both conflicts were the same. Mueller identified a recurring trend in public responses to national conflicts. This trend flatly contradicted the notion that the media dominates policy formulation through biases of the editorial tone in reporting. Mueller called this tendency the

---

204  Dixon, T. L. (2006) "Psychological reactions to crime news portrayals of Black criminals: Understanding the moderating roles of prior news viewing and stereotype endorsement." *Communication Monographs*, 73, 163-187; Dixon, T. L. (2007). "Black criminal and White officers: The effects of racially misrepresenting law breakers and law defenders on television news." *Media psychology*, 10, 270-291; Campbell, R., Martin, C. R., & Fabos, B. (2005). *Media and Culture: An introduction to mass communication*. Boston: Bedford/St Martin's.

205  William M. Darley, "War Policy, Public Support, and the Media." *Parameters*, 2005; Ron Stienman, *Inside Television's First War*. Columbia MO: University of Missouri Press, 2002. Data was based on 1,733 ABC, CBS and NBC evening Newscasts broad on the Gulf War.

206  Ditton, Jason and Derek Chadee (2006). "People's Perceptions of their Likely Future risk of Criminal Victimization." *British Journal of Criminology*, May 2006; 46: 505-518; Peelo. Moia, Brian Francis, Keith soothill, Jayn Person and Elizabeth Ackerley (2004) "Newspaper reporting and the public construction of homicide." British. *Journal of Criminology*, Mar 2004; 44:256-275; William, Paul and Julie Dickinson (1993) "Fear of Crime: Read all about it? The Relationship between Newspaper Crime Reporting and Fear of Crime", *British Journal of Criminology*, Winter 1993; 33:33-56

---

"rally round the flag" phenomena.[207] There have been other researchers who have also seen this same tendency among the American public.

One of most noted theorists who wrote on this type of public behavior before the modern age was Carl von Clausewitz. Clausewitz describes this behavior as "moral forces."[208] Today, we would describe the phenomenon as a natural factor in human nature or public opinion. Clausewitz considers these moral forces or natural factors to be the most important elements in war. He described these factors as a natural "primordial hatred and enmity resident in the people toward those perceived as enemies."[209] He further describes this as "latent hostile intention" which manifests itself in an impulse to destroy the enemy. So then, this behavior basically suggests that it is a physiological expression amongst the public to respond in the way they do when their very notion of "being/reality" is threatened.

Clausewitz further states that this latent "hatred and enmity" are to be regarded as blind natural forces. William Darley and others who study the polling of public opinion, particularly as it relates to war, contend that what we describe today as public opinion regarding a war is better understood "not as a rational action, but primarily as a non cognitive passion guided by an instinctive faith that a population invests in the intellectual judgment and wisdom of trusted political leaders."[210] Clausewitz's theory implies that the intensity of public opinion reflects the character of national policy. Meaning, "If war is part of policy, policy will determine its character. The more ambitious policy becomes so becomes war. Within this consideration it is agreed that the aim of policy is to unify and reconcile all aspects of internal administration as well as spiritual values."

So what does all of this really mean? In a nutshell—public opinion is not simply significantly influenced by the stories told by the media, but is a natural response to the threat of a people's notion of reality. This reality is rooted in the fundamental philosophy of a nation's system, its macro system, if you will. So the question to ask at this point, to better understand the behavior of public opinion in America with respect to the wars, might be, "What is the basic philosophy of our capitalistic society?"

The Korean War, the Vietnam War, the Gulf War, and the Iraqi War all occurred at different times in this country's development, so-

---

207  Romer, D. Jamieson, K. H., & de Coteau, N. J. (1998) "The Treatment of persons of color in local television news: Ethnic blame discourse or realistic group conflict?" *Communication Research*, 25, 268-305; Also see Supra at 16 and 17

208  Supra at 198

209  Supra at 202

210  Supra at 203

cially as well as politically. The media had significantly matured between the times of each conflict, meaning that each entity had developed its own audience and voice. The hands of ownership and corporate takeovers were greatly felt during the wars.

Television was in its infancy during the time of the Korean War. It was big business mainly because it was new and revolutionary with singlehanded ownership. The impact of the media on the Vietnam War was significant in that it was the first time battlefield casualties were brought into the homes of the American people. No one questions why there was such an opposition to the Vietnam War—death in massive numbers, a drag on the country's economy—all for twelve very long years. With respect to the Gulf War, however, public opposition was interpreted as an inability of the American people to see their leader's necessary capability to perform, to strategically "think and do" to eradicate any threat toward the American people. Public opinion of the Iraqi War was presented much the same. The public wanted to know how it was relevant and why we needed that type of political positioning, i.e., What was the actual threat? Both wars, the Gulf and Iraq, drew public criticism and expressions of no confidence in leadership and its ability to interpret and execute the law or the spirit of the law through policy and legislative procedure.

Today, the major television networks are owned, primarily, by multibillion dollar entities with diversified interests from food to entertainment. Revenues, or in the television industry, ratings, are a key factor in what is provided to the American public. "What is the hottest seller to our audience?" as opposed to "What simply is the news on social policy and procedure?" The era of reporting the facts in a literary, informed style and demeanor is over, if it ever existed. Similarly, when the public is confident in its leadership, it will surge ahead with vigor, focused on protecting "the American way", particularly during a time of war. When public opinion changes, it is seen as and expression of either a loss of confidence in the leadership's ability to perform or the public's a loss of conviction that battlefield activity is the best ways to uphold the fundamental law of policy or the spirit of its intent. Is it possible that our policies are too ambiguous? Is it also possible that the media actually has NO impact on popular opinion, but that the policies are actually so ambiguous that it gives the appearance that the public is impacted by the media?

Every news outlet is struggling to capture and hold onto a fixed audience. This competition leads journalists to emphasize and sensationalize negative events. Indeed, when the Center for Media and Public Affairs conducted a nonpartisan evaluation of network news broadcasts, it found the following:

1. During the active war against Saddam Hussein, 51% of the reports about the conflict were negative.

2. Six months after the land battle ended, 77% of all reports were still negative.

3. In the 2004 general election 89% of all reports about the Saddam Hussein conflict were still negative.

4. By the spring of 2006, 94% of all reposts were still negative.[211]

Interestingly enough, this decline in media support was much faster during the advent of Saddam Hussein than during the Korean and Vietnam wars although it is natural that some of the hostile commentary could simply be reflective of the nature of the reporting.

The maturation process of the media seems to have run from single-handed ownership with a sincere public interest and a relatively unbiased approach to reporting the news, to a multi-billion dollar diversified corporation strategically selling to selected audiences to maintain high ratings.

## CONCLUSION

The distortion of the extent of crime and crime coverage in the news media is well documented. After all, it is in the financial interest of the media to present whatever sells. There are numerous studies that have focused on the extent to which crime is reported in local print media, the number of television news reports that focus on crime, and reports which compare newspaper coverage of crime in other countries.[212] There is also a growing body of research that has begun to examine the impact of racial and ethnic stereotyping in the various forms of media.[213] Most of these studies focus on U.S. television news programming and investigate media portrayals of race and crime. These studies have determined that minorities and people of color are often associated with criminality on local news programs, and that this type of portrayal can have a significant impact on

---

211  Media Spinning the Iraq War. Available at http://www. discoverthenetworks. org/viewSubCategory. asp?id=22

212  Greer, C. and Jewkes, Y. (2005) "Extremes of otherness: media images of social exclusion", *Social Justice*, 32(1): 20–31

213  Valentino, N. (1999). "Crime news and the priming of racial attitudes during evaluations of the president." Public Opinion Quarterly, 63, 293-320; von Hippel, W., Sekaquaptewa, D., & Vargas, P. (1995). "On the role of encoding processes in stereotype maintenance." Advances in Experimental Social Psychology, 27, 177-254; Wilson, B. J., Kunkel, D., Linz, D., Potter, J., Donnerstein, E., Smith, S. L., Blumenthal, E., & Berry, M. (1998). "Violence in television overall: University of California study." In M. Seawall (Ed.), National television violence study II (pp. 3-204). Thousand Oaks, CA: Sage; Wimmer, R. D., & Dominick, J. R. (2000). Mass media research: An introduction (6th ed.). Belmont, CA: Wadsworth; Wyer, R. S., & Srull, T. (1989). Memory and cognition in its social context. Hillsdale, NJ: Erlbaum.

how society perceives minorities in general but African-Americans in particular.

There is one common thread that stands out in all this research: there is an overrepresentation of violent crime—and the frequency with which violent crime is presented does not match official crime statistics. Unfortunately, what sells seems to be violent crime, especially those committed by young African-American males.

The media would no doubt argue that,

1. This is the type of crime that the public fears most.
2. Violent crime is cheap and easy to report.
3. Reporting violent crime requires no in depth investigative reporting and is therefore cost effective.
4. It has a wide audience appeal.

Of course these arguments give rise to yet another set of profound questions:

1. Why do crimes committed by young male minorities invoke such public fear?
2. Do similar crimes committed by other ethnic groups invoke the same degree of fear?
3. Are the crimes that the public fears most only committed by young minority males or are the crimes that the public fears most (that happen to be committed by young minority males) the ones that the media choose to focus on?

This raises yet another question, "Do the media really have the power to influence society's opinion about crime or is society so gullible that members of the public are just that easily influenced?

The bottom line seems to be that the over dramatization of the worst types of crimes sells newspapers and magazines and guarantees an audience to television news and crime-related programming—the larger the viewing audience, the greater the advertising revenue. This is not intended in any way to suggest that the media deliberately try to incite public fear or that the media attempt to support a punitive crime control agenda. However, it can reasonably be argued that the media's ability to exploit public fear may inadvertently promote some type of agenda—all in the name of profit.

### CRITICAL THINKING QUESTIONS

Review the Case Study presented at the beginning of the chapter, and answer the following questions.

1. Why would America show a kind of hatred toward O.J. that was unseen in other murder trials?
2. What were the key factors that divided the nation during the O.J. Simpson trial?
3. If what some of the researchers on public opinion polls say is true, what do you think the American public actually believed about this case to make them so angry and polarized?
4. What about the psychological and emotional feelings of a society; do they go away as the society matures, or are they passed into policy and legislation. How?
5. Is the question of race still an issue today in American legislation? How is it seen?

## CHAPTER RESOURCES

Ready for Review
Introduction: Social Overview
The Media, Politics and Crime
Media Impact on the Criminal Justice System
- Impact on Policing
- Impact on the Courts

Media Impact on Society and Race Relations
In the News: The Duke Lacrosse Drama
Race Ethnicity and Policy
Controversy: Media Impact on the Wars

## KEY TERMS

Media
Internet (World wide web)
Social Control

# Chapter 4. Race and the Death Penalty

## Objectives

- To evaluate the impact of race on prosecutorial decisions to seek the death penalty
- To evaluate the impact of the quality of legal representation on the disposition of a death eligible case.

### Case Study: Significant Death Penalty Cases

Many citizens consider it insensitive and unseemly, if not immoral, for a country, with our historical record on slavery and race discrimination, to persist in using a punishment that is administered and controlled almost exclusively by whites and serves no demonstrated function, but has a profound adverse impact, physically, psychologically, and symbolically on its black citizens.

—Prof. David C. Baldus, Professor of Law, College of Law, University of Iowa, and George Woodward, in: "America's Experiment with Capital Punishment", J.R. Acker, CAP, 1998.

Defendant Jack House was represented by attorneys who had never read the State's death penalty statute. The lawyers did not visit the crime scene nor did they interview the state's witness. Moreover, counsel did not conduct discovery of the State's evidence and barely spoke with their client. During the testimony of a key prosecution witness, one of the members of the defense team left the court room, but later cross-examined that very witness without having heard the original testimony and, because they were unaware that there was a sentencing phase to the trial, presented no mitigating evidence to argue against a death penalty.[214] After sentencing and during appeal, defense counsel failed to present new evidence that there were three credible witnesses who claimed to have seen the victim after the state's certified time of death, which meant that their client had an iron-clad alibi. One of the attorneys was later disbarred for his performance and the U.S. Court of Appeals characterized their performance as a state of preparation which qualified them as spectators only.[215]

Former death row inmate Gary Nelson was represented at trial by a sole practitioner who had never tried a death penalty case. The attorney's request for co-counsel was denied. No funds were provided for an investigator and the attorney neglected to request funds for an expert witness. Moreover, the attorney's closing argument was a meager 255 words. He was later disbarred for other reasons. Nelson's case caught the attention of a well-respected law firm and he was eventually cleared of all charges.[216]

In the case of Judy Haney, the defendant's court appointed attorney was so inebriated during the trial that he was held in contempt and temporarily jailed.[217] Despite this infraction, the proceeding was allowed to continue. Counsel later failed to present hospital records showing that the defendant was a battered wife, a fact which would have gone a long way in supporting her defense. Consequently, Haney was sentenced to death and today remains on death row.

Terry Collins served time in jail and was disbarred in 1998 after pleading guilty to forging birth certificates to help his DWI clients obtain drivers licenses. Collins represented five inmates currently on death row. All five inmates claim that Collins did not provide an adequate defense. In the case of Frank Chandler, Collins neglected to disclose to the court, and to his client, that he and his co-counsel had previously represented a key prosecution witness in various felony charges. This was clearly a conflict of interest that presented grounds for reversal.

David Tamer surrendered his law license for misappropriation of client funds, including those of death-row inmate Blanche Taylor Moore. Tamer later pled guilty to felony embezzlement and received a suspended sentence. He was disbarred following a three-year suspension for ethical violations and other misconduct. Tamer also had a

---

214  Death Penalty Information Center. "Ineffective Defense Counsel. Fight the Death Penalty in USA" available at http://www. fdp. dk/uk/couns-uk. htm

215  Ibid.

216  Ibid.

217  "The Forgotten Population: A Look at Death Row in the United States Through the Experiences of Women." Published December 2004 American Civil Liberties Union available at http://www. aclu. org/files/FilesPDFs/womenondeathrow. pdf

history of mental problems that impaired his ability to service his clients. In fact, in the weeks prior to Tamer's appeal on behalf of death-row inmate Willie Fisher, Tamer was hospitalized for depression. According to a report by the Common Sense Foundation, these types of atrocities are common.[218]

The case of Frank Lee Smith of Florida is another good example of the problems faced by indigent capital case defendants seeking exoneration through DNA evidence. Smith was convicted and sentenced to death for the rape and murder of an eight-year-old girl in 1985. His defense attorneys sought DNA testing but the state resisted. Smith avoided a lethal injection for 14 years. He did, however, eventually die of cancer on death row before DNA testing exonerated him. The prosecutor who argued against the test later said that the outcome of the case did not shake his belief in the death penalty because there will be times when guilty people go free, and innocent people will be wrongfully incarcerated.[219]

In 1989, the Texas Court of Criminal Appeals overturned the conviction of Charles Bradley when the Court found that the police and the prosecutors failed to investigate leads to other potential suspects, suppressed evidence placing other suspects at the crime scene at the time of the crime, failed to call witnesses to rebut the state's case, allowed the perjured testimony of a witness, and failed to notify the court that another man had confessed to the crime.[220]

## INTRODUCTION

In the past three chapters we have evaluated the concepts of race and ethnicity, and we have analyzed the impact of the media on perceptions of race, ethnicity and criminality as well as the impact of race and ethnicity on the decision-making process of the criminal justice system. We have also questioned whether the underlying ideology of each of the three parts of the criminal justice system (police, courts and corrections). In this chapter we will evaluate the impact of race on the administration of the death penalty. Specifically, this chapter will attempt to evaluate the impact of the race of the defendant and the race of the victim on decisions to sentence a defendant to death.

In as much as capital punishment is intended predominantly for those who commit violent crimes, it can be reasonably argued that for purposes of retribution, the state has the right to impose a level of

---

218 Death Penalty Information Center. Criminal Injustice Independent Weekly (Durham) October 16, 2002 Criminal Injustice By Bob Burtman, available at http://www.deathpenaltyinfo.org/node/533

219 Ibid.

220 O'Boye, S. (2000) Death row prisoner cleared by DNA test 11 months after he dies of cancer. Sun Sentinel, December 14th

pain and punishment equal to or greater than the pain suffered by the victim. On the other hand, deterrence, of which there are two types, seeks to provide some measure of service to society at large. Specific deterrence seeks to prevent individual offenders from continuing to commit crimes by exacting punishment for previous criminal activity.[221] The goal of incapacitation is met by removing an offender from society. Opponents of capital punishment argue that individual offenders can be prevented from continuing to commit crimes simply by sentencing offenders to life in prison without the possibility of parole, as opposed to putting them to death.[222]

General deterrence seeks to prevent crimes from being committed in the first place.[223] The fact that the state can inflict the death penalty, for example, is expected to deter potential offenders from committing capital crimes.

Opponents and advocates of capital punishment both rely on these conflicting perspectives to justify their positions. Opponents argue that the death penalty fails to deter crime and serves no other purpose in society.[224] They also argue that the death penalty cannot be applied fairly by a discriminatory criminal justice process. Additionally, opponents feel that the state should not involve itself in executions, since this action tells members of society that violence is an acceptable method of resolving disputes.[225]

Advocates of capital punishment claim that the growing body of research which supports the visible deterrent effect of death penalty laws is a clear indicator that capital punishment penalty prevents homicides.[226] Although these proponents admit to some questionable due process issues surrounding its application, they argue that these occurrences are either rare or can be corrected by legislative and administrative reforms. Their strongest argument, however, is based on public opinion.[227] Generally speaking, society favors capital punishment because of its retributive results.[228]

---

221  Ibid.

222  Paternoster, R. (1991). "Prosecutorial discretion and capital sentencing in North and South Carolina." In R. M. Bohm (Ed. ), *The death penalty in America: Current research* (pp. 39-52). Cincinnati, OH: Anderson; Keil, T. J. & Vito, G. F. (1995); "Race and the death penalty in Kentucky murder trials: 1976-1991." *American Journal of Criminal Justice*, 20(1), 17-36.

223  Albanese, J. S. (2001). *Criminal Justice*. Boston, MA: Allyn and Bacon; Champion, D. J. (1989). *The US Sentencing Guidelines: Implications for Criminal Justice*. New York: Praeger

224  Bedau Hugo Adam, & Paul G. Cassess (2005). *Debating the Death Penalty: Should America have Capital Punishment? The Experts on both sides make their case*. Oxford University Press

225  McCord, David, Barry Latzer (2010). *Death Penalty Cases: Leading U.S. Supreme Court Cases on Capital Punishment*. 3rd ed. Burlington, MA: Butterworth-Heinemann

226  Death Penalty Information Center (2003). "Understanding capital punishment: A guide through the death penalty debate." Death Penalty Information Center

227  Ibid.

228  Ibid.

Whether or not the death penalty has a deterrent effect is still questionable. Capital punishment therefore remains one of the most hotly debated issues in American politics today. Passions run high for both antagonists and protagonists. Indeed, despite the evidence that shows significant racial disparities and substantial error rates in the application and administration of the death penalty, the practice continues to attract strong support. Let's take a look at the numbers.

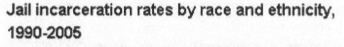

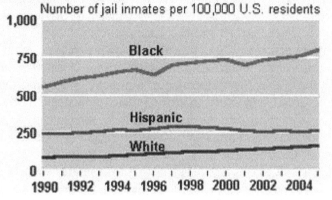

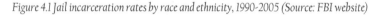

*Figure 4.1 Jail incarceration rates by race and ethnicity, 1990-2005 (Source: FBI website)*

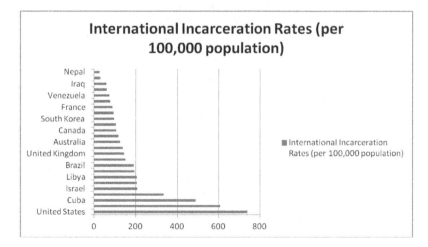

\\*Figure 4.2 International Incarceration rates 2009*

As mentioned previously, African-Americans constitute 12.3% of the national population and White-Americans constitute 74.5%.[229] Yet, African-Americans constitute 42% of the national death row population.[230] And the picture is even worse in certain states. For example, in Philadelphia, Pennsylvania, 83% of the death row inmates are African-American.[231] In a study conducted in Philadelphia to determine the impact of the defendant's race on the likelihood of his receiving a death sentence, it was determined that despite similar circumstances African-American males were almost four times more likely to receive a death penalty verdict than White-American males.[232] Moreover, recent social science research has revealed strong inconsistencies in prosecutors' decisions to seek the death penalty for African-American offenders based on factors other than the severity of the crime.[233] In a Kentucky study on prosecutorial decision making in capital sentencing, researchers identified quantitative proof of discrimination, especially based on the victim's race. Kentucky prosecutors were more likely to seek the death penalty in cases where the defendant was African-American and the victim was White-American.[234]

A national race-of-victim analysis has revealed that African-American victims account for almost 50% (47.1% for years 2000-2006) of homicide victims nationally,[235] but of the 500 inmates executed nationally, between 1977 and 1998, 81.8% of their victims were White-American[236]. Additionally, offenders whose victims are White-American are 4 1/3 times more likely to receive the death penalty, even when factors such as the heinousness of the crime, prior convictions, and a prior relationship between the victim and the offender are taken into

229   U.S. Census Bureau, Current Population Survey, 2009 Annual Social and Economic Supplement. Available at www. census. gov

230   Ibid.

231   Ibid.

232   Baldus, D. C., Woodworth, G., Zuckerman, D., Weiner, N. A., & Broffitt, B. (1998). "Racial discrimination and the death penalty in the post-Furman era: An empirical and legal overview, with recent findings from Philadelphia." Cornell Law Review, 83, 1638-1770.

233   Keil, Thomas, J. and Gennaro F. Vito (2006) "Capriciousness or Fairness? Race and Prosecutorial Decisions to seek the Death Penalty in Kentucky." Journal of Ethnicity Criminal Justice Vol. 4 Issue 3 pg 27-49; Wang, Xia, Daniel P. Mears, Cassia Spohn and Lisa Dario (2009). "Assessing the Differential Effects of Race and Ethnicity on Sentence Outcomes under Different Sentencing Systems." Crime and Delinquency, 2009

234   Ibid.

235   General Accounting Office (1990). "Death Penalty sentencing: Research Indicates Pattern of Racial Disparities." Washington, DC: GAO; John Blume, Theodore Eisenberg, and Martin T. Wells, "Explaining Death Row's Population and Racial Composition," Journal of Empirical Legal Studies, Volume 1, Issue 1,165-207, March 2004.

236   Ibid.

consideration.[237] Prosecutors are also more likely to seek a death sentence when the victim is

(1)  White-American,
(2)  of high social status,
(3)  not previously known to the offender, and
(4)  when the offender is represented by a public defender.[238]

This is particularly true for African-Americans capital case offenders.

APPLICATION OF THE DEATH PENALTY

Racial discrimination pervades the U.S. death penalty at every stage of the process. There is only one way to eradicate ethnic bias and the echoes of racism, from death penalty procedures in the United States—and this is by eradicating the death penalty itself.[239]

The one aspect of capital punishment that both antagonists and protagonists agree on is that it is blatantly racist.[240] Indeed, in capital cases, it appears as if the lives of White-American victims are valued far more than the lives of African-American victims. Prosecutors are more likely to seek the death penalty when the victim is White-American than when the victim is African-American, and juries are far more likely to hand down death sentences when the victim is White-American.[241]

Between 1930 and 1966, African-Americans represented 54% of all inmates put to death in the U.S. and 90% of all the people executed for rape.[242]When the case involves an African-American defendant and a White-American victim, the death penalty seems almost automatic. In fact, research shows that African-American defendants who kill White-Americans have a 25% probability of receiving the death

237  Amnesty International (2003) United States of America: Death by Discrimination-The continuing role of race in capital cases, available at http://www. amnesty. org/en/library/info/AMR51/046/2003/en; Baldus D. C., George Woodworth & Charles A Pulaski, Jr. (1990). *Equal Justice and the Death Penalty: A legal and empirical analysis.* Boston: Northeastern University Press

238  Phillips, Scott (2010) "Death more likely if victim is high-status." *Law and Society Review* 43-4: 807-837; Phillips, Scott (2009). "Legal Disparities in the Case of Capital Punishment." *Journal of Criminal Law and Criminology,* Vol. 99 No 3

239  Amnesty International (1999). "Unites States of America, Killing with Prejudice: Race and the Death Penalty in the USA" available at http://asiapacific. amnesty. org/library/Index/ENGAMR510521999?open&=of=ENG-393

240  Baldus, D., G. Wentworth and C. Pulaski (1990). *Equal Justice and the death penalty: A Legal and Empirical Analysis.* Boston, MA: Northeastern University Press; Paternoster, R. 1991. *Capital Punishment in America.* New York: Lexington Books; Radelet, M. 1981. "Racial characteristics and the imposition of the death penalty." *American Sociological Review* 46: 918-927

241  Ibid.

242  Bureau of Justice Statistics. (1992). Capital punishment 1991. Washington, D. C. : Government Printing Office

penalty, while White-Americans who kill African-Americans have a zero percent probability.[243]

Research done on 594 murder cases in the state of Georgia in 1990, revealed the following:

> (1) controlling for all legally relevant variables, the death penalty was sought in 45% of the cases involving White-American victims but only in 15 % of the cases with African-American victims.

> (2) prosecutors sought the death penalty in 58% of the cases of African-American defendants with White-American victims, but only 15% of the cases with African-American defendants of African-American victims.

> (3) fifty seven percent of defendants with White-American victims and 42% of the defendants with African-American victims were sentenced to death.[244]

The researchers concluded that race had a potent influence on the likelihood that the state would seek the death penalty as well as the likelihood that a jury would return a death penalty verdict.[245]

Earlier, in a 1984 study of 300 capital murder cases in South Carolina, researchers found the following,

> (1) In cases involving White-American victims, prosecutors were 2 ½ times more likely to seek death than in cases involving African-American victims.

> (2) In cases of African-American offenders with White-American victims the state sought the death penalty 49.5% of the time.

> (3) In cases involving African-American offenders with African-American victims, the state sought the death penalty only 11.3 % of the time.

> (4) In cases with White-American victims, prosecutors sought the death penalty with only one aggravating felony, while in cases involving African-American victims; they only sought the death penalty when the case involved several aggravating felonies.[246]

These statistics send the message that homicides committed against African-Americans have to be significantly more vicious and brutal to satisfy the criteria for the death penalty. It seems reason-

---

243   Porter, Gary (1997) "Crime control and the death penalty." *The Advocate*, Vol. 19, No. 6 (November 1997); Baldus, D. G. Wentworth and C. Pulaski (1990). *Equal Justice and the death penalty: A Legal and Empirical Analysis.* Boston, MA: Northeastern University Press

244   Porter, Gary (1997) "Crime control and the death penalty." *The Advocate*, Vol. 19, No. 6 (November 1997); Baldus, D. G. Wentworth and C. Pulaski (1990). *Equal Justice and the death penalty: A Legal and Empirical Analysis.* Boston, MA: Northeastern University Press

245   Ibid.

246   Supra at 289

able to argue that African-American capital case defendants are more likely to receive a death penalty verdict than White-American capital case defendants. In fact, although African-Americans represent 12.3% of the national population, they make up 41.6% of the national death row population, 29.4% of the Maryland population but 80% of the Maryland death row population, 10.8% of the Pennsylvania population but 60%of the Pennsylvania death row population, 32% of the Louisiana population but 63.5% of the Louisiana death row population and 15.8% of the Arkansas population but 60% of the Arkansas death row population.[247] Shockingly, of the 1200 executions that have taken place in the United States between 1976 and 2010, only 30 cases involved White-American defendants and African-American victims.[248]

Some argue that the biases and prejudices that permeate the criminal justice system have been found to be a significant factor in the decision making processes of police officers, prosecutors, judges, and jurors.[249] Indeed, although racism and bigotry have been written out of the law, it is arguable that it still exists in police precincts, courtrooms, and jury boxes. In fact, according ongoing research "among the more troubling findings, is that several of these factors (eyewitness misidentification, false accusations, false confessions, police and prosecutorial misconduct, inadequacy of counsel) are more pronounced in the conviction of innocent African-American men".[250] Researchers also claim that subtle elements or racism are even found in the area of forensic science.[251]

In 1963, a landmark Supreme Court ruling determined that a defendant in a criminal case who is deemed indigent must have counsel appointed to represent him.[252] Subsequent courts have upheld this ruling as one of the cardinal principles of criminal law and the criminal justice system, and it has become one of the mandates of the Sixth

---

247 NAACP Legal Defense and Educational Fund, Inc. Fall 2009, New York: NAACP Legal Defense and Educational Fund, Inc.

248 The Clark County Prosecuting Attorney. The Death Penalty. US Executions since 1976 available at http://www. clarkprosecutor. org/html/death/usexecute. htm

249 Ibid.

250 Johnson, D. (2008). "Racial Prejudice, perceived injustice, and the Black-White gap in punitive attitudes." *Journal of Criminal Justice*, Volume 36, Issue 2, Pages 198-206

251 Weitzer, Ronald (1996). "Racial discrimination in the criminal justice system: Findings and problems in the literature", *Journal of Criminal Justice*, Volume 24, Issue 4. pp 309-322

252 Thousands of newly released FBI documents show a pattern of racial bias and incompetence at the FBIUs once highly vaunted crime lab—this according to the National Association of Criminal Defense Lawyers. The FBI memos—part of 60,000 pages generated by an 18-month investigation by the Justice Department inspector general US office into the crime lab—also show repeated favoritism towards prosecutors. Access audio and video broadcast at http://www. democracynow. org/1997/12/3/fbi_crime_lab

Amendment to the United States Constitution.[253] Notwithstanding this significant show of support for equity, an indigent defendant still does not have the right to choose the counsel appointed to represent him[254] and current statistics indicate that indigent capital case defendants, minority capital case defendants, and capital case defendants whose victims are White-American are more likely to be sentenced to death than to receive a life sentence.[255] More importantly, there is disproportionate representation of indigent and minority offenders in prison and on death row.[256] And even in cases where representation is equal, issues such as prosecutorial misconduct still make the field an uneven one.

### Prosecutorial Misconduct

> It is as much the duty of the prosecuting attorney to refrain from improper methods calculated to bring about a wrongful conviction as it is to use every legitimate means to bring about a just one....a prosecutors proper interest is not that he shall win a case, but that justice is done.[257]

The highest duty of the American criminal justice system and those sworn to uphold the law is to protect innocent citizens from wrongful convictions and death sentences. Unfortunately, there is growing evidence that prosecutors in general, and criminal case prosecutors in particular, possess overwhelming advantages (both legal and illegal) which frequently corrupt the outcome of the cases they try.[258] The execution of illegal advantages is referred to as prosecutorial misconduct. Prosecutorial misconduct seems to fall into several categories, including but not limited to: courtroom misconduct; mishandling of physical evidence; failing to disclose exculpatory evidence; threatening, badgering or tampering with witnesses; using false or misleading evidence; harassing, displaying bias toward, or having a vendetta against the defendant or the defendant's counsel; and deliberate-

---

253  Gideon v. Wainwright, 372 U.S. 335 (1963), U.S. Supreme Court

254  U.S. Constitution Amend V; N. C. Constitution Art. 1, § 22; N. C. GEN. STAT. § 15-144 (1983)

255  State v. Thacker, 301 N. C. 348, 351-52, 271 S. E. 2d 252, 255 (1980)

256  Swarns, Christina (2004). "The Uneven Scales of Capital Justice: How race and class affect who ends up on death row." *The American Prospect*: Liberal Intelligence available at www. prospect. org/cs/articles?articleId=7882

257  Race and Crime-Data Source and Meaning available at Law. jrank. org/pages/1090/Race-Crime-Data-source-meaning. html

258  Berger v. United States, 295 U.S. 78, 88, 55 S. Ct. 629, 79 L. Ed. 1314 (1935). ; The National Centre for Prosecution Ethics: Quotes about prosecutors and the prosecution function. National District Attorneys Association Education Division: National College of District Attorneys. www. ethicsforprosecutors. com/quotes. html

ly excluding jurors based on race, ethnicity, gender, or other discrim-inatory grounds.[259]

Prosecutorial misconduct or unethical behavior is often guided by a desire to obtain a higher than average rate of conviction. It can also be fed by public outrage at the nature of a particular crime, or it can be fueled by a politician's desire to gain public support. Unfortu-nately, statistics show that instances of prosecutorial misconduct are more often found in cases involving indigent defendants than in cases involving those defendants who are able to afford private attorneys.[260]

The fact that the cases of prosecutorial misconduct are rarely pun-ished is perhaps the most significant reason why it continues to exist in courtrooms across the country. Prosecutors who are likely to en-gage in misconduct have been described as those who work in envi-ronments where the highest charges are always sought, criminal law is broadly interpreted, and the focus is not just on conviction, but on conviction with the highest possible penalty.[261] Research has also suggested that prosecutors may not necessarily have noble reasons for their misconduct and that bigotry, racism, and greed may also be determining factors.[262] Prosecutorial misconduct has become an in-creasingly common reason for reversal of sentences, and most fre-quently involves prosecutors failing to comply with rules of discov-ery and failing to turn over all evidence.[263] The disturbing part of this process is that prosecutors who engage in misconduct have absolute immunity from being sued, even if the misconduct is intentional.[264]

### WHAT THE NUMBERS SHOW

There is little argument that the criminal justice system discrimi-nates against indigent defendants. According to data collected by the Federal Death Penalty Resource Counsel Project indigent defendants are less likely to receive plea agreements in death penalty cases than are defendants who retain private counsel.[265] On the other hand, the data, presented in a BJS report on indigent defense counter argues

---

259  Police Prosecution and Judicial Misconduct http://truthinjustice. org/index. htm
260  "Is Prosecutorial Misconduct a Widespread Problem in Capital Cases?" Available at deathpenalty. procon. org/view. answers. php?questionID=0000993
261  Supra at 305
262  Ibid.
263  Ibid.
264  Gersman, B. (2010) "Bad Faith Exception to Prosecutorial Immunity for Brady Violations" available at
digitalcommons. pace. edu/cgi/viewcontent. cgi?article=1635&context=lawfaculty
265  Ibid.

that conviction rates for indigent defendants and those with private attorneys are about the same in federal and state courts.[266]

It is not surprising, therefore, that statistics show that those offenders who are represented by publicly-financed attorneys are found guilty and incarcerated at a higher rate than those defendants who paid for their own legal representation: 88% compared to 77% in federal courts and 71% compared to 54% in state courts.[267] Additionally, sentence lengths for convicted offenders are longer, on average, for those with publicly financed attorneys than for those who hired counsel.[268] And, of those offenders who were allowed bail, over 30% of those who had a public attorney and 75% of those with a hired attorney were released before adjudication.[269] Seventy-five percent of state and federal prison inmates who had a public defender or assigned counsel and 66% with their own counsel either pleaded guilty to the charges or did not contest them.[270]

So although it can be argued that in cases of public versus private legal representation, the outcome is statistically the same, it would appear that the type of representation is still significant as far as sentencing, rate of incarceration, severity of sentencing, pretrial release, release before adjudication, and granting of bail are concerned.

A report by the American Bar Association (ABA) concluded that in 93% of capital cases reviewed, race of victim and race of defendant discrimination was evident.[271] For example, over 80% of capital cases involved White-American victims although nationally, 50% of murder victims are African-American.[272] Once again this suggests that the lives of White-Americans are valued more than the lives of African-Americans. Moreover, critics of the death penalty have always argued that not only are the administrative policies applied arbitrarily, but only a small portion of those who commit the crimes are actually brought to justice.[273]

---

266  Access home page at http://www. fairness. com/resources/relation?relation_id=7382
267  Seigel, L. (2010) *Introduction to Criminal Justice*, Wadsworth CA
268  Bureau of Justice Statistics. (2001). Uniform crime report of Federal bureau of Investigation, indigent defense statistics, 1999. Washington, D. C. : U.S. Dept. of Justice, Offices of Justice Programs, Bureau of Justice Statistics.
269  Compendium of Federal Justice Statistics, 1998, Bureau of Justice Statistics report, NCJ 180258, Table 5. 1 available at http://www. findalawyerfast. com/lawyer-articles/defense-counsel-in-criminal-cases/ ; U.S. Department of Justice, Office of Justice Programs, Bureau of Justice Statistics Special Report. Defense Counsel in Criminal Cases. November 2000 NCJ 179023
270  Ibid.
271  Ibid.
272  Ibid.
273  American Bar Association (1991). Resolution 107, ABA House of Delegates: Chicago: Author

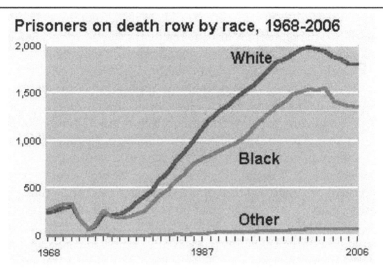

Figure 4.3 Prisoners on Death Row by Race, 1968-2006

| African-American | 1482 |
| White-American | 1605 |
| Hispanic | 347 |
| Other | 83 |

- 86% of White-American victims were killed by White-Americans
- 94% of African-American victims were killed by African-Americans

Persons Executed for Interracial Murders:

| White-American Defendant/African-American Victim | 12 |
| African-American Defendant/White-American Victim | 180 |

The importance of race as a factor in the imposition of capital punishment is well documented.[274] While some of the evidence concerning the death penalty reveals that the race of the defendant alone does not result in unwarranted disparity, there is other evidence to the contrary. According to the results of a study conducted by researcher David Baldus and his colleagues, the race of the victim appears to have a profound impact on the likelihood of being charged with capital murder and receiving the death penalty. Those who murdered

274 Bureau of Justice Statistics. (2007). "Homicide Report of Federal Bureau of Investigation", National Crime Victimization Survey; Dan Eggen. Study: "Almost Half of Murder Victims Black" August 10, 2007. Washington Post available at http://www. washingtonpost. com/ wpdyn/content/article/2007/08/09/AR2007080901964. html

White-Americans were found more likely to be sentenced to death than those who murdered African-Americans.[275]

Baldus and his colleagues presented research that indicated that the race of the defendant, when combined with the race of the victim, yields significant disparities in the application of the death penalty.[276] The Baldus study also concluded that African-Americans who killed White-Americans were sentenced to death 22 times more frequently than African-Americans who killed African-Americans, and seven times more frequently than White-Americans who killed African-Americans.[277] Again, this discrepancy appears to hinge on the exercise of prosecutorial discretion. Georgia prosecutors sought the death penalty in 70% of the cases involving African-American defendants and White-American victims, while seeking the death penalty in only 19% of the cases involving White-American defendants and African-American victims, and only 15% of the cases involving African-American defendants and African-American victims.

In short, African-American defendants charged with killing White-American victims were the group most likely to receive the death penalty. Until 1991, when Donald Gaskins, a White-American man, was executed in South Carolina for the murder of an African-American victim, no White-American person had been executed for the murder of an African-American person since the Supreme Court's 1976 decision in *Furman* v. *Georgia* holding that capital punishment is not necessarily unconstitutional.[278] In all, since 1976, only 11 White-Americans have been executed for the murder of an African-American victim, while 145 African-Americans have been executed for the murder of a White-American victim, and 80% of those, currently on death row are there for killing a White-American person.[279] The Baldus Study also revealed that of the seven individuals executed in Georgia between 1976 and 1986, all were convicted of killing White-Americans, and six of them were African-American, despite the fact that of all homicides in Georgia during that period, only 9.2% involved African-American defendants and White-American victims, and 60.7% involved African-American victims.[280]

---

275  See http://deathpenaltyinfo. org/race-and-death-penalty

276  Pokorak, J. (1998). "Probing the capital prosecutor's perspective: Race and Gender of the discretionary actors." *Cornell Law Review*, 83: 6.

277  David Baldus, et al., "Arbitrariness and Discrimination in The Administration Of The Death Penalty: A Challenge To State Supreme Court," 15 Stetson L. Rev. 133 (1986); Death Penalty Information Center (2010). Arbitrariness http://www. deathpenaltyinfo. org/arbitrariness

278  Supra at 290

279  Ibid.-

280  US Supreme Court Cases from Justia and Oyez available at Supreme. justia. com/constitution/amendment-08/06-capital-punishment. html

Statistics on the imposition of the federal death penalty are similarly disturbing. In 1988, Congress enacted the first federal death penalty provision. The 1988 law authorized the death penalty for murders committed by those involved in certain drug trafficking activities under 21 U.S.C. §848. From 1988 to 1994, 75% of those convicted under 21 U.S.C. 848 were White-American.[281] However, of those who were the subject of death penalty prosecutions under that law in the same period, 8% were Hispanic or African-American (33 out of 37) and only 11% (4 out of 37) were White-American. And, indeed, the first defendant scheduled to be executed under the 1988 law is Hispanic.[282]

Additionally, a congressional subcommittee studied the application of the 1988 law and concluded that "some of the death penalty prosecutions under [21 U.S.C. §848] have been against defendants who do not seem to fit the expected 'drug kingpin' profile," including, in several cases, "young inner-city drug gang members and relatively small-time traffickers," or individuals who committed murder at the behest of a higher-up who received a lesser sentence.[283] Moreover, these researchers argued that this arbitrary application is attributable to who the victim is and not how the victim is killed.[284]

The most significant policy implication of this research is that the current administrative procedure for capital punishment appears to support and encourage serious miscarriages of justice. This is especially important since the punishment of death is irreversible.

As of April 1, 2004, there were 3,490 inmates on death row in the United States.[285] All were convicted of murder; 55% are White-American and 43% African-American; 1.4% are female, and 2% received the death penalty for crimes committed as juveniles. Since 1973, 115 innocent people have been released from death row with 10 being released in 2003 alone.[286] Some of these individuals were released just days before their scheduled executions, and researchers have even suggested that at least 25 innocent people have been executed during this century alone.[287]

---

281 "How Racism Riddles the US Death Penalty" available at
www. ejusa. org/moritorium_now/broch_race. html
282 Ibid.
283 Reports and Curricular—Justice on trail: race and Prosecution Discretion available at
www. civilrights. org/publications/justice-on-trail/prosecutorial. html
284 "Racial Disparities in Federal Death Penalty Prosecutions 1988-1994." Available at
www. deathpenaltyinfo. org/racial-diparities-federal-death-penalty-prosecution-
1988-1994#fnB9
285 Death Row USA Spring 2004. Available at
naacpldf. org/content/pdf/puls/drusa/DRUSA_Spring_2004. pdf
286 Amnesty International USA—The Death Penalty Claims Innocent Lives. Available at
www. amnestyusa. org/abolish/innocence. html
287 The Use of the Death Penalty› A Paper Presented by the national policy Committee
to the American Society of Criminology. Available at www. asc41. com/polcypaper2. html

## In the News: The Shareef Cousins Saga

One of the most shocking cases of prosecutorial misconduct was the case of Shareef Cousins, a 16-year-old African-American who was charged with murder and armed robbery. The state's case was based solely on the eyewitness testimony of the victim's friend who testified that she was absolutely certain of Cousin's guilt and positively identified him at trial.[288] Cousins maintained that he was playing basketball at the time the murder was supposed to have occurred and even had several witnesses who could attest to this fact. Unfortunately, they did not appear in court and Shareef Cousins was convicted and placed on death row.

After the trial, the defense team received videotape from an anonymous source which contained the eyewitness's initial statement to the police in which she said that she could not identify the assailant because it was too dark in the alley and she had not been wearing her corrective lenses. Not only had the prosecution withheld this crucial evidence, but it was later discovered that the defendant's basketball teammates did, in fact, appear at trial to testify regarding his alibi; however, they were taken to the prosecutor's office to wait. The prosecutor claimed that he wanted the witnesses to be comfortable and since it was too hot in the designated waiting area, he felt that his office would be more appropriate. During subsequent questioning, the Assistant District Attorney admitted that the trial took place in the middle of winter.[289] Despite the District Attorney's admission of blatant prosecutorial misconduct, none of the parties involved in this miscarriage of justice were ever punished.

## Race, Ethnicity and Policy

Professional standards for trial lawyers have evolved along with the court system. The American Bar Association (1989), for example, recommended that the lead attorney in a capital case have a minimum of five years criminal defense experience, have served as legal counsel on at least nine jury trials, and have served as legal counsel in a case where the death penalty was being sought.[290] Unfortunately, most states have failed to demand the same standards for its capital case attorneys. In fact, court administrators acknowledged the problem and established the Indigent Defense Services Commission to manage

---

288 Amnesty International Canada: Extreme Prejudice—Racism and the Death Penalty. Available at www. amnesty. ca/usa/racismphp

289 Stormy Thorming-Gale and Kira Caywood. (1999). "Shareef Cousin: Will Justice be done?" http://www.justicedenied.org/vIissue2.htm#Shareef Cousin

290 1989 Recommendations—ABA Section of Individual Rights and Responsibilities. Available at www. abanet. org/irr/feb89a. html

the process in a fair and ethical manner.[291] Whether appointed or re-tained, trial attorneys in capital cases are, in effect, handling two cas-es: one to determine the guilt or innocence of their client and a second, to determine if their client should be sentenced to death.[292] As such, these attorneys must be, at the very least, experts in jury selection techniques, and experienced in the selection and utilization of expert witnesses as well as the use of psychiatric and forensic evidence.

The possession of this talent is critical since researchers have con-cluded that it is not the facts of the crime that determine the penalty but the quality of legal representation.[293] According to the American Bar Association, the overwhelming majority of death row inmates re-ceived substandard legal representation at trial.[294] In fact, ABA statis-tics show that 90% of capital case defendants nationally, are indigent when arrested.

In California, the state with the largest death row population (513), less than 2% were represented by retained counsel.[295] In some states less than 10% of death row population was represented by re-tained counsel.[296] The United States legal system currently hosts one legal aid lawyer or public defender for every 4300 citizens who live below poverty lines. This compares to one lawyer for every 380 citi-zens in the general population.[297]

The reality of the situation is that accepting indigent defendants as clients places an insurmountable financial burden on attorneys in general and discourages them from investing the time and effort nec-essary to properly represent indigents especially in capital cases. Ad-ditionally, the more experienced attorneys in private practice who are court appointed to perform mandatory, pro bono service tend to be even less committed because of the absence of a financial incentive.[298]

---

291  Indigent Defense Services. Available at www. aoc. statew. nc. us. www/ids/

292  Lyon, A. Defending the Life or Death Case
    works. bepress. com/cgi/viewcontext. cgi?article=1000&context=andrea_lyon

293  The Future of Capital Punishment in the State of New York
    www. nyclu. org/context/future-of-capital-punishment-new-york-state

294  Testimony of Stephen F Hanlon on behalf of the American bar Association before the Sub Committee on the Constitutional Civil Rights and Civil Liberties. Committee on the Judiciary of the US House of Representatives for the Hearing on the Impact of Federal Habeas Corpus Limitations on the Death Penalty Appeals. Available at judiciary. house. gov/hearings/pdf/Hanlon091208. pdf .

295  Death Penalty Watch—Capital Punishment Statistics from ACLU. Available at https://www.aclu.org/capital-punishment

296  O'Shea, K. (1999). *Women and the Death Penalty in the United States 1900-1998 Connecticut* : Praeger Publishers; Colbert, D. Professional Responsibility in Crisis. Available At digitalc-ommons. law. umaryland. edu/cgi/viewcontent. cgi?article=1621&context=fac_pubs

297  "The Future of the Death Penalty in the US: A Texas Sized Crisis." Available at www. deathpenaltyinfo. org/node/682sxn6

298  Bureau of Justice Statistics—State and Local Defender Offices. Available at bjs. ojp. usdoj. gov/index. cfm?ty+tp&tid-215

Racial disparity exists when the proportion of racial or ethnic groups within the criminal justice system is greater than their proportion of the general population. Racial disparity also exists when racial or ethnic differences result in dissimilar treatment by the criminal justice system. Generally speaking, racial disparities within the criminal justice system would be the result of the decision-making process that exists at various points in the criminal justice system. At each point, the decision makers—law enforcement practitioners, lawyers, and judges—are the ones to ensure that the system treats all men fairly.

Racial disparity in the use of public defenders, while unintended, is still a major area of concern for criminal justice practitioners. While 69% of White-American state prison inmates reported they had lawyers appointed by the court, 77% of African-American and 73% of Hispanics had publicly financed attorneys.[299]

In federal prison, African-American inmates were more likely than White-Americans and Hispanics to have public counsel: 65% for African-Americans, 57% for White-Americans, and 56% for Hispanics.[300]

The *National Law Journal* (1999) also found that capital case defendants from low socioeconomic backgrounds receive substandard legal service and that more than 50% of the death row inmates in six Southern states were represented by lawyers who had never before handled a capital case.[301] These statistics also show that those offenders who are represented by publicly-financed attorneys and are found guilty, are incarcerated at higher rates than those defendants who paid for their own legal representation: 88% compared to 77% in federal courts and 71% compared to 54% in state courts.[302]

Another issue that can have a significant effect on the quality of legal representation is the fact that court-appointed counsels rarely receive adequate financial support to ensure legitimate representation for indigent defendants. As a result, defendants with court-appointed counsel have weaker cases against the prosecution because the court-appointed lawyer is less likely to obtain expert witnesses and conduct competent investigations. It is obvious that stricter guidelines must be put in place to prevent the inconsistencies that continue to

299   Mauer, Marc and Tracy Huling (1995). "Young Black Americans and the Criminal Justice System: Five Years Later." The Sentencing Project. Available at http://www.sentencingproject.org/doc/publications/rd_youngblack_5yrslater. pdf

300   National Law Journal (1999) "A Good Year for Those who fight to Save the Innocent from Death." In *Criminal Justice Weekly* 2, 1, 24-25

301   The Legal System—The Price of Defending the Criminal Poor. Available at social. jrank. org/pages/1360/Legal-System-Price-Defending-Criminal-Poor-html

302   With Justice for Few: The Growing Crisis in Death Penalty Representation. Available at www. deathpenaltyinfo. org/node/742

plague the sentencing process. It is not fair that two people who commit similar crimes receive different sentences especially if race and legal-competency issues are the deciding factors.

An even more significant variable in this equation is the ethical and moral character of the attorneys that indigent defendants are forced to accept, or defendants of low socioeconomic status are forced to retain. It is no longer surprising to find drug addicts, thieves, or sex offenders in criminal courtrooms sitting as counsel for the defense.[303]

### INADEQUATE REPRESENTATION: THE ISSUE OF INCOMPETENCE

Inadequate counsel is one of the leading factors in cases of wrongful conviction and execution.[304] Yet, as a matter of law, the court determines that defenses attorneys are effective as long as they are breathing. At least 1% of all felony convictions are mistaken or wrongful convictions.[305] Research on the death penalty has also identified over 350 miscarriages of justice since 1900, when defendants were convicted of capital crimes despite proof of their innocence. Of these defendants, 139 received the death penalty and 23 were in fact executed.[306]

In 1984, the U.S. Supreme Court set forth its first opinion on the court's ability to overturn death sentences based on a claim of ineffective assistance of counsel. In the case of *Strickland* v. *Washington* (1984), the Court declared that errors by trial counsel were not sufficient to warrant a reversal of a conviction unless the defendant could prove that the errors had actually prejudiced the outcome of the case.[307] In reaching this decision the Supreme Court argued that the government was not responsible for, and hence not able to prevent, attorney errors. This decision was a blatant slap in the face for defendants in capital cases especially since, at that time, there were no universal standards of competence for attorneys in capital cases. This belies the contention of the criminal justice system that the death penalty is only applied to those who have received a fair trial and who have been afforded every opportunity to appeal their sentences. Since the advent of Strickland (1984), the American Bar Association has not

303  ACLU Death Penalty Campaign—Reason #3 to Support a National Moratorium on Executions
www. prisonpolicy. org/scans/aclu_dp_factsheet3. pdf
304  The Constitutional Failure of Strickland Standard in Capital Cases under the Eighth Amendment. Available at
www. law. duke. edu/shell/cite. pl?63+Law+Contempt. +Prob+179(Summer)+2000#H1N3
305  Crime Control and the Death Penalty. Available at
www. e-archives. ky. gov/pubs/Pub_Adv/Nov97/crime_control. htm
306  Ibid.
307  Strickland v Washington, 466 U. S 668 Volume 466: 1984. Available at supreme. justia. com/us/466/668/

only established a defendant's right to counsel, especially in a capital case (American Bar Association, 1988), but has also established the minimum requirement for legal representation in all capital cases.[308] Today, existing federal and state procedures also require lawyers in capital cases to be knowledgeable, competent, and diligent in ensuring a fair trial for their clients.

Unfortunately, the socioeconomic background of most capital case defendants determines the type of representation he or she can afford, and the quality of the representation is directly related to the outcome of the case. Although all states provide some form of public defense, few states provide adequate funding for, or access to, the resources necessary to ensure proper preparation for capital cases. Scholars and practitioners continue to argue that this issue of disparate representation is the most significant downfall of the U.S. criminal justice system.[309] Inadequate funding and resources to gather evidence, interview witnesses, and obtain scientific evidence are significant handicaps to capital case defendants, and these problems typically plague the defendant all the way through the appellate process.

Statistics also show that individuals accused of capital crimes are typically unable to afford private counsel and are often represented by public defenders who lack the skills, resources, and commitment to handle such serious matters.[310] In other words, defendants in the most complex criminal cases are usually represented by the most inexperienced counsel. According to Stephen Bright of the Southern Center for Human Rights, "the death penalty is not for the worst murder but for the worst lawyer."[311] Bright continues, "It is not the facts of the crime, or the guilt or innocence of the defendant, but the quality of legal representation that distinguishes a case where the death penalty is imposed from another similar case where it was not."[312]

Bright argued that capital cases involving indigent defendants are often marked with incompetent investigations and even outright witness perjury, as well as prosecutorial manipulation of evidence and of the jury. He also points out that the discretion that judges and juries hold in the imposition of the death penalty enables the penalty to be applied in a prejudicial manner, especially if the accused is poor and

---

308   American Bar Association Standing Committee on Legal Aid and Indigent Defendants Special Committee on Death Penalty Representation. Available at
www. abanet. org/leadership/recommendations03/107. pdf

309   Reports and Curricula: Justice on Trail Racial Disparities in the American Criminal Justice System. Available at www. civilrights. org/publications/justice-ontrial

310   Bright, S. Council for the Poor; the Death Sentence not for the worst crime but for the worst Lawyer. Available at www. schr. org/files/resources/counsel3. pdf.

311   Ibid.

312   Ibid.

lacking in political clout.[313] Ironically, it is this very exercise of discretion that protects those who hold social position, or are members the racial majority.

Indeed, the single most common factor leading to erroneous death sentences may very well be the failure of authorities to provide adequate resources for the defense of individuals on trial for their lives. In case after case, research has determined that public defenders are guilty of conducting little or no pre-trial investigation, are severely under-funded by the state, or have never handled a capital case. Moreover, these inexperienced attorneys must face experienced prosecutors who not only have greater resources at their disposal but who are also more familiar with judges and courtroom tactics.[314]

It has become increasingly apparent that the right to counsel, in and of itself, is a nonexistent right unless the counsel is competent and adequate. Evidence gathered seems to suggest that ineffective or inadequate assistance of counsel is more detrimental to defendants in capital cases than in any other type of case.[315] Ineffective assistance of counsel, for example, has resulted in sentencing reversal 11 times or 12.5%. [316] Since it is unlikely that defense attorneys make deliberate errors, or are deliberately incompetent, it would appear that death penalty verdicts are more likely influenced by the socioeconomic biases inherent in the criminal justice system.

Defense attorneys, whether public defenders or retained counsel, also appear to carry significant proportions of the responsibility for cases of wrongful conviction. When the testimony of state forensic experts, state eyewitnesses, and law enforcement officials are presented as evidence against a wrongfully accused indigent person, the public defender stands alone against the credibility and financial resources of these formidable opponents. As documented cases of wrongful conviction show, the odds are invariably stacked against the indigent and his or her public defense. Over the past 15 years, a growing list of researchers have determined that inadequate defense representation contributes exponentially to the incidence of wrongful conviction.[317]

---

313   Ibid.
314   "Fatal Flaws: Innocence and the Death Penalty in the USA." Available at
      www. amnesty. org/en/library/asset/AMR51/. . /amr510691998en. pdf.
315   Death Penalty in Tennessee: A View from the Federal Bench. Available at
      www. hawaii. edu/hivaids/The_Death_Penalty_in_Tenn_View_from_the_Fedpdf
316   Ibid.
317   Wrongful Convictions resources. Available at
      lawinfo.  com/en/Articles/Post-Sentencing-Criminal-Defense/Federal/wrongful-conviction.
      html

Supreme Court Justice Ruth Bader Ginsburg has also acknowledged the problem created by the poor quality of defense that many death row inmates have received. In April 2001, while articulating her support for a State of Maryland bill that was expected to place a moratorium on executions, she said,

> "I have yet to see a death case among the dozens coming to the Supreme Court on eve-of-execution stay applications in which the defendant was well represented at trial. . . . People who are well represented at trial do not get the death penalty."[318]

At about the same time Supreme Court Justice Sandra Day O'Connor, in her speech to the Minnesota Women Lawyers' Group said, "Perhaps it's time to look at minimum standards for appointed counsel in death cases and adequate compensation for appointed counsel when they are used."[319] The general consensus appears to be, therefore, that capital defendants are relegated to lawyers who are notoriously inexperienced, often over-worked, lack training in capital litigation, or, as in the cases mentioned in this chapter, are so downright incompetent that an eventual reversal is inevitable.

Notwithstanding these incidents of incompetence, judges have been found to be anything but generous with reversal rulings. The burden of proof rests with the defendant and is tough to meet. Defendants must not only show that the lawyer's work was substandard, but defendants must provide evidence that the substandard work had a direct bearing on the outcome of the case.[320]

Socio-economic factors also seem to influence the criminal justice system at all levels. Some researchers claim that since the individuals in the positions of authority typically maintain conservative perspectives and represent the status quo, indigent defendants are assumed to possess non-conforming or deviant (yet legal) characteristics.[321] In essence, since indigent defendants do not possesses the typical appearance, demeanor, level of articulateness, place of residence, material possessions or social status, these facts actually shape the case and the interpretation of the individual in the position of authority.[322]

---

318  The Death Penalty in 2001 year End Report. Available at www. deathpenaltyinfo. org/ YearEndReport2001. pdf.

319  Ibid.

320  Effective Assistance of Counsel in Capital Cases. Available at www. press. umich. edu/ pdf/0472099116-ch2. pdf; The Effects of Social Class on the Adjudication of Criminal Cases: Class Linked Behavior Tendencies, Common Sense and the Interpretive Procedures of Court Appointed Defense Attorneys. Available at caliber. ucpress. net/doi/abs/10. 1525/si. 1994. 17. 1. 1?journalCode=si

321  Ibid.

322  Liebman, J., Fagan, J., West, V 2000 A Broken System: Error in rates in Capital Cases, 1973-1995. Available at http//papers. ssrn. com/paper. taf?abstract_id=232712

Liebman, Fagan, and West (2000) analyzed 5760 capital cases between 1973 and 1995 and found epidemic error rates in the sentences imposed. Appellate courts have also found serious errors in about two thirds of these cases.[323] In 75% of these cases new trials resulted in a resentencing of life in prison as opposed to a sentence of death. Some 7% were exonerated, and only 18% were resentenced to death.

The most common identifiable errors were incompetent defense lawyers and prosecutorial misconduct. In 37% of the cases, appellate courts ruled that defense attorneys performed so poorly at trial that the defendant did not receive a proper defense, and in 16% of the cases, it was determined that prosecutors suppressed mitigating or exculpatory evidence to the detriment of the defendant's case. Overall, the rate of judicial error in the American capital punishment system was estimated at 68%. In other words, the courts themselves found serious reversible error in nearly 70% of the almost six thousand capital sentences that were reviewed.

There is little question that in a case where a defendant faces the possibility of the death penalty, a competent attorney can mean the difference between life and death. In a system where a person is executed, not due to the nature of their crime, but because of the adequacy of their representation, the death penalty cannot be anything other than arbitrary and discriminatory.

> "When we execute a capital defendant in this country, we rely on the belief that the individual was guilty, and was convicted and sentenced after a fair trial, to justify the imposition of state-sponsored killing. . . . My 24 years of overseeing the imposition of the death penalty from this Court have left me in grave doubt whether this reliance is justified and whether the constitutional requirement of competent counsel for capital defendants is being fulfilled."[324]

+++

DO NOT COLLECT $200
Dr. Deborah H. Barnes

I grew up in the South during the Civil Rights Era where symbols of privilege and prohibition were emblematic of a social segregation that was imposed by law, custom, and behavior. We learned what we could be and do from public discourses that set the limits of social mobility, via signs declaring "whites only" and "no colored served" and in textbooks that excluded people of color. Even the games we played

---

323  Ibid.

324  Justice for Few: The Growing Crisis in Death Penalty Representation. Available at www. deathpenaltyinfo. org/node/742

fostered subtle messages of restriction and consequence. Monopoly, for example, directed unlucky players to *"Go to jail. Go directly to jail. Do not pass go. Do not collect $200."* We saw through no fault of our own it was possible to lose the game if we did not have sufficient property or capital to free us or to support us during our detention. As teens and young adults the message was reinforced when it became clear that jail was a foreseeable consequence for those who could not escape its seemingly arbitrary tow. Since graduating with the Ph.D. in English from Howard University, I have spent most of my academic career exploring the overt and subtle messages attached to cultural ideations of race, class, and gender. I am most intrigued by ethnographies which more recently are proffered as "infotainment"—cultural fact dramatically presented. With the first episode, I succumbed to *The Wire's* vividly honest portrayal of life in inner-city Baltimore—a city I knew intimately. The show represents, I believe, a more subtle, twenty-first century version of the overt social discourses I was exposed to as a child. In both, the upshot of not knowing one's place is the same: death or imprisonment.

Author Horatio Alger (1834-1899) wrote more than one hundred dime novels for boys in the latter half of the nineteenth century. His wildly popular "city stories," valorized the plight of street urchins like Ragged Dick [1] who overcame great adversity to achieve wealth and fame. These urban "rags to riches" stories quickly became metaphors for the America Dream: in the land of opportunity, any man could pull himself up by his bootstraps and make something of his life. In Alger's fictive world, upward mobility is predicated, more often than not, on fortunate accidents or luck rather than entitlements of birth. When opportunity knocked, up-and-comers who were determined to prosper would, by necessity, answer with pluck, hard work, self-denial, and a developing sense of morality. Using this formula, anyone, most Americans believed, could achieve anything.

Stringer Bell, a lieutenant in the Barksdale drug ring on the highly acclaimed HBO drama series, The Wire [2], is a contemporary, version of Alger's urban hero though with a different outcome. His story is situated in Baltimore's Franklin Terrace housing project, a crime-ravaged segment of an industrial city on the decline. We are told nothing of Stringer's past or of his life other than he is the childhood friend of and right-hand man to Avon Barksdale, a local drug lord. Stringer's upward mobility takes off once he corporatizes the crew's heroine trade, modeling his business tactics after those employed by area businessmen, bureaucrats, and politicians. Determined to transcend the drug-slinging, gun-wielding gangsterism of his crew, he opts to play the role of narcotics financier and quasi-legitimate businessman. He breaks into the real estate development game using drug profits to purchase abandoned row houses, storefronts, and failing businesses on the city's Westside and for bribes. To insure his social advancement, he enrolls in a local community college where he learns the rigors of technology, economic theory, and law—competencies that keep him one step ahead of his enemies on both sides of the law. His willingness to mentor or to buy off (rather than kill) adversaries and competitors who would impede his social mobility signals his elevation of the street game to a corporate level.[3]

Stringer's evolution from motherless thug to ambitious businessman is fully realized by season three of the series six year run. By then, he is in bed with everyone who matters: rival druglords, gangsters, businessmen, the police, politicians, and the real estate board. Strategically, he covers all the bases and plays all the angles—or so he believes. Feigning a pose of legitimacy, civility, and goodwill, Stringer easily launders Avon's money. He makes hefty political contributions that are designed to emancipate him from the narcotics trade and secure his entrée into the rarified game of waterfront renewal. Before long, however, Stringer falls victim to vertical hold when his assent is thwarted from above and below. He meets a calamitous end when he is swindled out of $ 250,000 by a State Senator and then assassinated by rival gunsels out to settle a score—all under the watchful eye of police surveillance.[4] What worked for Ragged Dick, was beyond the reach of Stringer Bell.

Nowhere are the tensions governing social immobility and criminality more vividly wrought than in The Wire. The show marshals Alger's city story into the twenty-first century by offering a compellingly authentic, multi-faceted view of Baltimore's mean streets—streets made meaner by the spate of heroin and crack that ravages the city's inner core. Most of Avon's gang fall victim to arrest and incarceration if they're lucky and lethal gunplay if they're not. Consequently, the Westside housing projects where Barksdale gang holds sway are little more than staging areas for a ubiquitous criminal justice system that is, on any given day, both solution and problem for the city's woes. Few of the show's civil servants want to "protect and serve" the inner city or facilitate its "law and order." Since law enforcement's motives are mostly ignoble, their often halfhearted (or vicious) pursuit of criminals and innocents alike is little more than a "game" they play for hire. The Wire taps into "the game,"—Baltimorean slang for the exigencies of (criminal) street life—as it is played on both sides of the law.

The symbiosis of crime and punishment may explain why urban youth seem destined for incarceration. Indeed, nothing has had a greater impact on the lives of Black, urban, youth than the war on drugs, a verity The Wire reflects. Soldiers in the Barksdale crew are picked up, beaten up, and locked up with such regularity and indiscretion that they cannot (and do not expect to) escape the criminal industrial complex that predetermines their lives. A full-scale war was declared on drug traffickers, dealers, and users in the mid-1980s by the police, the courts, and a for-profit prison system. The Wire exposes the street-level impact of federal drug policies that fueled the war on drugs and increased penalties for drug offenses, as it reduced support for prevention and treatment. We see that inner city, impoverished youth have few authentic life choices that do not include exposure to illegal drug activity. Narcotics trafficking is frequently the only viable means of earning money in places where Blacks are underemployed, unemployed or locked out of social and economic opportunity. The few who successfully reject criminal activity often find themselves policing the very jails and prisons that incarcerate their loved ones and neighbors.

*The Wire* does not condone the drug trade or romanticize the disenfranchised youth who can find no other way to make their fortunes in the city. Neither does it aggrandize the brutal criminal justice system subtending society's civility and order. It demonstrates, instead, the ways poverty, crime, civil bureaucracies, and business work together to enforce a form of vertical hold that stymies the options and opportunities of the urban poor. It reveals the structural constraints preventing the sort of personal potential and uplift Horatio Alger had touted one century before. There is no high road for the urban poor, no bootstraps by which they might lift themselves up as the allegory of Stringer Bell shows. Unlike Ragged Dick, there is only one way out of the game for Stringer Bell.

## REFERENCES

1. *Ragged Dick, or, Street Life in New York*. Horatio Alger, Jr. 1st ed. Boston, 1868.
2. David Simon, HBO 2002-2008
3. Stringer will use enforcers to win territory and exercise dominion especially in the first two seasons, but he does not kill anyone himself. In time the police discover Stringer's campaign contributions to local and state politicians who grease the skids for his entrée into the high stakes game of waterfront renewal.
4. Season 3, Episode 36, ("Middle Ground")

Dr. Deborah H. Barnes
Associate Professor and Associate Dean
of University Studies
North Carolina A & T State University

+++

## CONTROVERSIES

> Be it resolved that because social science research has demonstrated the death penalty to be racist in application and social science research has found no consistent evidence of crime deterrence through execution, the ASC publicly condemns this form of punishment and urges its members to use their professional skills in legislatures and the courts to seek a speedy abolition of this form of punishment.
>
> American Society of Criminology, Resolution of the Death Penalty, ASC Annual Meeting, Montreal, 1987.

### Racial and Class Disparities

The existence of racial disparity in the application of the death penalty has become an increasingly controversial issue. Although very few persons convicted of murder actually receive the death penalty, according to the statistics, race and class bias seem to influence who receives a death sentence and who is executed.[325] This also raises the question of what factors actually influence a prosecutor's initial decision to pursue the death penalty.

A Justice Department study reported that in nearly 62% of the cases in which the prosecutor sought the death penalty the defendant was a member of a minority group.[326] Other researchers have also conducted numerous analyses of death penalty cases and found that both the race of the offender and especially the race of the victim are directly associated with the probability of a defendant receiving a death penalty verdict.[327] Although this acknowledges discrimination in the application of capital punishment and could be the basis for declaring the death penalty unconstitutional the U.S. Supreme Court in McClesky v. Kemp (481 U.S. 279 [1987] refused to use an apparent discriminatory application of capital punishment as a basis for declaring the death penalty unconstitutional.[328] In this case, data was presented to support an argument that persons who were convicted of murdering White-Americans were 11 times more likely to be sentenced to death than were persons who killed African-American. The data was also used to show that although prosecutors requested the death penalty in 70% of the cases where the defendant was African-American

---

325 "The Death Penalty in Black and White: Who lives, Who dies, Who decides". Available at www. deathpenaltyinfo. org/article. php?did=539

326 The Use of the Death Penalty—A Paper Presented by the National Policy Committee to the American Society of Criminology. Available at www. asc41. com/policypaper2. html

327 Race and the Death Penalty Part 1: Who gets the Death Penalty in America www. racismreview. com/. . /death-penalty-part-i-who-gets-the-death-penalty-in-america

328 McCleskey v. Kemp, 481 U.S. 279 (1987)

and the victim was White-American, they only sought the death penalty in 15% of the cases where the defendant was African-American and the victim was African-American.[329]

*Mitigating Factors*

It is important to recognize that class bias also plays an important part in the decision-making process of any attorney. It has actually been evaluated as a component of the evidence.[330] As a result, class-related factors are more likely to weigh heavily against the typical indigent defendant than against a non-indigent defendant. The low socio-economic status of indigent defendants will be less likely to counter-weigh any evidence against them.[331] This raises three important questions.

> (1) Why is the social class of a defendant more than just an extra-legal factor in the adjudication process?

> (2) Why does social class play such an important part in shaping the evidence and the outcome?

> (3) Why is indigence (poverty) synonymous with a death sentence?

The answer to these questions and the ultimate solution to these problems would be to change the social consciousness of the individuals charged with the responsibility of judging defendants. More directly, this society is faced with the monumental task of initiating fundamental changes to its current mode of application of the death penalty. The Constitution Project (formerly known as the National Committee to Prevent Wrongful Executions) issued a report urging federal and state legislatures to adopt immediate remedies."[332] Additionally, in August 2001, The American Psychological Association (APA) officially took the position that the use of the death penalty must end until its several deficiencies have been resolved.[333]

The specific deficiencies identified by the American Psychological Association include (a) the unfair and incompetent legal representation afforded individuals being tried in the majority of death penalty cases, (b) the number of death row inmates exonerated by DNA testing, (c) selective bias in the process of jury selection that favors death penalty sentencing, (d) racial disparities based on the race of the victim as well as the race of the defendant, (e) a lack of evidence that the

---

329  Ibid.

330  Prevention vs. Control. Available at www. justiceblind. com/death/dpfouranew1

331  Ibid.

332  The Constitutional Project—Mandatory Justice: Eighteen Reforms to the Death Penalty. Available at www. constitutionproject. org/pdf/MandatoryJustice. pdf

333  The Use of the Death Penalty. Available at www. asc41. com/policypaper2. html

death penalty has any deterrent effect, and (f) the presentation of re-search which shows that the murder rate tends to increase and not decrease immediately after state-sanctioned executions.[334]

A few states have already implemented policy and administrative changes in response to the growing problem. A number of states in-cluding North Carolina and Illinois have taken steps to restrict the use of the death penalty. In fact, 18 states have signed into law a bill that forbids the execution of mentally retarded defendants.[335] Texas, on the other hand, has vetoed a similar bill.[336]

*International Trends*

But why does a country as advanced as the Unites States still use such a barbaric system of punishment? Capital punishment is not common in developed nations; it is used predominantly in Arab na-tions, in most of Asia, many parts of Africa, and the United States.[337] Although comprehensive data on the use of the death penalty world-wide is difficult to collect and verify, it is nonetheless clear that an in-creasing number of countries have either abolished the death penal-ty or have placed restrictions on its application. As of 2001, an esti-mated 108 countries had already abolished the death penalty in law or in practice, a significant increase from 1980 when only 62 countries were so classified.[338] Of these 108 nations, 75 have abolished the use of the death penalty for all crimes while another 13 have abolished its use for non violent crimes. Of those countries that maintain its use, 20 currently have the authority to abolish it but have chosen not to do so.[339] It is cause for concern that, with respect to a topic as impor-tant as life or death, the U.S. is to be compared to predominantly de-veloping countries.

In the final analysis, the death penalty has not been proven to ef-fective in deterring capital crimes. Some research even argues that the states that utilize the death penalty have actually seen a 48-101% in-crease in the number of murders committed from 1980-1999 in com-parison to non-death penalty states.[340]

---

334   Ibid.

335   Ibid.

336   Amnesty International Death Penalty Statistics 2009 available at http://www. amnesty-usa.   org/death-penalty/international-death-penalty/death-penalty-statistics2009/page. do?id=1691051

337   Capital Punishment—world body life history person human. Available at www. deathreference. com›BI-ce

338   Ibid.

339   How the System Itself is Violent. Available at www. defendingjustice. org/. . /18Fact%20 Sheet%20— How%20the%20System%20Itself%20is%20Violent. pdf

340   Voices: Ending Racial Injustice and Prosecutorial Misconduct. Available at www. southerstudies. org/2009/07/post-44. html

## CONCLUSION

No matter how careful courts are, the possibility of perjured testimony, mistaken honest testimony, and human error remain all too real. We have no way of judging how many innocent persons have been executed, but we can be certain that there were some (Marshall, J., concurring).[341]

As can be seen from the many studies presented, there is a questions of whether the race of the offender and/or the race of the victim have any impact on the outcome of death eligible cases. While some studies identify an interactive effect between victim race and victim gender such that killers of White-American women are especially at risk of receiving death sentences, other studies argue that the introduction of control variables via logistic regression equations yield no gender or race interactions as predictors of sentencing outcomes.[342] Despite contradictory findings, the general consensus seems to be that cases with African-American defendants and White-American victims are more likely to be death noticed and death sentenced than comparable cases in which the defendant was not African-American and the victim was White-American.[343]

Capital cases are no doubt the most emotionally and financially draining cases in the criminal justice system. In no other litigation are the stakes as high as life or death. Moreover, the procedural bureaucracy of federal and state criminal procedures require lawyers in capital cases to be extremely knowledgeable and extraordinarily diligent to ensure that their clients receive fair hearings.

To date, nearly 68% of all death penalty appeals have been reversed, and studies show that executions have more to do with economics, race, geography and just plain bad luck, than criminal innocence or guilt.[344] Wrongful convictions can and do occur in capital case trials and innocent people can and do receive death sentences. Lack of adequate legal representation, coerced or false confessions, testimony from jailhouse snitches, uncorroborated witnesses, prosecutorial and police misconduct, juror misinterpretation and misunderstand-

---

341 "Race and Sentencing—A Meta Analysis of Conflicting Empirical Research results" www. sciencedirect. com/science?_ob=ArticleURL&_udi=B6V75-3V544X3-6&_user=10 _coverDate=11/12/1998&_rdoc

342 Race and the Death Penalty. Available at www. capitalpunishmentincontext. org/issue/race

343 The Justice Project: Statement by the Justice Project on the 100th Death Row Exoneration www. thejusticeproject. org/press/ststement-by-thejustice-project-on-the-100th-death-row-exoneration/

344 "The Death Penalty in Black and White: Who Lives, Who Dies and Who Decides" www. deathpenaltyinfo. org/article. php?did=539

ing of the law, and judicial error and prejudice all combine to result in wrongful convictions.

The racial disparities in the administration of capital punishment have drawn increasingly critical reaction from legal and civil rights groups both nationally and have even attracted international criticism. In 1996, the International Commission of Jurists, whose members include respected judges from around the world, visited the United States and researched the use of the death penalty. Their report was sharply critical of the way the death penalty is being applied, particularly with regard to race:

> The Mission is of the opinion that . . . the administration of capital punishment in the United States continues to be discriminatory and unjust—and hence arbitrary'—, and thus not in consonance with Articles 6 and 14 of the Political Covenant and Article 2(c) of the Race Convention.[345]

Additionally, the U.N. Special Rapporteur on Extrajudicial, Summary or Arbitrary Executions filed a report with the U.N. Commission on Human Rights after his visit to the U.S. stating that "...economic status appear[s] to be [a] key determinants of who will, and will not, receive a sentence of death."[346] In addition to this strong criticism, in a March of 1998 Inter-American Commission on Human Rights stated that the United States had violated international law and should compensate the relatives of William Andrews, who was executed in Utah in 1992, because of racial bias in his case.[347]

In 1987, the Supreme Court of Georgia narrowly rejected a challenge to the racially biased application of the death penalty in Georgia.[348] Since then, civil rights groups and many newspaper editorials have called for the passage of the Racial Justice Act to remedy this issue on a national level. Although this proposed legislation was passed by the U.S. House of Representatives in 1990 and again in 1994, it was ultimately defeated on the theory that any such racial inquiry would weaken the efficacy of the administration of the death penalty.[349] Only Kentucky has passed and upheld similar legislation on the state level. It is as a result of this and other inequities in the administration of capital punishment, that the American Bar Association, which had earlier recommended the passage of the Racial Justice Act, eventually called for a complete moratorium on executions.[350] Other bar associations such as the Pennsylvania Bar, the Ohio Bar, the Chi-

345  Ibid.
346  Ibid.
347  Ibid.
348  Ibid.
349  Ibid.
350  Ibid.

cago Council of Lawyers, the Massachusetts Bar and the Philadelphia Bar have either endorsed the ABA's resolution or passed similar resolutions. Over 100 other organizations have also endorsed motions to stop executions, at least until a greater sense of justice can be restored to the process.[351]

In the final analysis, the general consensus is that court-appointed counsels should be better compensated to encourage a better quality of representation of indigent defendants. By providing court-appointed counsels with better financial resources, defendants will have stronger representation. Improved access to financial resources will also allow the court-appointed lawyer to obtain expert witnesses and conduct competent investigations. Additionally, in an effort to eliminate bias and discrimination during the process of sentencing, sentences should be more narrowly assigned to the various crimes such that jurors and judges have less room to include their personal beliefs and biases. The issue of racial disparities must also be addressed. On the state level racial disparities are most obvious in the predominant selection of cases involving White-American victims. On the federal level, cases selected have almost exclusively involved minority defendants.

This criminal justice system should conduct on-going studies of the use of capital punishment to determine the degree of bias in its application. For those jurisdictions that choose to use the death penalty, data should be collected to analyze each jurisdiction's decision-making process to seek or not seek the death penalty. This data should analyze prosecutorial decisions to seek the death penalty, assignment of counsel for the defendant, and the appeal process and decisions. This data should be made readily available to social scientists and other interested parties to facilitate an unbiased determination of the extent of racial, gender, and class bias.

Juries in all capital cases should be required to consider the option of a sentence of life-without-the-possibility-of-parole. This should always be an option to the counts in all capital punishment cases. Although most states do allow for juries to automatically consider this option, three states do not. For states that already provide for that option, they should be encouraged to give the option due consideration for capital cases. DNA testing of evidence should be required for all capital cases to establish guilt or innocence and biological samples should be preserved in all pending death penalty cases. Convicted defendants should be afforded the right to DNA testing not only where innocence is claimed but also where there is a possibility of an erro-

---

351  Ibid.

neous sentence (e.g., death as opposed to some lesser sentence). Such testing should be paid for by the state.

Stricter guidelines must be put in place to prevent the inconsistencies that are prevalent in the sentencing process. It is not fair that two people who commit similar crimes should receive different sentences simply because a difference in socioeconomic status is the determining factor in whether a public defender is appointed or a private attorney is retained. In other words, every criminal must have the same quality of representation and every criminal act must attract the same specific punishment

Race should not influence which cases are chosen for capital prosecution. Likewise, race affects the makeup of the juries which determine the sentence. In other areas of the law, protections have been built in to limit the effects of systemic racism when the evidence of its impact is clear. With the death penalty, however, attempts at corrective measures seem to have been blocked. Opponents claim that any limitations placed on the current administration of capital punishment would slow the wheels of the judicial progress.[352] As a result, those in danger of being affected by these atrocities are being paid lip service.

Those who die because of this racism are not the kind of people who usually evoke the public's sympathy. Many have committed horrendous crimes. But crimes no less horrendous are committed by White-American offenders or against African-American victims, yet it appears that the killers in those cases are generally spared death. The death penalty today is a part of a system which imposes society's concern over the problem of crime on a select few. The existing data seems to suggest that many of the death sentences are a product of racial discrimination.[353] How can we expect to maintain our vow of equal justice under the law, when we ignore the racial injustice inherent in the manner in which this nation takes lives?

CRITICAL THINKING QUESTIONS

a.   In each of the cases, what is the impact of the race of the accused on the disposition of the case?

b.   What is the impact of the race of the victim on the disposition of the case?

c.   What is the impact of the quality of legal representation on the outcome of the case?

---

352   Ibid.
353   Ibid.

d.  Was there any evidence of prosecutorial misconduct in the case proceedings?

# CHAPTER 5. RACE, ETHNICITY AND TERRORISM

## OBJECTIVES

- To identify the various forms of terrorism
- To conduct a comparison of ethnic and racial profiling as it relates to acts of terror
- To evaluate the impact of race and ethnicity on the concept of terrorism

## CASE STUDY: 9/11

On September 11, 2001, four airplanes were hijacked in the airspace above the United States. Two of these aircrafts were flown into the towers of the New York City World Trade Center, and then three buildings collapsed; one plane hit the Pentagon in Washington DC, and the fourth plane is reported to have crashed in a field in rural Pennsylvania after passengers and members of the crew attempted to retake control of their plane. Approximately 3,000 people from some 90 countries died in the September 11th attacks. The attacks were deemed acts of terrorism and the United States immediately declared a War on Terror.

This event had such an impact on the world that stock exchanges were closed for almost a week, with airlines and insurance carriers suffering the greatest financial losses. It was suggested that the suspected hijackers had links to Al-Qaeda ("the base"), a radical Islamic organization. And on March 19, 2003, a U.S.-led coalition invaded

Afghanistan to depose the Taliban who had been accused of harboring terrorists. The United States also passed the USA Patriot Act[354].

As at the time of publication, over 8 years later, the war on terror continued with over 4,000 American lives lost in combat, over 30,000 Americans wounded, and up to 100,000 in combat and an astounding 1,200,000 Iraqi deaths resulting from the U.S. invasion.[355]

## INTRODUCTION: WHAT IS TERRORISM? WHO IS A TERRORIST?

Terrorism has been defined by Title 22 of the U.S. Code as politically motivated violence perpetrated in a clandestine manner against noncombatants.[356] Experts on terrorism further expand the definition to include a statement that "the act is committed in order to create a fearful state of mind in an audience different from the victims."[357] Terrorism has also been defined, as the "deliberate, negligent, or reckless use of force against noncombatants by state or non-state actors for ideological ends and in the absence of a substantively just legal process."[358]

There are different types of terrorism, for example grievance terrorism which is perpetuated by an individual or group seeking redress or power for a particular grievance.[359] Then there is institutional terrorism, which is usually employed by powerful entities to maintain or preserve the status quo.

Other kinds of terrorism include national terrorism, revolutionary terrorism, reactionary terrorism, and religious terrorism, to name a few. Social-revolutionary terrorism and nationalist-separatist terrorism continue to be the two predominant types active today. Also known as ethno-nationalist terrorism, these groups fight to establish a new political order based solely on ethnic dominance or homogeneity. They are carrying on the mission of their forefathers who have been dishonored or been damaged by the regime.

Although individuals who can be described as terrorists have always existed, the United States first took a serious interest in the

---

354  The Patriot Act expands the authority of US law enforcement agencies for the purpose of fighting terrorism in the United States and abroad. http://www.thepeoplehistory.com/october26th.html#2001

355  Rodin, D. 2004. "Terrorism Without Intention", *Ethics* 114(4): 752-771: 755

356  Ward, N (2001). "The Fire Last Time-The 1920 Wall Street Bombing." *American Heritage*. http://www. freerepublic. com/focus/f-news/577915/posts

357   Davis, M (2006) "Car Bombs With Wings-History of the Car Bomb" (part 2). Tom Dispatch. http://www. tomdispatch. com/post/print/76824/Tomgram%253A%2520%2520Mike%2520Davis%252C%2520%2522Return%2520to%2520Sender%2522%2520%2528Car%2520Bombs%252C%2520Part%202%2529

358   Crank, J. & Gregor, P. (2005). *Counterterrorism after 9/11*. Cincinnati: LexisNexis Anderson.

359   Leonnig, C and Frankel, G. (2005) "U.S. to Send 5 Detainees Home from Guantanamo." *Washington Post*. http://www. washingtonpost. com/wp-dyn/articles/A982-2005Jan11. html

concept during the Vietnam War. U.S. soldiers were trained to seek out and kill North Vietnamese soldiers, but Viet Cong sympathizers were hard to identify, so that it was easiest to say that every man, woman and child of North and South Vietnam represented the enemy. Similarly, in typical modern-day terrorist scenarios, we have no way of determining who, among the local population, is acting defensively and who is acting offensively.

American history in the 20th century has been punctuated by acts of terrorism both at home and on U.S. territory abroad. Most notable are:

1. 1901–The assassination of President William McKinley
2. 1920–A horse cart filled with dynamite exploded near the intersections of Wall and Broad Streets in New York City's financial district killing 40 and wounding about 300 others.[360]
3. 1976—Croatian terrorists fighting against Yugoslavia hijacked a TWA plane and killed a New York police officer
4. 1993–A truck loaded with over 1000 pounds of dynamite exploded in the basement of the World Trade Center killing 6 people and injuring over 1000 others.[361]
5. 1998–Bombings of the U.S. embassies in Tanzania and Kenya
6. 2000–Bombing of the USS Cole in Yemen[362]

Despite acts of terrorism that have spanned the globe over the last century, terrorists have been stereotyped as men of Middle Eastern descent. Nonetheless, terrorists can emerge from any political group. In fact, some of the Taliban prisoners held at Guantanamo Bay are Australian and British.[363]

Today, terrorist groups include:

a. Separatists –Tamil Tigers in Sri Lanka
b. Racial hegemonic groups – Ku Klux Klan, and
c. Environmentalists – Earth Liberation Front[364]

More recent terrorist groups include:

a. The Irish Republican Army, which attacked civilian targets in England to protest continued British presence in northern Ireland,

---

360  Supra at 401

361  Supra at 404

362  Human Rights Watch (2002) "Opportunism in the face of tragedy: repression in the name of anti-terrorism", http://www. hrw. org/campaigns/september 11/opportunismwatch. htm, 22 November:12)

363  Yamada, K. (n. d) Desert reclaims Japanese-American Camp. http://www. asu. edu/studentaffairs/studentmedia/archives/bulldog/971212/japan. html

364  Etzioni and Marsh, J., 2003, *Rights vs. Public Safety after 9/11*, Lanham, MD: Rowman & Littlefield

b.   Palestinians who have targeted Israelis and others across the world in their continued protest over Israeli occupation of what they believe to be the Palestinian homeland, and of course,

c.   Al Qaeda, a fundamentalist Islamic group that is opposed to all Western secular power and is responsible for the attacks on the World Trade Center as well as numerous other attacks worldwide.

In the aftermath of the 9/11 attacks, the Federal Bureau of Investigation (FBI) and Immigration and Naturalization Service (INS) quickly embarked on a sweeping process that involved arresting, detaining and questioning thousands of non-citizens for months without charging them. It is being argued that those detained were enemy combatants, not deserving of the liberties enshrined in the U.S. Constitution.[365]As a result Middle Eastern males (and anyone who appeared to be Middle Eastern), were, in essence profiled. Indeed, in its report Presumption of Guilt: Human Rights Abused of Post-September 11th Detainees (2002), Human Rights Watch discovered a growing use of profiling on the basis of actual or perceived nationality, religion and gender. In other words, being a Muslim non-citizen was enough to invoke the suspicion of the FBI or INS. The Human Rights Watch had this to say:

> Using nationality, religion, and gender as a proxy for suspicion is not only unfair to the millions of law-abiding Muslim immigrants from Middle Eastern and South Asian countries, it may also be ineffective law enforcement technique. The U.S. government has not charged a single one of the thousand-plus individuals detained after September 11 for crime related to terrorism. Such targeting has also antagonized the very immigrant and religious communities whose cooperation with law enforcement agencies produce important leads for the investigation.[366]

To others, this type of action invokes disturbing reminders of the World War II detainment of some 110,000 Americans of Japanese ancestry.[367] Today, America has been accused of going too far by creating secret detention centers and engaging in secret proceedings—concepts that go against the very fabric of democracy and liberty. Moreover, a series of subsequent events from which more substantive evidence was gathered gives rise to suggestions that profiling terrorists

---

365   Benjamin, D. and S. Simon. 2002. *The Age of Sacred Terror*. New York: Random House. : 407

366   Mark Juergensmeger, "The Religious Roots of Contemporary Terrorism," in The New Global Terrorisms: *Characteristics, Causes and Controls*, ed. Charles w. Kegley (Upper Saddle River, NJ: Prentice hall, 2003), 185-193.

367   Harris, David, (2002) *Profiles in Injustice: Why Racial Profiling Cannot Work*. NY: The New Press, 2002

based on national origin may actually be a flawed process. Some of more notable examples are,

a.    Zacharia Moussaoui, the so-called "20th hijacker," is a French citizen

b.    The "shoe bomber", Richard Reid, is a British citizen and,

c.    Jose Padilla (aka Abdullah Al Muhajir, "the dirty bomber," is a U.S. citizen of Puerto Rican descent.

It is somewhat ironic that those who come to this country seeking the freedom of which the U.S. boasts sometimes find that these freedoms and liberties may not apply, depending on the color of their skin and their ethnicity.[368]

Benjamin and Simon (2002), both of whom were once Directors of the National Security Council of the United States, analyze the causes of terrorism as follows:

- The United States is resented for its cultural hegemony, global political influence, and
- overwhelming conventional military power. Its cultural reach threatens traditional values,
- including the organization of societies that privilege males and religious authority. It offers
- temptation, blurs social, ethical, and behavioral boundaries and presages moral disorder.
- American's political weight is seen as the hidden key to the durability of repressive
- regimes that fail to deliver prosperity while crushing dissent.... American military prowess
- is used to kill Muslims, as in Iraq, or is withheld to facilitate their extermination, as in Bosnia.
- The American cultural challenge to Islamic societies stands for a broader Western
- commitment to secularization, the relegation of religion to the private sphere...[369]

The War on Terrorism is said to target those currently involved in terrorist acts, who have very specific characteristics:

1.    A clear and identifiable enemy.
2.    A political rather than a social agenda.
3.    Firmly believe their cause is just.

368   Harris, D. (1999). "Driving While Black: Racial Profiling on our Nations Highways"http:// www. aclu. org/racialjustice/racialprofiling/15912publ9990607. html
369   Benjamin, D. and S. Simon. 2002. *The Age of Sacred Terror*. New York: Random House. p.407

4. Terrorists believe their acts are justifiable and in many cases spiritually ordained.[370]

American society claims that terrorists are abnormal, yet throughout history we "normal" people have participated in executions, lynch mobs, military massacres and genocides. It is not the violence that qualifies terrorist acts as "terror." In reality, how different are normal citizens from abnormal terrorists?

*Ethnic Profiling*

Profiling, both racial and ethnic, has become a generic term used to describe the targeting of racial and ethnic minorities by law enforcement agencies. A profile is simply a set of characteristics—physical, behavioral, or psychological used to identify an individual or group of individuals.[371] Prior to the September 11th attacks on the United States, the rationale for racial profiling was to protect the public against drug traffickers and illegal immigrants, the vast majority of whom were identified as being minorities.[372] African-Americans and Hispanics were the primary targets of racial profiling. Since the terrorist attacks, however, Arabs and Muslims have increasingly become the targets of ethnic profiling.

Indeed, there are many similarities between the profiling of African-Americans, Arabs and Muslims. In each case, the race and or ethnicity of the target appears to be such a fundamental problem that the innocent minorities are sometimes denied their civil liberties as well as the equal protection of the law. Phrases such as "driving while black", "driving while brown", "flying while Arab" and "flying while Muslim", have all been coined as a part of the general approach to these specific minority populations.[373]

In fact, recent polls indicate that the majority of Americans would prefer if Arabs were screened more intensively at airports and the Federal Motor Carrier Administration, which inspects trucks carrying hazardous materials, has indicated that it began a process of scrutinizing its drivers more closely, and drivers of Arab descent should

---

370 Harris S. (2006). "Terrorist Profiling, Version 2. 0" *National Journal*. National Journal Group Inc.

371 Testimony of J. Michael Waller, Annenberg Professor of International Communication, Institute of World Politics, before the Subcommittee on Terrorism, Technology and Homeland Security Senate Committee on the Judiciary. Retrieved from Gilly, Gilinskiy and Sergevnin (2009). *The Ethics of terrorism: innovative approaches from an international perspective*. Springfield, IL: Charles C. Thomas Publishers Ltd

372 Ibid.

373 Ibid.

expect additional scrutiny.[374] Unfortunately, constitutional protection is not absolute, and the Supreme Court will allow discrimination on the basis of race or national origin if there is a "compelling interest". Surely, protection against terrorists is sufficiently compelling?

## In the News: Black Muslims

In 1996, Rodney Hampton-El (also known as Dr. Rashid), was arrested by the FBI and imprisoned for supplying bombs and automatic weapons as part of a plot that included attacks on major bridges and tunnels leading into Manhattan.[375] According to FBI reports, Hampton-El an African-American had been to Afghanistan where he joined jihad groups and returned to the U.S. to lead workshops on guerrilla warfare in Connecticut and New Jersey. He allegedly operated out of a Brooklyn Center called the Alkifah Center, which subsequently closed, but whose Jihad membership remained alive and helped form the nucleus of al Qaeda. The FBI claims that one of Alkifah's veteran members went on to establish an organization in Illinois called the Benevolence International Foundation with links to nine countries and a sizeable budget. Fenaam Arnaout, one of the founding members of this group has since been arrested for lying about ties to terrorism.[376]

The FBI maintains a very active list of self proclaimed potentially dangerous African-American Jihads. This list also includes one Abu Malik. Malik's name surfaced several times during the federal investigation of the 1998 East Africa Embassy bombings.[377] The FBI has described him as a self-proclaimed African-American jihadist who fought against the Soviets in Afghanistan in 1989. He has also been proclaimed as the most important of a handful of African-Americans who have allegedly been associated with al Qaeda for over 10 years.

Another African-American of interest, according to the FBI, is one Isa Abdullah Ali, whose birth name is Cleveland Raphael Holt aka Kevin Holt. A Washington D.C. native, Holt served in the U.S. Army in Korea, converted to Islam upon discharge, fought with the Afghans against the Soviets, and then ended up as a trash collector at Howard University.[378] Holt is even rumored to have worked with the Amal militia and Hezbollah in Lebanon. According to U.S. Intelligence, Holt, who is rumored to have joined a Jihad in Bosnia in 1966, is wanted for

---

374  Ibid.
375  Ibid.
376  Ibid.
377  Ibid.
378  Ibid.

questioning about alleged "terrorist activities" although no charges have been officially brought against him.[379]

According to the FBI, there appears to be growing evidence that extremist groups have, in a sense, infiltrated American's prison system and are recruiting under the guise of religion.[380] A case in point would be the three California residents who were investigated for their role in a plot to attack National Guard facilities. According to the FBI one of them had served time in a California State Prison and converted to a radical Islamic group called Jamiyyat Ul Islam Is Shaheeh.[381] The second was later arrested on unrelated charges and thereafter converted to Islam. The third was a Pakistani national. The men had apparently been recruited to join a Jihad against the United States.[382] The FBI also makes mention of a similar case involving an ex-gang member from Chicago who was held without charges as a suspected terrorist. He too, had converted to Islam while incarcerated.[383] There already exist many assumptions about the inherent danger of African-American men. Any obvious link between African-American men and Islam could be seen as potentially volatile.

### RACE, ETHNICITY AND POLICY: PROTECTING THE CIVIL LIBERTIES OF INDIVIDUALS VERSUS DEFENDING THE PUBLIC INTEREST

Questions of constitutionality with respect to the American response to terrorism are nothing new. In 1944, during World War II, for example, the issue of racial profiling was raised within the context of national security. At issue was the question of the violation of civil liberties—the U.S. government's issuance of an "Exclusion Order[384] which mandated that after May 9, 1942, all persons of Japanese descent were to move to a designated area on the West Coast because they were suspected of espionage.[385] The court's response was that this violation of civil liberties was allowable because it resulted from an activity necessary to protect the public as opposed to a violation resulting from racial antagonism. In the final analysis, the court agreed that all persons of Japanese descent were to be expelled from

---

379  Ibid.

380  Ibid.

381  Supra at 410

382  Korematsu v. United States, No. 22, 323 U.S. 214, 65 S. Ct. 193, 89 L. Ed. 194 (1944).

383  Ibid.

384  The 4th Amendment to the U.S. Constitution guarantees the rights of the people to be secure in their persons, houses papers, and effects, against unreasonable searches and seizures, shall not be violated, and no warrants shall issue, but upon probable cause.

385  United States v. Brignoni-Ponce, No. 95-157, 517U.S. 456, 116 S. Ct. 1480, 134 L. Ed. 2d 607 (1975)

the country because it was impossible to differentiate who was loyal to the United States from those where were not.[386]

Some thirty years later in 1975, the Supreme Court agreed that it was a violation of the 4th amendment[387] for patrol officers near the Mexican border to question motorists about their immigration status solely because the drivers looked Mexican.[388] On the other hand, the very next year the Supreme Court allowed some degree of racial profiling at a border checkpoint arguing that the goal was to protect the public interest against illegal immigration.[389] Eventually, in 1996, the Supreme Court placed the burden of proof of racial profiling on the defendant, in essence giving law enforcement agents discretionary powers to choose who to investigate.[390]

Today, there continues to be an ongoing issue surrounding the Al-Qaeda and Taliban suspects held at Guantanamo Bay-the issue being whether protecting the United States from terrorism is enough to detain the suspects indefinitely, without benefit of due process and in violation of the 14th Amendment to the U.S. Constitution.[391] Naturally, most of the suspects are Arab or Muslim who were arrested in Afghanistan or Pakistan on terrorism-related charges. These are non-U.S. Citizens and therefore are guaranteed no rights under the U.S. Constitution. But what are the implications for the many American-born Arabs and Muslims who were arrested in the United States, or who were in fact U.S. citizens? While some of the arrestees were indeed engaged in criminal activity, racial profiling seems to violate the assumption that "guilt is personal and not inheritable."[392]

Since the 9/11 attacks, Arabs and Muslims have become victims much like African-Americans claim they have been for some time. In

---

386   United States v. Martinez-Fuertes et al. No. 74-1560, 428 U.S. 543, 96 S. Ct. 2574, 45 L. Ed. 2d 1116 (1976)

387   United States v. Armstrong, No. 95-157, 517 U.S. 456, 116 S. Ct. 1480, 134 L. Ed. 2d 687 (1996).

388   The 14th Amendment to the U.S. Constitution guarantees no State shall make or enforce any law which shall abridge the privileges or immunities of citizens of the United States nor shall any State deprive any person of life, liberty, or property, without due process of law; nor deny to any person within its jurisdiction the equal protection of the laws.

389   As noted by Justice Jackson in Korematsu v. United States, No. 22, 323 U.S. 214, 65 S. Ct. 193, 89 L. Ed. 194 (1944).

390   The countries are: Afghanistan, Algeria, Bahrain, Bangladesh, Egypt, Eritrea, Indonesia, Iran, Iraq, Jordan, Kuwait, Libya, Lebanon, Morocco, Oman, Pakistan, Qatar, Somalia, Saudi Arabia Sudan, Syria, Tunisia, The United Arab Emirates, and Yemen. North Korea was also included in the list.

391   Talvi, S. J. A. (2003) 'It Takes a Nation of Detention Centers to Hold Us Back' (interview with Michael Welch, Associate Professor of Criminal Justice at Rutgers University) LiP Magazine, January 21

392   Verkaik, R. (2007). UK Provided Base for Rendition Flights, Says European Inquiry. Belfast telegraph (Ireland) June 2007. http://www. mindfully. org/Reform/2007/CIA-Secret-Prison9jun07. htm

fact, the U.S. government introduced the National Security Entry–Exit Registration System (NSEERS) which required all adult males from a very specific list of Arab and Muslim countries to be interviewed, fingerprinted, and photographed at U.S. ports of entry and other designated registration centers.[393] More than 82,000 students, tourists, businessmen and their relatives were affected, yet in the first few months of registration the FBI failed to uncover any links to terrorism. In fact, of the 1,000 who were initially detained, only 15 were charged with a criminal violation (mostly overstaying their visas), and none were charged with a terrorism-related crime.[394] In addition to arresting hundreds of Iranians and other Muslim men who voluntarily reported for registration as required, the few Canadians, Liberians, and Norwegians who showed up because of unclear instructions were also arrested, not to mention the two Canadian citizens who were born in Iran but migrated when they were children, who were also detained for several days.

It is important to note that many of the detainees held legal status and were in fact waiting to receive already-approved work permits that had been delayed by INS because of a backlog in processing the high volume of applications. Yet, notwithstanding their legal status and full cooperation, the Justice Department decided to deport as many as 13,000 Arab and Muslim men whose legal immigration status had expired but who had not yet received their work authorizations.[395] As a result, many Middle Eastern U.S. citizens and their families have fled the country, some seeking political asylum in Canada.

The ethnic stereotyping inherent in these directives is hard to overlook. In the end, the institution of selective registration, detention and deportation of immigrants has taken the form of a large, seemed to be nothing more than a fishing expedition. In essence, since 9/11, innocent Arabs and Muslims have been:

    a.    mistreated at airports,
    b.    arbitrarily detained on suspicion of being terrorists,
    c.    accused of having terrorist links and denied a free and fair trial,
    d.    held incommunicado.

Interestingly enough, the United States has also been accused of engaging in its own criminal activity and ignoring the sovereign rights of other countries. For example:

---

393  Craig Whitlock with the help of Dana Priest and William Magnuson,"CIA ruse on missing cleric misled Italians," Washington Post, December 5, 2005

394  Jones, Dale E. et al. 2002. Religious Congregations and Membership in the United States 2000:An Enumeration by Region, State and County Based on Data Reported by 149 Religious Bodies. Nashville, TN: Glenmary Research Center.

395  Ibid.

1.  Italy has accused the U.S. of kidnapping a radical Egyptian cleric and smuggle him out in a US military airplane.[396]
2.  Sweden and Germany have accused the U.S. of kidnapping and torturing their citizens in an effort to uncover terrorist activities.[397]
3.  Some Eastern European countries have accused the U.S. of operating secret prisons within their borders[398]

This practice called rendition is typically done with the knowledge of the host country, but apparently no permission was sought or given in these cases. The U.S. argues that this type of action (which is does not deny), is necessary to eradicate terrorism[399]. Many believe that a country's civilization can be measure by the way it treats its prisoners. If this is true, then what does America's treatment of its detainees say about us?

+ + +

ETHNICITY AND TERRORISM: PUTTING THE PIECES TOGETHER
(A brief narrative) by Dr. Faith Speaks

Since the beginning of time and especially the beginning of this country there has been an attack on those who possess difference in various aspects of humanness; race, gender, ethnicity, geography, financial and educational status, etc. The rule of the majority has usually been of those who have always considered themselves the "dominant" culture. Any other difference has not been tolerated for fear of "infiltration", which inevitably could mean domestic and international rule. Many instances in our society illuminate this fear which manifests itself psychologically, emotionally, behaviorally, and physically as, and translates itself into terrorism. Terrorism is understood in this discussion as that which holistically destroys the primary function of any one thing's basic nature, very being and purpose.

There is an historical backdrop to this paradigm of ethnicity and terrorism that, of course reaches back into the annals of our own social history. In other words, America's terroristic behavior is in no way, shape, or form immature. It has been written that in the wake of Pearl Harbor, 1942, Japanese who owned land in California were singled out by the state's District Attorneys to enforce the "Alien Land Law" against these Japanese landowners. Thus, residents were separated from their homes, businesses, and lands. At that time as in any time of

---

396  Welch, Michael (2002) *Detained: Immigration Laws and the Expanding I. N. S. Jail Complex.* Philadelphia: Temple University Press.

397  Statewatch: Monitoring the State and Civil Liberties in Europe available at http://www. statewatch.org/rendition/rendition.html

398  Edward Gilbreath, "How Islam Is Winning Black America", *Christianity Today*, 3 April 2000, 5253; Ilyas Ba-yunus, "Unifying Muslim North America", *Islamic Horizons*, May-June 1421/2000, 20.

399  Ibid.

war, America justifies racial discrimination. The American democratic ideal and racial equality—understood to be two very separate ideas—create an internal conflict for which no parallels exist.

America hides behind the constant rhetoric of "preserving the safety and security of the nation." Think, if you will, of post-9/11 and ·the country's effort to combat terrorist attacks on American soil. Who were these people we were after? Eventually, all persons of Middle Eastern descent were sought. The 1968 Supreme Court Decision of Terry vs. Ohio, otherwise known as the "Terry" stops which gave license to officers' subjectivity in stopping "suspicious persons only propelled the surfacing of bigotry and racism among our public servants toward Black and Brown people —once again in an effort to "serve and protect. This exhibition of valor among police officers became evident in 1999 and 2000 within the New Jersey state police which became the first major law enforcement agency to admit to the stop and detention of disproportionate numbers of Black men.

The Los Angeles Police Department (LAPD) and other agencies have been revealed as having patterns of routine practices that engage in racial profiling by officers. Now, let us be very clear, racial profiling, as it has been defined in governmental briefs and "legalese" refers to government activity directed at a suspect or group of suspects because of their race whether intentional or because of the disproportionate numbers of context based upon pre-textual reasons.( At this point I will refrain from my litany of the "pre-textual" reasons for the physical, psychological, and spiritual slaughter of African-American peoples and Native American peoples in the early years of this country which have been nurtured and have grown to be a well established characteristic in our society today.)

Pre-textual reasons may very well include all occurrences of racial and ethnic beliefs and the embodiment of the "different" racial experiences in American society. Better said in the fifties and sixties, "If you're Black get back, If you're Brown stick around, (your torture is delayed), If you're white, you're all right." This fundamental historical pre-text is one which plagues us to this very day!

Notwithstanding the reality, in March, 2001, Attorney General Ashcroft condemned racial profiling as an "unconstitutional deprivation of equal protection under our constitution."[400] Yet this very form of racial profiling is what we have seen in all of the historical tactics in our efforts to protect, and safeguard against infiltration and the threat of ultimate genocide.

France Cress Welsing discusses more intently and academically the European's fear of the threat of racial and ethnic annihilation. The current throws and ever growing concerns of the Immigration bills/laws passed and contemplated to rid America of its' illegal aliens, and

---

400  Justice Department Considers Racial Profiling For Terror Prevention available at http://www.huffingtonpost.com/2008/07/03/justice-department-consid_n_110625.html

the spirit of legal discontent against immigrants, legal and illegal living in America "taking all of the good jobs from the hard working American people.", are discussed so "matter of factly."

The pre-text to this, of course, is imbedded in the fabric of capitalism and the American ethic, the macro-system of better and best. "We hold these truths to be self evident that we are created better than others on the earth, and we can help them get right by making them conform and acculturative. Why then was America so convinced that the crimes of 9/11 were committed by those of Middle Eastern descent? Were they all Bin Laden's disciples? Were we really after Bin Laden? Who really was the culprit? No other factors warranted suspicion. In our recent debates and dialogue on naturalization and immigration what really are we saying and what is the bottom line? We see time and again the same pattern of behavior. Against whom, though?

Thurgood Marshall once said, "History teaches that grave threats to liberty often come in times of urgency when constitutional rights seem too extravagant to endure."[401] This nation, of the people, by the people, and for the people, has been put in direct conflict with the American democratic ideal of racial equality. Who did it?! Isn't it insanity to believe that we as a nation are acting out things that we really don't believe?

Where do we go from here?!

Dr Faith Speaks— Ethnicity and Terrorism— Putting the Pieces Together

a+++

## CONTROVERSY: AFRICAN-AMERICAN TERRORISTS

Over the last 50 to 60 years, the Muslim population in the United States has been rising subtly but significantly. Not only are people from the Middle East, South Asia and Africa immigrating in uncontrollably large numbers, but another more alarming phenomenon is taking place. The words "African-American" and "terrorist" which have hitherto been thought to be mutually exclusive are no longer being viewed as such. African-Americans are converting to Islam in massive numbers. By some estimates, as many as six million Muslims now live in the United States, with over two million of them belong-

---

401  Skinner v. Railway Labor Executives' Association, 489 U.S. 602, 635 (1989) (Marshall, J., dissenting).

ing to the African-American Diaspora.[402] A 1998 *Newsweek* article actually claims that up to 33% of African-American men in federal prison are now Muslim, and more importantly, most of them were converted while imprisoned.[403]

Notwithstanding the genuine religious overtones and the numerous programs converting the incarcerated and those in the armed forces to Christianity, a significant number of non-spiritually based conversions to Islam are occurring inside prison walls and have given rise to fears, real or therwise, of African-American-initiated terrorism. There have been news reports that African-Americans are training in terror camps in Pakistan and Afghanistan.[404]

It is not inconceivable that some African-Americans may nurse private hatreds toward the U.S. government, and out of that hatred, could be tempted to wreak their brand of divine retribution on other Americans; in a misguided reading of Islam, they might interpret that religion as supporting such actions.

But this sudden preoccupation with Islam is apparently not so sudden. As many as 20% of the Africans who were brought to the Americas from Africa during the slave trade have been identified as Muslim.[405] Muslim slave traders are credited with exporting over 17 million slaves to the coast of the Indian Ocean, the Middle East, and North Africa.[406] So it should be of no surprise that as many as 90% of the converts to Islam in the United States are said to be African-American.[407]

Although there appears to be a greater focus on the Nation of Islam, the majority of converts choose mainstream Islam, and this phenomenon is not just isolated to the North American continent only. In Britain, there seems to be an increasing number of young black men converting to Islam as well as a large Black Muslim (not to be confused with the Nation of Islam) population from Nigeria, Somalia, and Tanzania.[408] It is conceivable that the vast majority of Orthodox Muslims were introduced to Islam by one of the many Black Nationalist groups that rose and fell at some point in our nation's history.

---

402  Ibid.

403  Supra at 442

404  Ibid.

405  Armstrong, Rose-Marie (2003). "Turning to Islam— African-American Conversion Stories." *The Christian Century*, July 12, 2003, p. 19-23. The Christian Century Foundation

406  Ibid.

407  U.S. Dept. of State, (2005). Country reports on Terrorism 2004. U.S. Dept of State. Office of the Coordinator for Counterterrorism, April 2005, Washington DC

408  Waller, J. Michael (2003). Testimony before the United States Senate Committee on the Judiciary on Terrorist Recruitment and Infiltration in the United States: Prisons and Military as an Operational Base. Retrieved from http://judiciary. senate. gov/testimony. cfm?id=960&wit_id=2719

---

## AFRICAN-AMERICAN MUSLIMS AND FUNDAMENTALISTS

This movement can perhaps be traced back to the rise in the Black Power movement in 1966, which attracted thousands of African-American Christians who believed that God had allowed them to suffer too long at the hands of the oppressors.[409] Many African-Americans had begun to view Christianity as the religion of White-America and felt that conversion to Islam was their recovery of their ethnic heritage. African-American males, in particular, felt disconnected from the church because they felt that churches did not address their needs.[410]

They complained that the church addressed personal and spiritual matters but did not supply enough practical solutions for more important issues such as social and economical hardships.[411] The Christian church was accused of being more focused on demanding tithes and offerings from an already economically challenged group, while Islam was being praised for picking up the pieces and offering a sense of belonging and unity and providing immediate practical solutions such as money, housing and jobs.[412] Some African-Americans seem to be attracted to Islam simply because it is not Christianity.

Today, young African-American men are seeking empowerment and may be drawn to Islam despite the negative images projected by the extremists of 9/11. By living according to the strict tenets of Islam, African-American men feel that they are able to negate White-America's stereotype of black men on drugs, out of work or in jail.[413] For some young men, Islam presents a way to redefine their manhood.

The concept of a primarily African-American Islamic terrorist cell is indeed far-fetched. The US State Department's 2004 report refers to this new phase in the development of terrorism, one in which local groups inspired by Al Qaeda organize and carry out attacks with little or no support or direction from Al Qaeda itself.[414]

---

409  Carol L. Stone, Estimate of Muslims Living in America, in Yvonne Yazbeck Haddad, ed., *The Muslims of America* (New York: Oxford University Press, 1991), 25.

410  Martin, Susan Taylor (2002). "Are prisons a breeding ground for terrorists?" St. Petersburg Times, January 14

411  Ibid.

412  Frank J. Gaffney, Jr. is the founder, president, and CEO of The Center for Security Policy. During the Reagan administration, Gaffney was the Assistant Secretary of Defense for International Security, the Deputy Assistant Secretary of Defense for Nuclear Forces and Arms Control Policy, and a Professional Staff Member on the Senate Armed Services Committee, chaired by Senator John Tower (R-Texas). He is a columnist for The Washington Times, Jewish World Review, and Townhall. com and has also contributed to The Wall Street Journal, USA Today, The New Republic, The Washington Post, The New York Times, The Christian Science Monitor, The Los Angeles Times, and Newsday.

413  Ibid.

414  Testimony of Robert S. Mueller, III, Director, Federal Bureau of Investigation, before the Senate Committee on Intelligence of the United States Senate, February 16th 2005.

Yvonne Haddad, an academic who studies Muslims in America, has identified two loci of Islamic focus in the United States, the university and the prison.[415] Although it cannot be disputed that the conversion of many African-Americans to Islam is purely or primarily spiritual, this is not so in the case of some prison inmates. The possibilities for developing mischief have caused deep concern in some circles, and again it is important to study whether that alarm is well-founded or overblown.

In the current prison setting, some sociologists have accused Islamists of supporting intolerance and hatred of American society, culture, and government. The American correctional system apparently allows inmates to collaborate both amongst themselves and with the outside world to such an extent that fundamentalism is able to spread quickly. Dr. Theodore Dalrymple, a prominent British psychiatrist who works in British prisons, argues that Islam is attractive to inmates "because it revenges them upon the whole of society. . . . By converting to Islam, the prisoner is therefore expressing his enmity toward the society in which he lives and by which he believes himself to have been grossly maltreated."[416] Some FBI sources actually agree with these arguments. According to these sources, U.S. prisons are providing al Qaeda and other such organizations with a rich source of possible converts in the form of men who have already been convicted of violent crimes and have little or no loyalty to the United States.[417]

Moreover, according to a Global News Wire interview with Dr. Bilal Philips, a Jamaican-born Canadian, some U.S. officers welcomed lectures on Islam within their military camps because they believed it presented a much needed diversion to their soldiers.[418] According to Phillips, although the Christian missionaries tried to stop the trend, about 15 to 20 American soldiers were converting to Islam daily and one camp even became known as the "Conversion to Islam" camp.[419]

With this kind of rhetoric in the background, it is no surprise that the FBI also expressed great concern about the potential for extremist groups such as Al Qaeda to recruit radical American Muslim converts.[420] According to the FBI, the American prison system provides a ready pool of willing applicants.[421] They say that groups such as al Qaeda can exploit the newness of a prisoner's conversion to Islam and his less than thorough understanding of its message, while still incar-

---

415  Ibid.
416  Supra at 447
417  Ibid.
418  Ibid.
419  Ibid.
420  Ibid.
421  Ibid.

cerated, as well as his socioeconomic status and the difficulty with which African-American prisoners reintegrate into the community upon release.

Others have also expressed concern at an emerging pattern of alienation, radicalism and violence among African-American converts to Islam, particularly among those in prison.[422] Allegedly, several hundred African-American imams have been trained in Saudi Arabia to convert even larger numbers of African-American inmates not only to Islam but to also inculcate Islamic political objectives, i.e., injecting anti- Americanism into the general African-American prison population.[423]

There are several key organizations involved in Muslim prison recruitment. These include the National Islamic Prison Foundation (NIPF), which coordinates with area mosques to shelter and feed African-American Muslims who are released from prison with the customary $10, a suit of clothes, and a one-way bus or train ticket, and the Islamic Society of North America (ISNA), which brings prison chaplains and volunteers together to improve services offered to inmates, such as the provision of free literature, helping the families of those incarcerated and building halfway houses for those released. Maybe anti-American activism is not the main attraction, after all. In this view, Muslims are converting angry, suppressed and alienated African-American prison inmates, and providing them with jobs, security, and a sense of hope.

Over the past 30 years, Islam has become one of the most powerful forces in America's correctional system.[424] In New York State, for example, an estimated 17 to 20% of all inmates are Muslims and FBI estimates indicate that there are currently 350,000 Muslims in federal, state and local prisons—with an estimated 30,000 to 40,000 more being converted each year. According to the FBI, for the most part these inmates are non-Muslims when they come into first contact with the correctional system but once incarcerated, the majority turn to religion for spiritual fulfillment. The FBI also estimates that 80% of these religious converts turn to Islam and points out that this fact alone may be the major contributor to the exponential growth of Islam in the U.S.[425]

422  Tyner, Jarvis (2002). The Struggle against War, Racism and Repression. People's Weekly World Newspaper, February 16th. Retrieved on May 1, 2006 from http://www. pww. org/article/view/635/1/57/

423  Smith, Brent L., Kelly R. Damphouse, Freedom Jackson, and Amy Sellers. 2002. "The Prosecution and Punishment of International Terrorists in Federal Courts: 1980-1998." *Criminology & Public Policy* 1: 311-338.

424  Ibid.

425  Ibid.

On the other hand, research done by the Department of Justice, Bureau of Justice Statistics (National Census of the Jail Population indicated that these converts only account for 6-7% of the total number of prison converts.[426]

According to the FBI, for the most part these inmates are non-Muslims when they come into first contact with the correctional system but once incarcerated, the majority turn to religion for spiritual fulfillment. The FBI also estimates that 80% of these religious converts turn to Islam and points out that this fact alone may be the major contributor to the exponential growth of Islam in the U.S.[427]

If these numbers are indeed true, one contributor could be society's treatment of prisoners. Once incarcerated, inmates feel ostracized and abandoned not only by their family and friends but by society as a whole. This may leave them with a void that religion can fill, making them more susceptible to recruitment. According to FBI reports, prison converts actually acknowledge that not only does membership offer them protection, but they also become part of a network with which they can interact, and depend on both inside and outside of prison.[428]

## CONCLUSION

Terrorism has been described as "the foundation of fundamentalism with isolationism of information, government, and a political process".[429] Whether or not an act is considered an act of terrorism depends on whether a legal, moral, or behavioral perspective is adopted to interpret the act. If, for example, a legal or moral perspective is used, the perception of the interpreter is the determining factor rather than the act itself. If, on the other hand, a behavioral perspective is adopted, then the focus is on the act itself i.e., the behavior of the antagonists.[430] In the final analysis, regardless of the stance taken, terrorists are more often than not portrayed as ethnic minorities.

The Black Panthers, for example, was formed largely due to real social problems being experienced by the African-American population at that time.[431] Discrimination was rampant. The norm for African-Americans was a life in the ghetto, unemployment, poverty and

---

426   DOJ Bureau of Justice Statistics (National Census of the Jail Population. Available at http://www.adherents.com/misc/adh_prison.html#altformat
427   Vago, Steven (2006). Law and Society. Pearson Prentice Hall: NJ
428   Ibid.
429   Ibid.
430   Ibid.
431   Ibid.

segregation[432]. During that period a series of other "terrorist" groups rose and died. Groups such as the Black Liberation Army (BLA) and the May 19 Communist Organization (M19CO), the Revolutionary Armed Task Force, the Armed Resistance Unit and the Black Hebrew Israelites all claimed responsibility for many bombings in New York City and Washington D.C., including an attack on the U.S. capitol building in 1983.[433] Their motives varied, ranging from fostering Black Nationalism and separatism to the destruction of U.S. capitalism and imperialism.[434]

Traditionally, African-American converts claim to be economically subjugated by mainstream America, have no control over the resources necessary for their very survival and advancement, and as such are unable to respond to ever changing societal norms. Without the ability to compare their reality with the reality of mainstream America, it is conceivable that African-Americans can be more easily relegated to systematic fundamentalism.

Thus one could argue that the large number of converts is a direct result of society's treatment of African-Americans, the continuance of discrimination, racism, stereotyping and class struggle. Whatever else they are doing, fundamentalists are pouring much-needed money into African-American communities and providing African-American inmates with, social, moral, spiritual and financial support.[435]

From an economic perspective, the African-American community seems to be deteriorating into crisis mode. Statistics show that almost all African-Americans will have experienced some form of poverty or economic challenge during their lifetime.[436] Research claims that the poverty rate of African-Americans was 24.7% in 2008 which is almost three times that of Whites-Americans (8.6%).[437] Additionally, the unemployment rate for African-Americans for the past forty years has remained at about twice the rate for White-Americans, and for African-American youth, the unemployment rate is about 39.3%, compared to 23.3% for White-American youth as of March 2010.[438]

History has always shown that in cases where basic freedoms have been denied, the oppressed will turn to primitive actions such as violence. The genius in terrorism therefore is the ability to convert the

432  Ibid.

433  Brown, Steve & Coon, Chris (2003). Trojan Horse. Z Magazine Online V16 N 6. Downloaded from FrontPageMagazine. com on May 10th 2006.

434  Ibid.

435  Ibid.

436  U.S. Census Bureau http://www. census. gov/hhes/www/poverty/poverty08/pov08hi. html

437  Ibid.

438  Bureau of Labor Statistics: http://www. bls. gov/news. release/empsit. t02. htm

potential for violence into what appears to be a charismatic struggle. To do this, the terrorist must present himself as an advocate of social justice or something of a protagonist of the oppression of human rights. The protagonist or advocate must then initiate a method of mass systematic and societal transformation. In essence the current process of conversion has been described as something of a modern day "Trojan horse."

The war on terror bears a striking resemblance to the war on drugs. The strategies applied to both are directly linked to race and ethnicity. While the war on drugs has succeeded in incarcerating an unprecedented number of poor people (who happen to be disproportionately African-American and Hispanic), it has proven ineffective in reducing the consumption of illegal drugs. Similarly, the war on terror, and its reliance on ethnic profiling, has been minimally successful in relation to the vast amount of resources committed to the cause.

An obvious solution is the creation of a process of inclusion for racial, ethnic and religious minorities. However, the willingness to adopt an attitude of inclusion will, by necessity, American would have to admit that it has continued to be exclusive, and would have to actually be willing to change. This is a difficult, if not impossible, task—which may be why such crimes as terrorism will never totally diminish. It is perhaps the hypocrisy of the American power brokers and policy makers that perpetuate the division (real or perceived) between racial and ethnic minorities and mainstream American society. If the majority truly wishes to change, then they must be receptive to the outcome of the change even if it manifests itself in a reduction of their own level of power. We as a society cannot demand sacrifice while we live in luxury; just as we cannot demand peace while punishing those who define peace differently.

There are two major sociopolitical conditions that result in terrorism. The first is real or perceived oppressive rule and interference from an outside government and the second is real or perceived oppression and abuse from a domestic source. If African-Americans view themselves as socio-politically disadvantaged, oppressed and abused by White-America, then this could explain the ease with which African-American inmates are converted to Islam. More importantly, if African-Americans inmates are transitioning from a racially stereotyped group, to Islam, an ethnically stereotyped group, then their struggles will not end.

CRITICAL THINKING QUESTIONS

1.  Why would you say some people feel the need to resort to acts of terror?
2.  If the American government abolished the traditional mechanisms of due process, such as courts and appeals, would you feel the need to resort to violence to protect yourself?
3.  Should the U.S. government be allowed to bend a few laws to stop a potential terrorist? Is this justified by the war on terrorism? Why or why not?
4.  Should the U.S. government take it upon themselves to override the authority of foreign governments in the name of the war on terrorism?

CHAPTER RESOURCES

Key Terms
Patriot Act
Islam
Muslim
Middle Eastern
Terrorism
Ready for Review
Introduction
In the News
Race Ethnicity and Policy: Protecting the civil liberties of individuals versus defending the public interest
Biography: Ethnicity and Terrorism: Putting the Pieces Together
Controversy
African-American Terrorists
African-American Muslim or Fundamentalist
Class Struggle and racial Liberation

# CHAPTER 6. RACE, ETHNICITY AND HUMAN TRAFFICKING.

## OBJECTIVES

- To determine if the continued existence of Human trafficking is related to the race/ethnicity of the majority of victims and the offender
- To evaluate the relationship between human trafficking and poverty
- To evaluate the impact of supply and demand on the continued existence of human trafficking

### CASE STUDY: PENNY'S CHALLENGE

Penny was almost 29 when she was transported from Rwanda to the United Kingdom. She was told that she would be able to start a new life in the UK. Instead, she ended up held hostage in a small flat in London. She had unknowingly become a commodity in what is now being called the world's fastest growing illegal trade—in people.

When Penny agreed to meet the agent, to whom she was introduced by a friend, she was unaware that human trafficking even existed. Penny said she was so focused on getting out of the country that she never stopped to think of the possible consequences. Penny was told the journey to the UK would cost her £1,000 pounds, and the fact that she didn't have the money was not a problem. She would be given accommodation and a job when she arrived, enabling her to eventually pay the money back.

But the reality was very different. She was imprisoned by the agent and forced into sexual slavery. The one time she tried escape her captor tracked her down, gave her a severe beating, and then locked her in the flat. Eventually, Penny said, she was under his absolute control—mentally and physically. She said she couldn't even sneeze without her captor's knowledge[439].

Few stories like this one will surface because victims like Penny believe that authorities are more concerned about their illegal status than apprehending the offender. Penny, for example, was repeatedly imprisoned for not having the right paperwork while no genuine effort was made to apprehend her captor. And even those stories that surface do not paint an accurate picture of the reality of the phenomenon that is human trafficking. Somehow, somewhere, someone determined that if you can make money moving illegal products, then the people-product would be an easier product to move than even drugs or weapons.

### INTRODUCTION: WHAT IS HUMAN TRAFFICKING?

Article 3 of the UN Protocol to Prevent, Suppress and Punish Trafficking in Persons, Especially Women and Children (2000) says,

"(a) 'Trafficking in persons' shall mean the recruitment, transportation, transfer, harbouring or receipt of persons, by means of the threat or use of force or other forms of coercion, of abduction, of fraud, of deception, of the abuse of power or of a position of vulnerability or of the giving or receiving of payments or benefits to achieve the consent of a person having control over another person, for the purpose of exploitation. Exploitation shall include, at a minimum, the exploitation of the prostitution of others or other forms of sexual exploitation, forced labour or services, slavery or practices similar to slavery, servitude or the removal of organs;

(b) The consent of a victim of trafficking in persons to the intended exploitation set forth in subparagraph (a) of this article shall be irrelevant where any of the means set forth in subparagraph (a) have been used;

(c) The recruitment, transportation, transfer, harbouring or receipt of a child for the purpose of exploitation shall be considered "trafficking in persons" even if this does not involve any of the means set forth in subparagraph (a) of this article.[440]

---

439  Stephanie Holmes. Trafficking: A very modern slavery. BBC News Story from BBC News. http://news. bbc. co. uk/go/pr/fr/-/2/hi/europe/7243612. stm Published 2008/02/15

440  Supplementing the UN Convention Against Transnational Organized Crime (2000), hereafter referred to as the UN Trafficking Protocol. Retrieved from http://www2.ohchr.org/english/law/protocoltraffic.htm

Sometimes called "modern day slavery", human trafficking is defined by the United Nations as "the recruitment, transportation, transfer, harboring or receipt of persons, by means of the threat or use of force or other forms of coercion... for the purpose of exploitation."[441] Although human trafficking is a crime in and of itself, it is also a catch all phrased to describe a variety of illegal activities, including but not limited to:

a.   trafficking in women and children (for sexual exploitation),
b.   prostitution,
c.   Labor trafficking
d.   child exploitation,
e.   pornography,
f.   trade in body parts,
g.   illegal adoptions, and
h.   alien smuggling.[442]

After the illicit drug trading, human trafficking is the second largest and the fastest growing criminal industry in the world. The victims of human trafficking are mostly women and children who are ethnic minorities[443]. Interestingly enough, the traffickers, themselves are also predominantly ethnic minorities. The crime manifests itself in many forms including, but not limited to,

a.   sexual exploitation,
b.   forced labor (personal and commercial), and
c.   the removal and sale of human organs.

People are snared into trafficking by a variety of methods including,

a.   physical force
b.   false promises regarding job opportunities
c.   promises of marriage/marriages in a foreign country
d.   promises of a better life.

The U.N. estimates that some 2.5 million ethnic minorities are in forced labor at any given time, as a result of trafficking, including

---

441   Gender and Human Trafficking. United Nations Economic and Social Commission for Asia and the Pacific. http://www. unescap. org/esid/gad/issues/trafficking/index. asp

442   Christine Boutin. 141 CCDG 03 E—Organized Crime—Drug and Human Trafficking in Europe. (France). NATO Parliamentary Assembly. Retrieved from http://www. nato-pa. int/Default. asp?SHORTCUT=368

443   Economic and Social Commission for Asia and the Pacific. Gender and Development Discussion Paper Series No. 17. Violence against and Trafficking in Women as Symptoms of Discrimination: The Potential of CEDAW as an Antidote. Retrieved from http://www. unescap. org/esid/gad/Publication/DiscussionPapers/17/CEDAW%20discussion%20 paper%20no. %2017%20-%20revised%2023%20March%202006. pdf

some 1.2 million children[444]. The United States is a both source and destination country for thousands of minority men, women, and children trafficked for the purposes of sexual and labor exploitation. The Central Intelligence Agency (CIA) estimates that some 50,000 people are trafficked into or transited through the U.S.A. annually as

a.    sex slaves,
b.    domestics,
c.    garment and agricultural slaves[445]

The women and girls, largely from East Asia, Eastern Europe, Mexico and Central America are trafficked to the United States mainly into prostitution. Others, including some men, responding to fraudulent offers of employment in the United States, migrate willingly and unwillingly (legally and illegally) but are subsequently subjected to conditions of involuntary servitude at work sites or in the case of young boys, in the commercial sex trade. Additionally, an unknown number of American citizens and legal residents are trafficked within the country primarily for sexual servitude and, to a lesser extent, forced labor.[446]

Human trafficking has become one of the most controversial, if not dangerous forms of international trade in existence today. The mere fact that the practice is referred to as international trade is, in and of itself, cause for concern because it appears to give the practice some measure of legitimacy. With that being said, it is important to note that although trafficking for prostitution and sexual exploitation receives the most attention, labor trafficking and drug trafficking are just as prevalent.

Although trafficking of all kinds is usually associated with poverty, it is an industry that is fuelled by demand that emanates from wealthier countries. There are four components that make up the demand: 1) the men who buy commercial sex acts, 2) the exploiters who maintain the existence of the sex industry, 3) the destination countries, and 4) the culture that tolerates or encourages sexual exploitation.

Research indicates that in Europe the percentage of men who purchase sex acts varies from as low as 7% in the United Kingdom to as high as 39% in Spain.[447] Other percentages by country include Fin-

---

444  Supra at 488

445  Human Trafficking and Modern-Day Slavery. Adapted from U.S. State Department Trafficking in Persons Report, June 2007 retrieved from http://www. gvnet. com/human-trafficking/USA. htm

446  Ibid.

447  Donna M. Hughes, PhD, Reducing Demand for Victims of Sex Trafficking in the U.S. Women in Federal Law Enforcement. Washington, D. C. January 17. 2007 http://www. uri. edu/artsci/wms/hughes/256,1, Reducing Demand for Victims of Sex Trafficking in the U.S.

land, 13%; Norway, 11%; Sweden, 13%; Netherlands, 14%; Switzerland, 19%; and Russia, 10%.[448] The percentage of men who purchase sex acts appears to be higher in Asian countries, with reports of as much as 37% in Japan and 73% in Thailand.[449] In the United States, a national health study found that 16% of men had purchased a sex act, but only 0.6% of men did so on a regular basis.[450]

SCOPE OF THE PROBLEM

## The United States

Although the existence of the sex trade and human trafficking seem to be synonymous with certain Third World countries and minority populations, the problem is just as prevalent in the United States. Although exact figures are not available, researchers report that a rising number of Russian women are working in the U.S. sex industry[451]. Some are brought in on fiancé, student, or business visas; however, the majority enters the U.S. with tourist visas[452]. According to the U.S. Federal Bureau of Investigation (FBI) this is the work of organized crime groups that have infiltrated the United States.[453] The FBI estimates that there are at least 15 organized crime groups from the former Soviet Union who are operating in the U.S with well established and very intricate criminal networks in cities such as Chicago, Philadelphia, Los Angeles, and New York.[454] These groups are responsible for importing Russian women to work in nightclubs and massage parlors.

In a 1996 case involving the "Russian Touch Massage Parlor" in downtown Bethesda, near Washington, DC, eight young Russian women were tricked into prostitution after they answered advertisements in Moscow and St. Petersburg newspapers for positions in the U.S. as *au pairs*, sales clerks, and waitresses. Each woman had been charged US$1,800 by the "travel agencies" who facilitated their trip,

---

448  Ibid.
449  Ibid.
450  Ibid.
451  Caldwell, Gillian, S. Galster, and N. Steinzor, "Crime & Servitude: An Expose of the Traffic in Women for Prostitution from the Newly Independent States," A Report by the Global Survival Network, in collaboration with the International League for Human Rights, 1997; Janice Raymond and Donna Hughes. Sex Trafficking and Women in the United States: International and Domestic Trends. March 2001 Coalition against trafficking in women. http://www. uri. edu/artsci/wms/hughes/sex_traff_us. pdf
452  Ibid.
453  Ibid.
454  Johnson, C. (n. d) Trafficking in Russian Women: Sexual Exploitation as a Growing Form of International Trade. TED case studies retrieved from http://american. edu/ted/traffic. htm

and upon arrival their passports were confiscated while they paid off "debt." The women received no salary for their "work" at the parlor, and only made money from tips they received for sexual services given to clients.

The women were only rescued when the Immigration and Naturalization Service (INS), the FBI and the local police happened to raid the massage parlor for suspected tax evasion by the owner. Unfortunately, although the eight women were in a sense rescued from their plight, the rescuers promptly processed them as illegal workers.[455]

Unfortunately, the demand side of trafficking has not received the degree of attention it warrants. It is particularly challenging in the case of migrant labor. For example, in 2004 police and labor officials raided a makeshift garment factory producing jeans in Bangkok where 18 girls aged 11 to 14 were rescued.[456] Police reportedly found the girls hidden in a small space under the floor of a padlocked room. The girls had apparently been recruited for paid work and been dropped off at the factory by the recruiter. During the six months that followed, not only were the girls not paid, but they were forced to work from 6 a.m. to midnight, were poorly fed and were frequently beaten. The Thai couple running the factory were arrested and charged with human trafficking, unlawful detention and illegally hiring migrant workers.

At this point, one might be inclined to ask, "How does the global demand for cheap jeans, and therefore cheap labor, translate into modern-day slavery? Does the lack of adequate enforcement of laws encourage employers and recruiters to carry out these types of crimes? Or is it because the victims are "merely" migrant children and on some level there is tacit acceptance of treating migrants this way?"

Closer to home, in Houston, Texas, for example, Korean-owned nude-modeling studios are being supplied by flesh traders who typically bribe American soldiers based in South Korea.[457] The GIs are paid up to $5,000 to marry Koreans and bring them back to Fort Hood, Texas, where they divorce them for an equal sum. The women, who speak no English, are then threatened and forced to work in brothels in Houston, Detroit and other cities, supposedly to repay the marriage fees and airfare. Although local crackdowns have cut down the traffic significantly, it still continues with the Korean women being replaced with Salvadorans.

---

455  Ibid.

456  Elaine Pearson. The Mekong Challenge Human Trafficking: Redefining Demand. Destination factors in the trafficking of children and young women in the Mekong subregion. International Programme on the elimination of child labour. International Labour Office Bangkok.

457  Margot Hornblower Paris. "The Skin Trade." *Time Magazine* in partnership with CNN. Sunday June 24, 2001.

In Asia the sex trade has a long history. In the 1960s and '70s, Japanese men flocked in organized sex tours to Taiwan and South Korea. Then their preference changed to the Philippines and Thailand. In the 1980s, however, the traffic became two-way, with Filipina and Thai prostitutes migrating to Japan. Today, an estimated 70,000 Thai "hostesses" working in Japan as virtual indentured sex slaves in bars usually controlled by yakuza gangsters. The women, many of them uneducated villagers, are sold by Thai brokers for an average of $14,000 each and resold to the clubs by Japanese brokers for about $30,000— a sum they are obliged to work off, but rarely can.[458]

Each month the Thai embassy in Tokyo repatriates about 250 escapees yet the Japanese government remains indifferent to the plight of prostitutes—indeed, there are several recorded instances in which police, especially in rural areas, have handed escaping girls back to their abusers. In Ho Chi Minh City, by one report, the number of prostitutes has recently increased from 10,000 to 50,000 and Morocco has become a Mecca for Saudi sex tourists.[459]

Another tier of prosperous Asian countries is following in Japan's footsteps with South Korea and Taiwan developing their own sex-tour operations. Attesting to the growth of market economics, more than 240,000 people engaging in prostitution were arrested in China.[460] Sex tourism takes on ever more ingenious guises as well. In Bombay, a center for inexpensive medical treatment, Arabs are flocking for such common ailments as high blood pressure or skin infections— excuses to stay a week or a month and patronize the brothels that have sprung up around the hospitals. These establishments cater specifically to Arabs with rate of between $100 and $1,000 a night.[461]

*The Economics of Human Trafficking*

Although the practice of trafficking humans occurs worldwide, over the last decade there has been a sharp increase in incidence in places like Russia and the former Soviet Union. Organized crime and corruption throughout the newly independent Russia, for example, play a fundamental role in the incidences of human trafficking[462].

According to experts, Russia's "organized crime and corruption is a growing phenomenon (that) presents a formidable challenge to the international law enforcement, political and business communities..... and has a disproportionately negative effect on transitional and de-

---

458  Ibid.
459  Ibid.
460  Ibid.
461  Ibid.
462  Supra at 503

veloping countries, ...where the most severely impacted are the less privileged, particularly women, children, ...and those not part of the circle of corruption.[463]"

There is no argument that the growth of this industry is probably attributable to the declining economic conditions in that part of the world but experts also believe that the related massive growth in transnational organized crime and corruption is also a major part of the problem. Poor and rapidly deteriorating of economic conditions in Russia, for example, encourage and sometimes even force as many as 50,000 Russian women annually to seek overseas opportunities to better their lives and the lives of their families.[464] Additionally, those who have access to American television are drawn by the glamorous lifestyle. For others it's a case of "any lifestyle is better than the one I'm currently living."

While it is true that some Russian women choose to enter into the international sex trade knowingly, because they believe they will make a lot of money and eventually live a glamorous life, the overwhelming majority are tricked by criminal groups posing as employment agencies, travel agencies, and marriage firms. The victims enter into what they believe are legitimate agreements with these agencies who promise them jobs as entertainers, waitresses, or barmaids overseas, or who promise to find them husbands. Interestingly enough, a significant number of those who perpetrate this scam are of the same ethnicity as their victims which could be another reason why the rest of the world turns a blind eye.

Eventually, most of these women find themselves the victims of illegal trafficking, and are often sold involuntarily into prostitution. They become commodities of the international trade in human flesh, and find themselves coerced, deceived, and deprived of their basic human rights. The majority of these women are sold in countries such as Israel, Malaysia, Japan, Sri Lanka, Cyprus, Belgium, the Netherlands, Thailand, Macau, Germany, Switzerland, and the United States.[465]

An alarming number of these women are also subsequently raped and beaten, have their passports confiscated and are threatened with harm to themselves or their families if they try to break their "contracts" or seek help. They are then forced to work as prostitutes in

---

463 Stoecker, Dr. Sally, of American University's Transnational Crime and Corruption Center (TraCCC), "The Rise in Human Trafficking and the Role of Organized Crime," an expanded version of paper presented at the Third International Parliamentary Roundtable on "Contemporary Legal Policy in Countering Transnational Organized Crime and Corruption," held in Irkutsk, Russia, July 8-10, 2000. ; The Transnational Crime and Corruption Center, American University, Program Brochure
464 Supra at 502
465 Supra at 504

order to pay off travel "debts," which can sometimes be as high as $15,000. Some women are sold to other criminals who then add more to this "debt."[466]

But not all human trafficking is related to the sex trade and even Japan is not immune to the problem. More than 75,000 foreign "guest workers" are trafficked into Japan each year[467]. The guest workers arrive legally from China, Vietnam, Indonesia, Philippines, and Thailand and even as far as Brazil[468]. However, immediately upon arrival into Japan, their passports are confiscated. Over the next 12 months they are placed "in training" and as such, are not covered by Japan's labor or minimum wage laws.[469] They are forced to work long grueling hours seven days a week, often earning less than half of the legal minimum wage. Sixteen-hour shifts, from 8:00 a.m. to midnight, are not uncommon. You may be surprised to know that most of these guest workers are employed by Toyota—through the Toyota Tsusho Corporation—a part of the Toyota Group.[470] Here again both the traffickers and the victims are of minority ethnicities.

The United Nations (UN) recognizes human trafficking as a form of slavery and in a recent report estimated that as many as four million people are trafficked throughout the world each year, as part of a seven billion dollars illegal industry.[471] According to Dr. Sally Stoecker, project director and research professor at The Transnational Crime and Corruption Center (TraCCC), there are at least four factors that facilitate its continued growth:

1. Globalization of the economy;
2. Increased demand for personal services in the developed world;
3. The continuing rise in unemployment among women; and
4. The rapid and unregulated enticement and movement of human capital via the Internet[472].

---

466  Ibid.

467  Francis T. Miko & Grace (Jea-Hyun) Park. Trafficking in women and children: the U.S. and International response. Update March 18, 2002. CRS Report for Congress. Congressional Research Service The Library of Congress

468  Ibid.

469  Anita Lienert. "Toyota looking into allegations of human trafficking and sweatshop abuses." New York. Published June 19, 2008. http://www. insideline. com/toyota/toyota-looking-into-allegations-of-human-trafficking-and-sweatshop-abuses. html

470  Ibid.

471  Ruth Dearnley & Steve Chalke. "Prevention, Prosecution and Protection—Human Trafficking". *UN Chronicle*; Judge Mohamed Chawaki and Dr. Mohamed Wahab. Technology is a double-edged sword: Illegal human trafficking in the information age. Computer Crime Research Center. March 5, 2005.

472  Supra at 512

## WHAT IS THE UNITED STATES DOING TO STOP TRAFFICKING?

The U.S. Government has taken significant steps to combat the trafficking occurring at home. A few examples of domestic efforts are:

1. Congress has passed legislation so that Americans who sexually prey on children abroad can be prosecuted and sentenced for up to 30 years in prison[473].

2. The Department of Justice now focuses on increasing the number of trafficking victims rescued and the number of prosecutions and convictions of traffickers as opposed to prosecution of the victim.

3. The Department of Health and Human Services (HHS) has developed a certification process to qualify trafficking victims for the same assistance available to refugees.[474]

4. The Department of Defense has implemented a zero-tolerance policy against Defense personnel whose actions contribute to human trafficking and has also instituting mandatory service-wide training[475].

### Strategies

Human trafficking is transnational in nature therefore partnerships between countries are essential to winning the fight against modern-day slavery. As a result the U.S. has reached out to other countries and has agreed to provide some $528 million over a 7 year period to find programmatic assistance in efforts to end trafficking.[476] This money is specifically earmarked for initiatives including, but not limited to:

1. Creating rehabilitation and work training centers for victims
2. Providing special housing shelters for victims
3. Providing assistance in implementing legal reform
4. Launching information and awareness campaigns
5. Providing voluntary repatriation for displaced victims
6. Providing special training for immigration officials, medical personnel and social workers
7. Installing special monitoring systems to combat sex tourism

---

473  United States Department of State. "Facts about Human Trafficking. Democracy and Global Affairs." Retrieved from http://www. salvationarmyusa. org/usn/www_usn_2. nsf/0/56E8CA3E6B2D13E88525765D00572978/$file/Facts%20About%20Human%20Trafficking%20-%20Department%20of%20State. pdf

474  Ibid.

475  Ibid.

476  Audit of US/AID/Cambodia's Counter Trafficking in persons project. Audit report No. 9-000-10-002-P. December 10, 2009. Office of Inspector General U.S. Agency for International Development

8. Securing resources to rescuing victims from slave-like situations[477]

In 2000, the United States also passed the Trafficking Victims Protection Act (TVPA) and enhanced it in 2003 and again in 2007.[478] One of the key components of the law is the creation of the Trafficking in Persons Report. The Trafficking in Persons Report requires the Department of State to produce an annual report which assesses governmental response to trafficking in any country with a significant number of victims. Each country is rated and placed in a "tier" based on government efforts to combat trafficking.

- Tier 1 countries include: Australia, Denmark, Austria, Belgium, Canada, The United Kingdom, Norway, The Netherlands, New Zealand, Sweden, South Korea, and France
- Tier 2 countries include: Switzerland, Germany, The Czech Republic and Portugal, Japan
- Tier 2 watch countries included: Cyprus, Armenia, Russia, and China
- Tier 3 countries include: Greece, the Slovak Republic and Ukraine, Uzbekistan, Burma[479]

In 2004 President Bush verbally targeted Cuba as one of the leading offenders of human trafficking ranking in the top 10 with other countries such as North Korea, Burma, Sudan and Venezuela[480].

*What the Numbers Show*

Here is a disturbing but telling table adopted from the Spring 2006 issue of the Iowa Review published by the University of Iowa Center for Human Rights.

| | |
|---|---|
| 0 | Number of shelters in the United States for trafficking victims who, commonly aliens without English language proficiency, are misled to relocate by false promises of lucrative new jobs, only to find themselves having to repay travel expenses and work permit indebtedness, typically as low-skilled workers in slavery-like circumstances (Coalition to Abolish Slavery and Trafficking, 2005; Human Rights Watch, 2000) |

---

477 Supra at 522

478 Tracy Smith, Kim Kennedy. "Against their will—The Realities of Human Trafficking: In the end, it's the customers who keep teen sex rings a viable source of profit." CBS, The Early Show. September 12, 2007

479 Department of State United States of America. Trafficking in Persons Report 2009. http://www. state. gov/documents/organization/123357. pdf

480 Bush Speech on Human Trafficking Targets Castro

Remarks at Official Event Are Tailored for Cuban Exiles in Florida and Religious Conservatives. By Dana Milbank Washington Post Staff Writer Saturday, July 17, 2004; Page A02. http://www. washingtonpost. com/wp-dyn/articles/A54840-2004Jul16. html

| | |
|---|---|
| 75 | Percentage of all human trafficking dedicated to sexual exploitation, the victims commonly being forbidden to refuse "customers" on pain of punishment by their "employers" for resisting, even when they are sexually or otherwise physically abused — a circumstance of especial vulnerability for trafficked persons, who, has "illegal immigrants," tend not to report their abuse for fear of prosecution and/or deportation and potential further victimization upon their return home (U.S. Department of State, 2005; Human Rights Watch, 2001) |
| 227 | Minimum number of nightclubs engaged in the forced prostitution of trafficked women and girls in Bosnia — victimized females who, upon arrival at their first destination, usually are initiated into their new life by gang rape, as illustrated by a 14-year-old girl raped by seven men her first night, whose mouth was taped shut to silence her screaming upon the request of her first "customer," who paid extra to rape a virgin (Community Action Publishers, 2002; BreakPoint, 2004) |
| 2,700 | Minimum number of mail-order bride agencies worldwide, approximately 500 in the United States, with American mail-order customers being generally white, older, and prone to patriarchal values that cause their usually foreign, non-white, younger brides to be made economically dependent and put at risk of physical abuse — a condition that is facilitated by U.S. immigration policy, which gives to the husbands virtual total control over their foreign wives' immigration status, including their eligibility for "conditional resident status" (Perspective, 2002) |
| 14,500 | Minimum number of foreign women and children annually trafficked into the United States (different sources estimating as high as 50,000), with U.S. citizens making up the rest of the U.S. forced labor work, much of it hidden but nevertheless reported in as many as 90 U.S. cities from which, according to one estimate, some 200,000 American children are at high risk of being trafficked into the sex industry each year (Human Rights Watch, 2001; UN Office on Drugs and Crime, 2005) |
| 600,000 | Minimum number of persons annually trafficked across international borders and thereafter commonly trapped into bonded labor or debt bondage (where they must work to "repay" loans about which they are unaware or misinformed) or forced labor (where they work under threat of violence), half of these victims being children under age 13, 43% of them from East Asia and the Pacific (U.S. Department of State, 2005; International Commission for Women of African Descent, 2004) |
| 2,000,000 | Minimum number of persons annually trafficked within their own country (different sources estimating as high as 7 million) and subjected to the same mistreatment and rights violations that are suffered by foreign trafficked laborers (International Commission for Women of African Descent, 2004) |

| | |
|---|---|
| 9,000,000,000 | Minimum estimated U.S. dollar profits resulting annually from human trafficking (different sources estimating as high as $32 billion), increasingly at the hands of organized crime due to the high profits and the fewer risks compared to arms or drugs trafficking, thus making human trafficking the fastest-growing criminal industry in the world at this time (U.S. Department of State, 2005; Public Health Association of Australia) |

Source: *The Iowa Review (Volume 36, Number 1) Spring 2006. The University of Iowa Center for Human Rights.*

Are we doing enough to address this issue? If the targeted victims were non minorities, would our response be any different?

## IN THE NEWS: ZOE'S ARK

In October 2007, Chadian authorities arrested 9 French citizens as they attempted to take 103 children from Chad to Paris. Zoe's Ark, a Paris-based non-governmental organization said they were rescuing the children from Darfur, a war-torn region in the Sudan. Initially, the UN Refugee Agency reported that some of the children, aged one to nine were orphaned and sick and being evacuated to receive health care. One humanitarian worker in Chad allegedly said that some of the children had bandaged limbs. But later the UN High Commission for Refugees (UNHCR) said the children were found to be in good health. Later, the Chadian Minister of the Interior and Public Safety told the media that the children were not all orphans. In fact, some of the children were believed to be Chadians and not Sudanese.

Despite the fact that members of Zoe's Ark had documents showing that the children were orphans, Chadian authorities felt that the evacuation of the Chadian and Sudanese children (an act which was allegedly being carried out unbeknownst to local authorities), simply was not normal and that only the Office of the UN High Commissioner for Refugees (UNHCR), is responsible for movement of any Sudanese refugees settled in the east of Chad. Furthermore, neither Chad nor Sudan allow international adoption. Moreover, Zoe's Ark had no official authorization to take the children.

The head of Zoe's Ark told a French newspaper that the organization was not setting up adoptions and meant no harm when it planned the operation, which is now being termed an illegal kidnapping and possibly child-trafficking. The group's website says it seeks to help children gain refugee status abroad while hostilities are ongoing in their home countries. "International law allows it as much as morality requires it," the website states.[481]

According to Zoe's Ark, 300 families had agreed to host children, paying up to 2,400 Euros (US$3,450) each. Delphine Philibert, who on 26 October was still waiting at the airport for the 5-year-old boy she was to take home, told Le Parisien she was shocked by the way events had been portrayed. "It is absolutely heinous that the authorities suspect we played a role in child-trafficking," Philibert said. "The volunteers at [L'Arche de Zoé] are so dedicated. It's sacrilege to treat them as child traffickers."[482]

The children were placed in the custody of the Chadian Ministry of Social Affairs. The UN Children's Fund (UNICEF), UNHCR, the Red Cross and Chadian officials cared for the children until they could be returned to where they came from. The Chadian Prime Minister vowed to punish those who had tried to move the children. Media reports said France had also denounced L'Arche de Zoé's operation.[483]

## RACE, ETHNICITY AND POLICY

When the American Congress was officially exposed to the reality of human trafficking in 1999, many people were outraged. At that Congressional hearing, a woman from Nepal testified that she had been drugged, abducted and forced to work at a brothel in Bombay while an activist shared tales of how the women overseas were being beaten with electrical cords and raped.[484]

The U.S. State Department, which monitors crimes of this nature, demanded action—up to 50,000 trafficking victims pouring into the United States every year was unacceptable.[485] The very next year, Congress passed a law putting into motion a worldwide war on human trafficking. The war began toward the end of the Clinton administration and became a top Bush administration priority. Rep. Christopher H. Smith (R-N.J.) was so openly furious about what he called the "tidal wave" of victims that he vowed to crack down on modern-day slavery.[486]

481 IRIN News. Chad: French NGO accused of trafficking children. 26 October 2007. IRIN Humanitarian News and Analysis: A project of the UN Office for the Coordination of Humanitarian Affairs. http://www. irinnews. org/Report. aspx?ReportId=75019

482 Ibid.

483 BBC News. Chad 'kidnapping' angers Sarkozy. Monday 29 October 2007 http://news. bbc. co. uk/2/hi/africa/7066770. stm

484 "Human trafficking—really such a big issue?" September 30, 2007 By Jerry Markon, *Washington Post* http://articles. sfgate. com/2007-09-30/news/17262541_1_ human-trafficking-task-forces-victims

485 Ibid.

486 "Human trafficking—really such a big issue?" September 30, 2007 By Jerry Markon, *Washington Post* http://articles. sfgate. com/2007-09-30/news/17262541_1_human-traf-

But the government couldn't find the victims; at least not in the U.S. The evidence and testimony presented to Congress indicated that this was mostly an international problem and that since the law was passed, human trafficking was no longer become a major domestic issue. In fact, over a 7-year period only 1,362 individuals have been identified in the U.S. as being victims of human trafficking—not the 50,000 a year the government had estimated.[487] Although there have been several estimates over the years, the number that helped fuel the congressional response was really an unscientific estimate by a CIA analyst who relied mainly on clippings from foreign newspapers.[488] Since then, much lower numbers have been presented to Congress (14,500 to 17,500 a year).[489]

Despite these much lower numbers, the U.S. government still spent $28.5 million in 2006 to fight human trafficking in the United States, a 13% increase over 2005's spending.[490] Steven Wagner, who helped the Department of Health and Human Services distribute millions of dollars in grants to a variety of community groups eager to find and assist victims, said, "Those funds were wasted....Many of the organizations that received grants didn't really have to do anything... They were available to help victims. There weren't any victims."[491]

How could the numbers be so wrong?

Despite discrepancies, the government's determination to find and help victims of trafficking continues unabated, and it is a lucrative business—the Bush administration even hired a public relations firm, a highly unusual approach to fighting crime. Ketchum, a New York-based public relations firm, received $9.5 million and has been awarded $2.5 million more.[492]

Unfortunately, the U.S. government has not yet established an effective mechanism for determining the number of victims, nor has the government established a reliable method of conducting ongoing analysis of trafficking related data that resides within the various government entities. Despite the fact that federal agencies have now

---

ficking-task-forces-victims; US Estimates Thousands of Victims, Efforts to Find Them Fall Short September 24, 2007 Adapted from: Jerry Markon. "Human Trafficking Evokes Outrage, Little Evidence: U.S. Estimates Thousands of Victims, But Efforts to Find Them Fall Short." *The Washington Post.* 23 September 2007

487  Supra at 533

488  US Estimates Thousands of Victims, Efforts to Find Them Fall Short September 24, 2007. Adapted from: Jerry Markon. "Human Trafficking Evokes Outrage, Little Evidence: U.S. Estimates Thousands of Victims, But Efforts to Find Them Fall Short." *The Washington Post.* 23 September 2007

489  Ibid.

490  Ibid.

491  Ibid.

492  Ibid.

undertaken anti trafficking activities, the U.S. government has still has not developed or coordinated a much needed strategy for combating trafficking abroad or developed a way to gauge the effectiveness of the strategies used.

Ironically, the U.S. Department of State is responsible for assessing foreign governments' compliance with minimum standards to eliminate trafficking in persons, but the U.S. remains unranked. Moreover, the methods used to determine the final ranks in the annual Trafficking in Persons Report are incomplete. Although the creation of the annual Trafficking in Persons Report has increased global awareness, encouraged reluctant governments to take action, and raised the risk of sanctions against governments that do not make significant efforts to comply with the standards, the process does not comprehensively describe compliance with the standards, lessening the report's credibility and usefulness as a diplomatic tool. This chapter's contributing author's piece speaks directly to the inadequate monitoring of minimum standards of compliance and hints at some type of statistical manipulation.

+++

THE PURPLE ROSE MARKETS OF MUMBAI AND MANILA: GLOBALIZATION AND FEMALE SEX TRAFFICKING IN INDIA AND THE PHILIPPINES
   Dr. James G. Crawford

In a recent public awareness campaign, the anti-trafficking organization GABRIELA chose the Purple Rose to symbolize victims of the Philippine sex industry. These hybrid blooms were made exotic by human will, their natural beauty distorted "for the pleasure and profit of others."[1] This essay describes the contemporary female sex trafficking markets of India and the Philippines. It argues that one consequence of globalization is an increase in the exploitation of women and girls in the brothels of Mumbai and Manila. Poverty, labor mobility, porous borders, and electronic finance and communication have combined, in hot-house fashion, to yield more Purple Roses than ever.

India has more than 1,000 red-light districts, where from 2.3 million to 8 million females are involved in prostitution. One quarter of these prostitutes are children who are often presented for customer selection in cages.[2] One 14 year-old girl rescued from a Mumbai brothel of 218 children had been sold at age 9 for $600 by her father. After five years in the trade, she, like most of girls in the house, was HIV positive.[3] More than 40% of Indians live in absolute poverty. Rural parents often sell their female children into debt-bondage as urban domestic servants, but the girls often are sold to city brothels. Once "corrupted," they are unfit for marriage, and face ostracism from family and society. They must continue selling their bodies until age or disease renders them unmarketable.

Mumbai is the center of the South Asian flesh trade. Many of its women and girls are smuggled into India across un-policed borders with Nepal and Bangladesh. Hindu men pay a premium for light complexioned Nepali females, who are also Hindu, while the Bangladeshi sex traffic satisfies Muslim men preferring Muslim prostitutes. Poverty drives young women to seek jobs in India or drives families to sell their children to recruiters promising legitimate wage work. Trafficking of persons is illegal in India, but consensual prostitution is not, complicating law enforcement. A three-tier market exists in Mumbai, and it grows as India's place in the world economy grows. At the top are foreign customers, predominantly Arab men, who pay a premium for virgins and typically take women or girls to hotel rooms for "dates." Then there is the middle "Bungalow" market where Indian businessmen pay for private rooms in tasteful and discrete houses in Mumbai's safer districts. The bottom and largest tier is for working class Indian men, the truck drivers, day laborers, soldiers, and tradesmen. As the value of a victim of the prostitution ring declines with age and use, she is passed down market and must work harder to earn her keep. Sex can be bought on the streets of Mumbai's Kamathipura district for as little as 100 rupees, less than three U.S. dollars. Some victims here have been forced to serve as many as thirty-five clients a day.[4]

Not only is India a destination for smuggled Purple Roses, it is also a source market. For decades, Indian females have been taken to Persian Gulf countries, often after sham marriages to Arab men. As the stream of legal migrant laborers has increased into this oil-rich region, so has illegal trafficking of women and girls. Saudi Arabia and Kuwait have been joined by Bahrain and the United Arab Emirates as importers of women and girls from South Asia.[5]

To the east, the Philippines ranks with Thailand and Cambodia as a leading sex tourism destination. Manila's brothels draw pedophiles from throughout the world on "sex tours" advertised via magazines and the internet.[6] Of the 300,000 Filipinas engaged in prostitution an estimated 75,000 are minors. Most of these young victims of the sex trade are drawn from the country's 200,000 street children, displaced by worsening poverty in rural districts.[7] Although prostitution is illegal in the Philippines, corruption and the government's need for foreign currency cause officials to turn a blind eye to the trade. Indeed, in the decade since the East Asian financial crisis of 1997, declining agricultural and manufacturing employment and IMF and World Bank structural adjustment programs have combined to make tourism and supporting entertainments a main source of Filipino foreign exchange.

Manila, like Mumbai, is a source of Purple Roses for external markets and tastes. For decades Filipinas have been routinely smuggled into Japan, Thailand, Malaysia, South Korea, and Australia. In recent years they have been trafficked globally to brothels in Nigeria, Ivory Coast, and Saudi Arabia. The Philippines' domestic sex industry grew from an American military presence. To protect off-duty personnel, U.S. medical officers inspected Filipino prostitutes for STDs during the Vietnam era. This regulated vice built the red-light districts of Olongapo outside Subic Bay naval station and Angeles City outside Clark air base. Today, the "R and R" privileges of U.S. armed forces in the Asia-Pacific region maintains prostitution even after the cancellation of these base leases in 1992. English-speaking Filipinas populate the bars and brothels outside American bases in South Korea and Okinawa.[8]

Instead of American soldiers and sailors, the flesh peddlers of Olongapo and Angeles City now cater to a more diverse global clientele, drawing Japanese, European, and mainland Asian customers. At the low end of the scale, a man who pays a Filipina hostesses' "bar fee," can take her off premises for sex acts. The house keeps the money to offset the woman or girl's debt. More discriminating customers can book online packages that include air fare, lodging, food, drinks and a full menu of female entertainments. Many business firms send their male employees to Manila in groups on sex junkets as a perk, a practice winkingly promoted by the Philippine government's tourism board.[9]

Contemporary globalization fosters sex trafficking through eased travel restrictions, enhanced internet booking and payment services, and the increased mobility of labor markets disrupted by declining wages and international competition. For nations with struggling economies, the money remitted by overseas workers and male tourists' cash staves off financial disaster. But at what cost? A candid look at the brothels of Mumbai and Manila should give globalism boosters pause. Far from creating a flat world of opportunity or a level playing field, the neo-liberal policies of the past two decades have bolstered the marketing of human flesh and its attendant miseries. The suffering of the world's most vulnerable has worsened. "Forced by poverty, commodified and enslaved by globalization," GABRIELA laments, "women and children have become Purple Roses."

## REFERENCES

1. GABRIELA quoted in Vidyamali Samarsinghe, *Female Sex Trafficking in Asia: The Resilience of Patriarchy in a Changing World* (New York: Routledge, 2008) p. 121.
2. *Illicit Trafficking*, p. 149.
3. "Rights India: Life after Exploitation for Child Sex Workers," *Inter Press Service*, 24 October 2000.
4. Samarsinghe, pp. 78-9 & 81.
5. "Kuwait Deports 1,000 This Year for "Practicing Prostitution,"" *Agence France Presse*, 4 August 1998; "Report Alleges Exploitation of Women by Arabs," *Associated Press*, 28 April 1981.

6. *Handbook of Transnational Crime and Justice*, Philip Reichel, ed. (Sage Publications: Thousand Oaks, Calif., 2005) p. 397. Sheldon X. Zhang, *Smuggling and Trafficking in Human Beings: All Roads Lead to America* (Westport, Connecticut: Praeger, 2007) p. 138.

7. *Illicit Trafficking: A Reference Handbook* Robert J. Kelley, Jess Maghan, and Joseph D. Serio, (Santa Barbara, California: ABC-Clio, 2005), p. 149.

8. "15 Filipinas Rescued from Africa Sex Den," *Straits Times* Interactive (Singapore), 18 March 2001. "Filipino Women in Malaysian Sex Dens," *Asian Migration News*, 1-15 June 2000. "Filipinas Sneaked in as Pilgrims to Work in Mid-East," *Straits Times*, 3 November 1999. Samarasinghe, 177-78.

9. Samrasinghe, pp. 145-7.

The contributor, Dr. James G. Crawford, is assistant professor of History and University Studies at NC A&T State University. He holds a 2003 doctorate in History from the University of North Carolina in the field of U.S. Foreign Relations.

+++

## CONTROVERSIES: SUPPLY AND DEMAND

Human trafficking is a dehumanizing crime that turns people into mere commodities. An issue that is sometimes overlooked in addressing human trafficking is the fact that its very existence is based on supply and demand. On the supply side there are push factors such as

a.   poverty

b.   lack of employment opportunities,

c.   lack of education

d.   well established criminal networks, and

e.   corruption

Poverty and a lack of employment opportunities make people desperately vulnerable and easy targets for trafficking.

Meanwhile, on the demand side, the issue becomes more complex. Over the past decade there has been a boom in the number of sex tourism operators, most of whom advertise internationally via the internet. These types of businesses encourage and support the demand that continues to drive human trafficking. Unfortunately, the types of customer attracted to the sex tourism industry are not interested in whether the women (and sometimes young girls and boys) are there against their will.

Demand can take two forms:

1)    the demand of the trafficker or "wholesaler" who is only motivated by greed

2) the demand of the customer whose motivation is of a more deviant kind—desires for sexual, mental and physical control of another human being

Demand also drives profitability. The growing demand for commercial sex acts and cheap labor have created a profit-incentive for traffickers to entrap even more victims. So in essence, demand drives supply.

One UNESCO study estimated that some 2,000,000 Thai women work as prostitutes and that 800,000 are adolescents and children. Demand for sex with young girls comes mainly from Asian tourists. Demand for young boys from Westerners[493]. Another UNESCO report estimates that over 10,000 boys, between 6 and 14, work as prostitutes in Sri Lanka, serving mainly foreign men.[494]

Of course one would think that it would be obvious to the average citizen that if an 11-year-old boy or girl is involved in this type of activity, it MUST be a case of forced participation. However, in the event it is not so obvious, educational campaigns need to be launched to expose these pleasure-seeking customers to the pain that comes with their pleasure.

In a 2-year study conducted by the Global Survivor it was pointed out that Germany, Switzerland, Japan, Macau, and the United States receive substantially higher numbers of trafficked women than elsewhere.[495] With respect to child prostitution, statistics are hard to come by. Studies published by UNESCO last year on the phenomenon cite Colombia, Brazil, Benin, Thailand and the Philippines as countries in which child prostitution is rampant. In Latin America and Africa, street children often operate independently, while in Thailand and the Philippines, countries with vast industries marketing sexual services, the children are usually recruited to work in

---

493  "The Sex Market: Scourge on the World's Children." Marlise Simons. Published April 9, 1993, *New York Times*. http://www. nytimes. com/1993/04/09/world/the-sex-market-scourge-on-the-world-s-children. html; George Gerbner, Hamid Mowlana, Herbert I. "Schiller Invisible crises: what conglomerate control of media means for America and the World": *Critical Studies in Communication and in the Cultural Industries*. 1996. Colorado: Westview Press http://books. google. tt/books

494  Ibid.

495  GSN, Trafficking of NIS Women Abroad: Moscow Conference Report (Washington, DC: GSN, 1998)

brothels. Laws explicitly ban prostitution of minors in most countries, but enforcement is uneven.

Child prostitution in the Middle East is more carefully concealed and therefore more difficult to track. But reportedly boys and girls from Bangladesh and India have in some cases been sold by their families and taken to the United Arab Emirates, Oman and other countries to work in brothels or appear in pornographic films.[496]

Experts also note that "sex tours" of Asian and Latin American cities marketed in the West often involve adolescent girls. And while the bulk of sexually explicit magazines and photographs marketed around the world involve adults, delegates said that an increasing number depict children.[497]

With respect to supply and the continued existence of human trafficking, it is interesting to note that while 116 out of 192 members of the United Nation have ratified the 2005 Anti-Trafficking Protocol, of the governments that do not yet have any legislation, several (like India, Pakistan, and Japan) have been identified as large suppliers of trafficked victims[498]. One wonders if the governments of these countries are genuinely interested in stemming the problem. One also has to wonder if the lack of action is in any way related to the socioeconomic status or race/ethnicity of the victims. In other words, if a rash of wealthy American or European women were suddenly trafficked, would the international community take more immediate and forceful action?

The United States, for example, is both a source and destination country for thousands of men, women, and children trafficked for the purposes of sexual and labor exploitation (effectively satisfying both supply and demand factors). Women and girls, largely from East Asia, Eastern Europe, Mexico and Central America are trafficked to the United States into prostitution.

Yet, the U.S. crackdown on human trafficking has typically focused on foreign nationals to the exclusion of U.S. Citizens trafficked within the continental U.S.

There is now a new debate on whether numbers should now include U.S. citizens forced into prostitution overseas as well as at home.

---

496 "The Sex Market: Scourge on the World's Children." Marlise Simons. Published April 9, 1993, *New York Times.* http://www. nytimes. com/1993/04/09/world/the-sex-market-scourge-on-the-world-s-children. html
497 Ibid.
498 Supra at 488

*Decreasing Demand*

In 2003, the United States passed the Prosecutorial Remedies and other Tools to end the Exploitation of Children Today (PROTECT) Act and the 2003 Trafficking Victims Protection Reauthorization Act. The PROTECT Act increased penalties to a maximum of 30 years in prison for anyone convicted of engaging in child sex tourism. Since the passage of the PROTECT Act, there have been approximately 64 convictions of child sex tourists. The Department of Homeland Security also developed the "Operation Predator" initiative to combat child exploitation, child pornography, and child sex tourism.[499]

In 2004, the International Organization for Migration (IOM) identified marketplace demand as a major cause of human trafficking[500]. This begs the question, "If demand has such an impact on the problem, why are those who demand the service, not prosecuted? Why, is the crime not viewed as negatively as violent crime? And, in view of the mental and physical atrocities endured by the victim of this crime, why is the crime itself not categorized as "violent"?

Researchers at the IOM argue that the problem is underlying racism, xenophobia and prejudice against foreign workers[501]. Meaning that racially and ethnically different individuals particularly those from 3rd world countries are not perceived as equal human being and so using and abusing them does not present as harsh a reality to the racial and ethnic majority population as it would, had the victims been one of theirs. Indeed, those who could afford to demand this type of service would more than likely belong to ethnic majority races/ethnicities and would therefore not be considered criminals by their peers. Similarly, there are also those Ethnic minorities with the resources to demand this type of service, for whom the race/ethnicity of the victim is immaterial.

As far as trafficking is concerned, racism, xenophobia and prejudice amongst ethnic minorities and against foreign workers have made it easier for clients and employers to justify the unethical and illegal practice of trafficking in illegal labor. According to the International Organization for Migration, "The racially/ethnically different worker is not perceived as an equal human being and so can be used

---

499   Office of the Press Secretary July 9, 2003. Homeland Security. http://www. dhs. gov/ xnews/releases/press_release_0210. shtm

500   Niurka Pineiro. International Organization for Migration. Press Briefing Notes. 06 January 2004. Geneva-Migration Research Series-Is Trafficking in Human Beings Demand Driven?; Study Finds Deman is a factor driving Human Trafficking: Work examines sex industry and domestic labour in Europe and Asia. http://www. america. gov/st/washfile-english/2004/January/20040106152916retropc0. 8637964. html

501   Ibid.

and abused in ways that would be impossible with respect to work-ers of the same race/ethnicity."[502]

The U.S. Government also funded organizations to initiate public awareness and deterrence campaigns which targeted U.S. sex tour-ists abroad. These campaigns include

1. public service announcements,
2. internet messages,
3. brochures,
4. posters and billboards.

The United States has also made additional efforts to prevent the U.S. Military and Civilian Police from contributing to trafficking. The Department of Defense (DoD) has taken an aggressive stand against any of its own who engage in any activity that may contribute to the phenomenon of trafficking in persons and anti-trafficking training is now mandatory for all U.S. service members. The Department of State has also taken measures to prevent its civilian police contrac-tors from engaging in sex trafficking and related activities while de-ployed in such countries as Iraq, Afghanistan, and Haiti and, have ini-tiated a training program, in which civilian police candidates not only receive information about human trafficking, the local situation, and U.S. anti-trafficking laws and policies, but for which U.S. police con-tractors are required to sign a certificate stating that they are aware of U.S. law and possible consequences for engaging in or facilitating sex trafficking.[503]

Prostitution is a contributing factor to trafficking in persons and the commercial sex trade. People who buy sex—usually men—fuel the demand for sex trafficking which in effect feeds the demand for sexual slavery. Since there is such a direct relationship between pros-titution, sexual slavery and human trafficking, State and local au-thorities across the country have created strategic deterrents some of which follow:

1. Cities, such as San Francisco, Brooklyn, and Tacoma, oper-ate "john schools" that provide educational programs for first time offenders arrested for buying sex. These programs in-form men of the risks while reinforcing the message that prostitution is not a victimless crime.
2. In November 2006 the city of Atlanta launched a "Dear John" public education campaign to educate potential sex buyers

---

502  Ibid.

503  Trafficking in Persons Report Office to Monitor and Combat Trafficking in Persons. June 4, 2008. Stopping Human Trafficking, Sexual Exploitation and Abuse by International Peacekeepers.

about their role in fueling the commercial sexual exploitation of children.

3. The city of Portland, Oregon has instituted vehicle forfeiture laws to seize the cars of offenders who use their cars to find persons in prostitution and engage in sexual activity in their cars. Other jurisdictions in Oregon provide for courts to suspend or revoke the offender's driver's license.

4. In San Diego, men charged with soliciting are required to appear before a panel comprised of community members, prosecutors, public health workers and social services staff all from the local community.

5. Men charged with soliciting in Indianapolis, Indiana, are required to return to the community in which the offense occurred to publicly face area residents and perform community service work there. Additionally, police agencies and local governments publicize the names and photographs of both the arrestees and the convicted in local media outlets and on the Internet.

6. In 2003 in Omaha, Nebraska, billboards with the slogan, "If you are convicted of soliciting a prostitute, you will see your name here" publicized the names of 6–12 offenders at a time.

7. In Akron, Ohio, the "Operation John Be Gone" Web site, which posted the photographs of men charged with soliciting persons in prostitution, drew more than 100,000 hits in its first year online[504].

### CONCLUSION

Despite all the information that is now available about human trafficking, a thorough understanding of this phenomenon is incomplete which only makes it more difficult to control it. In Russia, for example collaboration between traffickers and law enforcement officials is not secret (at least to the victims and their families)[505] Indeed, a 2-year undercover investigation conducted by Global Survival Network (GSN) revealed that in the receiving countries the problem tends to be minimized not only at the local police level but also at the national level as well[506]. In fact one of the ongoing complaints is that many governments tend to respond to the problem as a problem of illegal immigration effectively transforming the victim into a crim-

---

504 Center for problem oriented policing. "Responses to the problem of street prostitution." http://www. popcenter. org/problems/street_prostitution/3
505 Supra at 544
506 Supra at 544

inal.[507] As such, most victims are reluctant to testify against their captors, which make prosecution challenging.

Moreover, human trafficking is perceived by the rest of the world as a crime involving third world countries, a crime involving ethnic and racial minorities, certainly a crime of poverty. And that's as far as the thought goes. Very few citizens in first world wonder about the demand by first world countries that drives the supply of third world people. Does the fact that human trafficking is a crime of poverty make it any less of a crime? Does the fact those who demand the service are of predominantly majority races/ethnicities have any impact on how the crime is prosecuted? Indeed, there seems to be some similarity in how human trafficking is prosecuted to how drug trafficking is prosecuted. In drug trafficking, the dispensable and easily replaced "petty salesmen" on the street corners are targeted as opposed to the major traffickers so the cycle continues. In human trafficking, the supply chain is targeted, few traffickers are caught, prosecution is rare and punishment not sufficiently severe. Meanwhile, the demand is not addressed and, as long as there is demand, there will be supply.

If human trafficking is such an atrocity then why are the criminals not brought to task and when they are, why are they punished so lightly? Is human trafficking any better or worse a crime than robbery, drug trafficking or embezzlement? How important is the severity of the crime in the determination of the sentence and how much of an impact does race/ethnicity of the criminal and/or the victim have on the manner in which the crime is treated? Moreover, in the case of human trafficking, how much culpability should the customer bear since there would be no supply without demand?

## CRITICAL THINKING QUESTIONS

1. Why are minorities, women and children exploited in the sex and labor markets?
2. Why are those who demand the services provided predominantly the wealthy or of non minorities?
3. If the victims of Human Trafficking were non minorities would the industry be allowed to flourish as it does now?
4. From an economic perspective what would be the advantages/disadvantages of allowing the industry to grow unabated?
5. Why are minorities predominantly the victims and traffickers of Human Trafficking in all its forms?

---

507 Seminar on Human Trafficking & Illegal Migration as a development issue in Sub-Saharan Africa. 27 September 2006. African Tourism and Development Organization.

6. Why are those who demand the services provided predominantly the wealthy or of non minorities?
7. If the victims of Human Trafficking were non minorities would the industry be allowed to flourish as it does now?
8. From an economic perspective what would be the advantages/disadvantages of allowing the industry to grow unabated?

CHAPTER RESOURCES

Key Terms
Human Trafficking
Alien Smuggling
Child Exploitation
Forced Labor
Garment and Agricultural slaves
Illegal Adoptions
International Organization of Migration
Human Trafficking
Labor Trafficking
Trade in body parts

Ready for Review
Objectives
Case Study
Introduction: What is Human Trafficking
Scope of Problem
  • In the United States
  • The Economics of Human Trafficking
What is the U.S. doing to stop Trafficking?
  • Strategies
What the numbers show
In the News: Zoë's Ark
Race, Ethnicity and Policy
  • The Missing Victims
Biography
  • The Purple Rose Markets of Mumbai and Manila: Globalization and Female Sex Trafficking in India and the Philippines By Dr. James G. Crawford
Controversy
  • Supply & Demand
  • Decreasing Demand
Conclusion

# CHAPTER 7. RACE, ETHNICITY AND THE CONCEPT OF CRIME— AN ALTERNATE PERSPECTIVE

## OBJECTIVES

- To evaluate the social impact of street crimes versus crimes against humanity
- To determine if certain acts are perceived as being more serious crimes because of the race or ethnicity of the offender
- To determine if certain acts are perceived as being less serious crimes because of the race or ethnicity of the victims
- To evaluate whether the race of the offender or victim determines the speed and force with which authorities react to crimes against humanities.

## CASE STUDY: WAR CRIMES

On September 2, 1998, the International Criminal Tribunal for Rwanda (a court established by the United Nations) issued the world's first conviction for the crime defined as genocide. Jean-Paul Akayesu was found guilty of genocide and crimes against humanity, for acts he engaged in and oversaw while he was the mayor of the Rwandan town of Taba.[508]

---

508   United States Holocaust Memorial Museum. Rwanda: The First Conviction for Genocide. Retrieved from http://www. ushmm. org/wlc/article. php?lang=en&ModuledId=10007157

Akayesu was born in 1953 in a Taba commune and was an active member of the local football team. He was the father of five children, and taught at a local school. As mayor he was well respected by his community and widely considered a man of high morals, intelligence, and integrity. Akayesu became politically active in 1991 and was elected bourgmestre (mayor) of Taba in 1993. He held the position until 1994.

As mayor and leader of the village, Akayesu was treated with respect and deference by his townspeople. He oversaw the local economy, controlled the police, administered the law well, and generally led social life in the village. When the Rwandan genocide began on April 7, 1994, Akayesu was initially able to keep his town out of the mass killing. He refused to let militia operate in his town and protected the local Tutsi population. But following an April 18th meeting of mayors with the interim government leaders (who allegedly planned and orchestrated the genocide), a fundamental change took place in the town and apparently within Akayesu himself. He seemed to have calculated that his political and social future depended on his joining the forces carrying out the genocide. Akayesu exchanged his business suit for a military jacket, literally donning violence as his modus operandi. Witnesses said they saw him incite townspeople to join in the killing and turn former safe havens into places of torture, rape, and murder.[509] As the war's tide turned, Akayesu escaped to Zaire (now the Democratic Republic of the Congo) and later to Zambia, where he was arrested in October 1995. In a trial held before the International Criminal Tribunal for Rwanda he was convicted of genocide, the first such conviction in an international court and the first time rape was considered a component of genocide. Akayesu is serving a life sentence in a prison in Mali.[510]

## INTRODUCTION: WHAT IS A CRIME?

For the past 6 chapters we have evaluated a variety of crimes and the race and ethnicity of the offenders and the victims typically involved in those types of crimes. We have looked at violent crimes and society's tendency to associate certain types of crimes with certain races and ethnicities. We have looked at Terrorism and the assumptions that all terrorists are of Middle Eastern descent. We have looked at human trafficking and its tendency to target 3rd world victims. In Chapter 8 we will end our discussion with an alternative perspective of crime. We will also touch on White Collar Crime and evaluate the

---

509  Ibid.
510  Ibid.

data that shows that most White Collar criminals are White-American and male. We will conclude with a reevaluation of what is a crime and who is a criminal.

Crime is an act which, when committed, breaks the law. That would include obvious crimes like property crimes (for example, stealing someone's money or breaking someone's windows), or crimes against persons (for example, beating or sexually assaulting someone, or child sexual abuse), and not so obvious crimes like crimes against humanity.

According to Black's Law Dictionary, a crime is:

A positive or negative act in violation of penal law; an offense against the State or Unified States. A crime may be defined to be any act done in violation of those duties which an individual owes to the community, and for the breach of which the law has provided that the offender shall make satisfaction to the public.[511]

Webster's dictionary defines crime as

> an act or the commission of an act that is forbidden or the omission of a duty that is commanded by a public law and that makes the offender liable to punishment by that law; especially : a gross violation of law: a grave offense especially against morality.[512]

For crimes against persons and property the process is fairly simple if not always successful: identify the crime, the criminal, the victim and exact swift and severe punishment. For crimes against humanity, however, the distinctions are not so clear. The criminals are often individuals in positions of power, the list of victims usually run into the tens of thousands and the crimes......well, let's just say that a crime is a crime regardless of who commits it.

So how do we determine which crimes are so heinous that one should take precedence over another. For example, should a drive by shooting, in which 4 people die, have a greater impact on society than the case of the government of a country murdering 200,000 of its citizens because of their race or ethnicity? What makes one case less important than the other—the race/ethnicity/socioeconomic status of the victims or the race/ethnicity/socioeconomic status of the criminal? Before we attempt to answer these questions, let's evaluate some of the "other" types of crime. We'll begin with White Collar Crime.

---

511  Black, Henry Campbell. *Black's Law Dictionary.* 8th ed. St. Paul, Minn. : West Pub. Co., 2004.
512  Hacker. 2008. In *Merriam-Webster Online Dictionary.* Retrieved April 7, 2008, from http://www. merriam-webster. com/dictionary/hacker

## WHITE COLLAR CRIME

An examination of the range of crime statistics reveals that just as African-Americans are disproportionately likely to commit certain crimes (homicide), White-Americans are disproportionately likely to commit others. Although some of these are nonviolent, financial crimes like those for which executives such as Martha Stewart, Bernard Ebbers (WorldCom), Dennis Kozlowski (Tyco), and Kenneth Lay (Enron) were convicted, harm millions of Americans who end up losing their pensions, their paychecks, their health insurance, and their livelihood. Ironically, these crimes are referred to as "White-Collar Crimes".

According to Sutherland, a White Collar Crime a crime committed by "a person of respectability and high social status in the course of his occupation."[513] Sutherland goes on to say that "conventional generalizations about crime and criminality are invalid because they explain only the crime of the lower classes, at most."[514]. Sutherland also says that,

> The theory that criminal behavior in general is due either to poverty or to the psychopathic and sociopathic conditions with poverty can now be shown to be invalid for three reasons. First, the generalization is based on a biased sample that omits almost entirely the behavior of white-collar criminals. Second, the generalization that criminality is closely associated with poverty obviously does not apply to white-collar criminals because without small exception, by and large, they are not poor. Third, the conventional theories do not even explain lower class criminality.[515]

To the average citizen, a white collar crime may not be a crime at all. A perfect example would be the case of the demise of Enron. In December of 2001, Enron imploded in a wave of accounting fraud and proceeded to declare the largest bankruptcy in U.S. history. Within months of Enron's demise, others began to come out of the woodwork. WorldCom's financial wrongdoings resulted in a bankruptcy even larger than Enron's and numerous other companies issued "restatements" of their financial results, including Tyco, Global Crossing, Quest, Xerox, Adelphia, Micro Strategy, AOL-Time Warner, K-Mart, Halliburton, Lucent Technologies, Rite Aid, and Waste Management to name just a few.

513  Sutherland, Edwin H. (1949). *White Collar Crime.* New York: Dryden Press
514  Ibid.
515  Sutherland, Edwin H. "White Collar Criminality." *American Sociological Review*, Vol. 5, No. 1 (Feb 1940), pp 1-12

The Enron scandal implicated accounting firm Arthur Andersen, which was eventually closed down because it was already the subject of a Securities and Exchange Commission "cease and desist" order for misleading financial statements. Additionally, other major financial institutions like Citigroup and J. P. Morgan Chase were implicated for helping firm's book loans as revenue.

Not unexpectedly, prosecutions got off to a slow start, especially with Enron, because, according to the New York Times "Attorney General John Ashcroft and virtually the entire legal staff of the United States attorney's office in Houston [were] disqualified from the Enron criminal investigation".[516] You see, Enron, and its Chairman Ken Lay, were major donors to the Bush campaign, and Ashcroft himself had received substantial donations from them for his own failed 2000 Senate campaign. Besides, the US Department of Justice's resources were being better used against real crimes like Operation Pipedream, which resulted in the February 2003 indictment of 55 individuals for selling drug paraphernalia over the internet. This, you see, was real crime. This was the type of crime that really hurt people, the type of crime of which the public should be scared. The Kenneth Lays of the Enrons and the like weren't real criminals and did not commit real crimes.

Well let's talk a bit about what Mr. Lay and Enron did do that was not so criminal. Mr. Lay and his company were allegedly responsible for massive fraud and manipulation of the California energy crisis. In the end just as the company was beginning to collapse, Lay insisted that he and Enron had nothing to hide. Yet, a special committee of Enron's board found "a systematic and pervasive attempt by Enron's Management to misrepresent the Company's financial condition." Additionally, while Lay was advising employees to continue buying the stock, he cashed out his own shares to the tune of about $103 million. Moreover, he began to take cash advances from the company that he repaid with stock (to the tune of $19 million). We must not forget that Mr. Lay was paid $103 million in salary, bonuses, incentives, annuities and cash advances.

The reality is that Mr. Lay would have been in more trouble had he smoked crack—especially if he was a minority in the inner city –than he was in for getting rich while misleading thousands of employees and stockholders who eventually lost their retirement accounts. Indeed, Forbes magazine commented "If the president wants to make the case that his administration will not tolerate corporate wrongdo-

---

516   David Johnston. "Enron's collapse: the investigation; justice dept's inquiry into Enron is beginning to take shape, without big names." *New York Times*. January 16 2002

ing, what better way than to indict his old friend and former Enron CEO, Kenneth Lay? [517]

Despite the financial and emotional harm victims such as Enron's may have suffered, it is still arguable that White Collar Crime is not violent crime. Genocide and Ethnic Cleansing, on the other, are a different matter.

## THE CRIMES OF GENOCIDE AND ETHNIC CLEANSING

The term "genocide" did not exist before 1944. It is a very specific term, referring to violent crimes committed against specific groups or people with the intent to erase them from existence. The term was created by a Polish-Jewish lawyer who sought to describe Nazi policies of systematic murder particularly as it related to the European Jews. He formed the word "genocide" by combining geno-, from the Greek word for race or tribe, with -cide, from the Latin word for killing. In 1948 the United Nations established "genocide" as an international crime. It defines genocide as:

> ....... any of the following acts committed with intent to destroy, in whole or in part, a national, ethnic, racial or religious group, as such:
> a.  Killing members of the group;
> b.  Causing serious bodily or mental harm to members of the group;
> c.  Deliberately inflicting on the group conditions of life calculated to bring about its physical destruction in whole or in part;
> d.  Imposing measures intended to prevent births within the group;
> e.  Forcibly transferring children of the group to another group[518]

Discussions of genocide or ethnic cleansing tend to evoke thoughts of the Holocaust of World War Two—the most egregious and infamous case of the mass killing of people based on their ethnic or religious background. For many people, that is the full extent of what genocide means. Today, however, the word genocide draws upon an even more complex body of history and scholarship. By narrow definition, genocide can only occur when there is a deliberate attempt to

---

517  Dan Ackman. "Where are the Indictments?" *Forbes Magazine*. 07 August 2002.

518  Convention on the Prevention and Punishment of the Crime of Genocide. Adopted by Resolution 260 (III) A of the UN General Assembly on 9 December 1948. Article 2. ; Analysis: Defining Genocide. BBC News Story. February 03, 2010. http://news. bbc. co. uk/2/hi/3853157. stm

completely destroy all members of a particular group. As such, there are few clearly identifiable examples of genocide.

The phrase "ethnic cleansing" on the other hand, has been defined as "the elimination of an unwanted group from society, by genocide or forced migration."[519] This definition is narrower than that of genocide alone, and encompasses mass killings and forced removals in far greater number and scope.

The U.S. State Department, in a recent report on Kosovo, concluded that ethnic cleansing "generally entails the systematic and forced removal of members of an ethnic group from their communities to change the ethnic composition of a region."[520] Ethnic cleansing may involve death or displacement, or any combination thereof, where a population is identified for removal from an area. If these crimes are more criminal then why are these types of crimes perceived more lightly than our street crimes which are typically committed by minorities and the poor?

By using the above definitions, most mass killings and forced relocations fit into one or both of the two discrete categories that are presented. Acts of genocide, as the more broadly defined term, have been recognized by the United Nations nine times this century. These examples include the purge of Armenians by the Turks beginning in 1915, Jews killed in the Ukraine in the late 1910s as well as during the Nazi regime, Cambodians under the Khmer Rouge in the 1970s, Bosnian Muslims in the former Yugoslavia early this decade, and the slaughter of the Tutsi minority by the Hutu majority in Rwanda in 1994. At least ten additional examples of ethnic cleansing were not recognized by the U.N., due to the criteria used to determine what qualifies as genocide. Interestingly enough, while genocide is globally recognized as a crime against humanity, ethnic cleansing is not.

Both "genocide" and "ethnic cleansing"—as words and concepts—have drawn criticism. Some suggest that the word genocide is used too frequently and too loosely and can only incite unnecessary panic [521]. Others argue that overuse may be necessary in view of the three examples of genocide in the 20th century alone:

1. Armenians killed by the Turks (1915–1918);
2. Extermination of Jews, Gypsies, and homosexuals by Nazis during World War II (1933–1945);

519  Karyn Becker (n.d.) genocide and Ethnic Cleansing. Model United Nations Far West. Retrieved from http://www. munfw. org/archive/50th/4th1. htm ; Annan, Kofi. Press release on the Occasion of the fiftieth Anniversary of the 1948 Convention on the Prevention and Punishment of the Crime of Genocide. SG/SM/6822, December 8, 1999

520  Ibid.

521  Ibid.

3. Slaughter of the Tutsi minority by the Hutu majority in Rwanda in 1994.

"Ethnic cleansing" has also been used to describe a group of people of similar nationality, race, or religion who are experiencing any kind of action which they consider objectionable. Illegal Jewish settlers in the Palestinian controlled territory of Israel, for example, believe themselves to be victims of ethnic cleansing when their own government decides to evacuate them in the name of preserving peace.[522] Others feel that they are simply forced from their home countries because of prejudices that make their lives difficult or intolerable, even though they may not actually fear for their physical safety.[523]

These examples demonstrate the difficulty in relying on the phrase "ethnic cleansing" to be self-explanatory. The given definition of ethnic cleansing might encompass these situations, but at the same time, may also diminish the seriousness often entailed in the use of the phrase.

The phrase ethnic cleansing has been drawn into the discussion often to identify examples of mass killings of persons with a distinctive commonality. In the former Yugoslavia, for example, a variety of groups—Bosnians, Serbs, Muslims, and Kosovars—have fallen victim to relatively, and perhaps specifically, organized campaigns of ethnic cleansing in this decade alone. More recently we have seen a wave of violence in East Timor, which may yet be described as ethnic cleansing when more complete information becomes available. Throughout history there have been countless examples of genocide and ethnic cleansing around the world. Even today there is no shortage of instances of death and destruction wrought upon those who suddenly find themselves of the wrong ethnicity, religion, nationality or political belief. The time appears ripe for a reconsideration of the instrument which was to have brought such cases to a halt more than a half century ago. Rwanda, for example, was a more definitive example of current day genocide than most situations. The lack of immediate and forceful international reaction begs the question of whether the race/ethnicity of the victims was the underlying cause of world inaction.

Rwanda is certainly not the only example of the international community turning a blind eye to the slaughter. Two million Cambodians were killed in the 1970s in what came to be considered genocide [524]. There is also the case of the indiscriminate killing of Kurds in northern Iraq at the hands of Saddam Hussein. While not genocide by

522  Ibid.
523  Ibid.
524  Ibid.

technical definition, this group was targeted because they threatened the totalitarian power and authority of Hussein.

Along with these crimes come cries of racism from those who believe that decisions not to intervene are based primarily on the skin color or ethnicity of those being massacred and those responsible for the massacre. Although efforts have been made to punish those who are responsible for genocide, even these endeavors—particularly in places like Rwanda and the former Yugoslavia—have come about only in this decade. Therefore, those responsible for recognized acts of genocide over the last three decades have gone unpunished which is probably why the crime continues unabated even today

In a world that can imprison millions of poor and minority criminals, are we to simply accept that the people responsible for these crimes are unreachable? Or is the degree of effort dependant on the race of the victim—or the race of the criminal, for that matter?

*Cambodia*

In the Cambodian genocide (1975–1979), some 1.7 million people or 21% of the country's population [525] were killed in one of the worst (yet little publicized) human tragedies of the last century. The events of this modern day tragedy are not much different from the Ottoman Empire during the Armenian genocide[526], in Nazi Germany [527] and more recently in East Timor, Guatemala [528], Yugoslavia, and Rwanda [529]. In this case Khmer Rouge regime[530] headed by Pol Pot exerted the use of extremist ideology and ethnic animosity, not to mention a blatant disregard for human life, to produce repression, misery, and murder on a massive scale.

On July 18, 2007, Cambodian and international co-prosecutors of the newly established mixed UN/Cambodian tribunal in Phnom Penh found evidence of "crimes against humanity, genocide, grave

---

525  Yale University. Cambodian Genocide Program. Retrieved from http://www. yale. edu/ cgp/cgpintro. html ; The Dith Pran Holocaust Awareness Project, Inc., Spreading the word of the Cambodian Genocide. http://www. dithpran. org/

526  Adalian, Rouben (1997). *The Armenian Genocide. In Century of Genocide: Eyewitness Accounts and Critical Views.* Samuel Totten, William S. Parsons and Israel W. Charny eds. pp. 41-77. New York and London: Garland Publishing Inc.

527  Black, Peter. "Forced labour in concentration camps". In a *Mosaic of victims: Non-Jews persecuted and murdered by Nazis'* edited by Michael Berebaum. New York: New York University Press, 1990, pp. 46-63

528  Stoll, David (1999). *Rigoberta Menchu and the story of all poor Guatemalans.* Boulder Colorado: Westview Press

529  Supra at 557

530  Supra at 574

breaches of the Geneva Convention, homicide, torture and religious persecution."[531]

## Bosnia & Croatia

More than one hundred thousand civilians were killed in Bosnia and Croatia during the Bosnian war[532]. Tens of thousands of women were raped, some of them more than a hundred times, while their sons and husbands were beaten and tortured in concentration camps like Omarska and Manjaca. Millions lost their homes due to a process called "ethnic cleansing."

The Serbian military commander in Bosnia, (a war criminal sought by the War Crimes Tribunal) sometimes issued specific orders to his subordinates to shell a particular village more than others, because there were fewer Serbs and more Muslims living there. Sometimes, refugees of one ethnic group previously "cleansed" from their homes by another ethnic group were made to live in the freshly "cleansed" territory of that other ethnic group.

Ethnic Cleansing created more than two million refugees and displaced persons in former Yugoslavia during the war in Bosnia. This number increased with the expulsion of Serbs from Croatia and with the ferocious atrocities committed by Serbs against the Albanian majority in Kosovo [533].

At the beginning of 1997 there were still more than 21,000 people in Bosnia missing. As of May 1, 2005, ten years after the war had ended, there were 14,444 persons, for whom the International Committee of the Red Cross requested tracing, and for whom no additional information was received.[534]

## Sudan

In 2004 the Sudanese government started the first genocide of the 21st century in Darfur Sudan not by its actions but by its inaction. A brutal system of ethnic cleansing was being practiced against the Black people of Darfur, by a group known as the Janjaweed. Janjaweed militiamen were primarily members of nomadic "Arab" tribes who have been at odds with Darfur's settled "African" farmers, who are darker-skinned. Until 2003, the conflicts were mostly over Darfur's scarce water and land resources. However, when two non-Ar-

531  Yale University. "Cambodian Genocide Program." Retrieved from http://www. yale. edu/cgp/cgpintro. html

532  Burg, Steven L. (1997). *Genocide in Bosnia-Herzegovina? In Century of Genocide: Eyewitness Accounts and Critical Views.* Samuel Totten, William S. Parsons and Israel W. Charny, eds. Pp 424-433. New York and London: Garland Publishing Inc.

533  Ibid.

534  Ibid.

ab groups, the Sudan Liberation Army and the Justice and Equality Movement, took up arms against the Sudanese government, alleging mistreatment by the Arab regime in Khartoum, the Janjaweed became more aggressive. They began pillaging towns and villages inhabited by members of the African tribes from which the rebel armies draw their strength. The government did not intervene, despite mild international pressure. As a result, the Janjaweed has terrorized the Darfur region by raping women, burning over 1000 villages, killing Muslim religious leaders, destroying mosques, ruining food stocks, and murdering men women and children alike.

The situation has resulted in over 1 million dead and 2 million displaced Black Sudanese who continue to flee the Darfur region, their homeland. Unfortunately, peace talks have failed and the Sudanese government has refused to allow any outside forces to intervene. And now, the Sudanese government seems to be preparing to start the second genocide in southern Sudan[535]. The Sudanese President Omar al-Bashir is backing away from the peace agreement, and prodding Arab militias to revive the war with the South Sudan military forces. Small-scale armed clashes have already broken out and it looks increasingly likely that Darfur will become simply the prologue to a far bloodier conflict that engulfs all of Sudan.[536]

### Chad

In November 2005 Genocide Watch declared a Genocide Warning for the country of Chad. This warning was renewed in April 2006 and again in January 2008. Sudanese government backed Janjaweed militias have crossed the Chad border from Sudan, where they have raided dozens of black African Chadian villages, murdering, pillaging, and displacing civilians, just as they have done in Darfur, Sudan. These Sudanese supported "rebels" have made three attempts to overthrow the Chadian government by force, including two invasions of the Chadian capital, Njamena. Sudan's government denies its support for the Janjaweed and for the rebel forces, but Sudanese government bombers and helicopter gunships have bombed villages in both Darfur and Chad and the "rebels" are armed and based in Sudan[537].

Although the Deby government in Chad was "re-elected" in 2006 in a vote boycotted by all opposition parties, and is known to be deeply corrupt, having broken its agreement with the World Bank

---

535  Nicholas D. Kristof. "Southern Sudan: A Genocide Foretold." *The New York Times* February 28, 2008

536  Ibid.

537  Chad: Genocide Warning: Chad. Genocide Watch: The International Campaign to end Genocide. http://www. genocidewatch. org/chad. html

to spend revenues from Chadian oil on education and health, a take-over by Sudanese backed rebels would be far worse. It would expose refugees from Darfur to the murderous Janjaweed, would prevent deployment of European Union troops to protect them, and would help Sudan finish its genocide against black African peoples in Darfur and Eastern Chad[538]. Meanwhile, the rest of the world sits back and observes. Would the inaction have been the same had the victims or offenders been non-minority?

### In the News: Body Parts for Sale

"He's a Doctor. He can't be a criminal!"

While society waged its war on Drugs focusing on minorities and the poor, another type of crime (perhaps not even perceived as being a crime) was taking place. In March 2004 the Director of the Willed Body Program at the University of California, Los Angeles (UCLA) was arrested for the illegal sale of body parts[539]. The investigation that ensued unwittingly revealed that a dismembered cadaver (as opposed to a whole one) could be sold to the pharmaceutical and medical industries for upwards of $200,000.

As the investigation continued it became shockingly clear that illegal "chop shops" were not just confined to stolen automobiles but that there was an underground network of body part traders who utilized university medical centers as "fronts" for their business. Unfortunately, it seems as if advances in surgery and other medical techniques have fueled an underground trade in transplantable tissues and organs that has quickly became a multi-billion-dollar a year business.

Among the unmentioned acts linked to this type of trafficking is the kidnapping of homeless children (for their transplantable tissues and organs) along the border between the U.S. and Mexico and the forced removal of organs from prisoners in third-world countries for sale in the U.S. How much more or less of a crime is this than murder, drug dealing and rape? What impact does the status of the criminal have on the perception of the crime? What about the impact of the victim's status?

The UCLA investigation had been ongoing for 6 years and another arrestee, Ernest Nelson, a body parts dealer claimed to have paid Reid over $700,000 for permission to enter the UCLA body freezer and literally chop up some 800 cadavers and harvest their parts. The cadavers stored at the university were supposed to be used exclusive-

---

538  Ibid.
539  "Superseding Indictment Returned in UCLA Body Parts Case." May 16, 2008 available at http://da. lacounty. gov/mr/archive/2008/051608a. htm

ly by medical students for study yet according to documents provided by Nelson high level UCLA administrators had knowledge of and approved the secret sale of the body parts.

According to investigators, Reid and his employees at the UCLA Medical Center appeared to have avoided detection by keeping some of the donated cadavers "off the books" and by possibly accepting cadavers that were never recorded. Interestingly enough, around the same time, there were numerous reports of homeless persons vanishing from the downtown Los Angeles "Skid Row" area located close to UCLA. There had been unexplained disappearances of UCLA students as well.[540]

One must realize that the pharmaceutical and medical industries pay very well for a host of body parts including skin, scalps, fingernails, tendons, heart valves, skulls and bones, which then find their way into research, manufacturing of drugs, and replacement surgery. Additionally, medical device and instrument manufacturers often use these harvested body parts in training seminars for doctors. For example, in 2004, Johnson & Johnson was named in court documents as having contracted with Nelson for certain human tissue samples.[541]

In addition to such scandals as the University of California Medical Center being used to "launder" cadaver parts, there are numerous underground clinics that perform transplants involving illegally obtained organs.[542] Indeed, it is suspected that many of these organs are being taken from children kidnapped along the U.S./Mexico border and transplanted into wealthy American patients in underground clinics in Mexico and Texas[543]. But how much of a crime is this? The victims were after all only children from a 3rd world country. Surely, this type of crime cannot be compared with drug dealing and rape and drive by shootings in gang wars?

RACE, ETHNICITY AND POLICY: INTERNATIONAL CRIMINAL COURT

After the Second World War, the United Nations General Assembly recognized the need for a permanent international court to deal with the kind of atrocities that had taken place during the war. Today, the magnitude of the atrocities that exist have given more impetus to the creation of a permanent mechanism to bring justice to the perpetrators of such crimes as,

---

540  Steven DiJoseph. "Illegal Harvesting and Sale of Body Parts, Tissue and Organs. Dr. Frankenstein would have been proud." April 8, 2006. Newsinferno. com: News that matters. http://www. newsinferno. com/archives/1064

541  Ibid.

542  Ibid.

543  Ibid.

1. genocide,
2. ethnic cleansing,
3. sexual slavery,
4. sale of body parts, and
5. environmental crime
6. Acts of Aggression

The International Criminal Court was established in 1998 as an entity independent of the United Nation and was given the power to try individuals rather than States and to hold them accountable for crimes against the international community. Seated in The Hague, in the Netherlands, the Court does not have the power to try those accused of committing crimes which occurred in the past. The Court only has jurisdiction over crimes committed after July 1, 2002[544].

The Court also has jurisdiction over War crimes which includes grave breaches of the Geneva Conventions and other serious violations of the laws and customs that can be applied in international armed conflict, and in armed conflict "not of an international character", as listed in the Statute, when they are committed as part of a plan or policy or on a large scale.[545]

What about terrorism and drug trafficking? There was significant interest in including terrorism in the Court's mandate, but it was decided not to do so. Today, in addition to various treaties prohibiting many specific acts of terrorism, and in the aftermath of 11 September 2001, the Member States of the UN have undertaken the drafting of a comprehensive convention against terrorism. It was the interest of a Member State (Trinidad and Tobago) in establishing an international court to prosecute crimes of drug trafficking that revitalized the process culminating in the establishment of the International Criminal Court. During the negotiations in Rome, however, delegations realized that, because of the magnitude of the problem of drug trafficking, to include it in the Court's mandate, especially in view of the investigations that would be required, would very likely result in the Court's limited resources quickly being overwhelmed.

It is important to note that the International Criminal Court is in no way meant to replace the authority of national courts. But there may be times when a State's court system collapses and ceases to function. Similarly, there may be governments that condone or participate in an atrocity themselves, or officials may be reluctant to prosecute someone in a position of great power and authority. The Court's jurisdiction is very carefully set out in the Statute. The Court can only exercise its ju-

---

544 International Criminal Court Fact sheet. http://www. un. org/News/facts/iccfact. htm
545 Ibid.

risdiction when a national court is unable or unwilling to genuinely do so itself. The first priority always goes to national courts.

There are many safeguards to prevent frivolous or politically motivated prosecutions from taking place, with ample, repetitive opportunities for challenges. When a State ratifies the Statute, it agrees to accept the jurisdiction of the Court over the crimes listed in the Statute. The Court may exercise its jurisdiction in situations that meet one of the following conditions:

1. one or more of the parties involved is a State Party;
2. the accused is a national of a State Party;
3. the crime is committed on the territory of a State Party; or
4. a State, not party to the Statute, may decide to accept the court's jurisdiction over a specific crime that has been committed within its territory, or by its national[546].

The International Criminal Court is a separate entity from the United Nations. Its expenses are funded by assessed contributions made by States Parties and by voluntary contributions from Governments, international organizations, individuals, corporations and other entities. In special circumstances funds could be provided by the UN, subject to the approval of the General Assembly, when they relate to expenses incurred due to "situations" referred to the Court by the Security Council. The contributions of the States Parties will be assessed based on the scale adopted by the United Nations for its regular budget, but any States that wish to do so may voluntarily contribute additional funds. The Netherlands is the host country for the Court.

The creation of the ICC was seen a step forward in global efforts to halt the proliferation of mass killings and other egregious violence. This pattern has been recurring throughout this century, and despite rhetoric to the contrary, little serious effort has gone into abating these tragedies. Clearly, past attempts have not been successful, and the reasons behind that remain unclear. What must future efforts entail in order to successfully avoid this scourge? How many more people will have to die at the hands of their neighbors and countrymen before the human considerations outweigh the political ramifications? What will be required to finally end what should have been but a memory at the dawn of the 21st century?

Interestingly enough, the United States opposed the ICC from the beginning, surprising and disappointing many people[547]. Human rights organizations and social justice groups around the world, and from within the US, were very critical of the U.S.' stance given its

---

546  Ibid.
547  Anup Shah. "United States and the International Criminal Court." *Global Issues.* September 25, 2005. retrieved from http://globalissues. org/Geopolitics/icc/us. asp

dominance in world affairs[548]. The U.S. did eventually signed up to the ICC just before the December 2000 deadline to ensure that it would be a State Party that could participate in decision-making about how the Court works. However, by May 2002, the Bush Administration effectively "unsigned" itself and threatened to use military force if U.S. nationals were held for committing any crimes that fell under the jurisdiction of the ICC[549]. Today, the U.S. continues to pressure many other countries to sign agreements not to surrender U.S. citizens to the ICC with threats of termination of economic aid and withdrawal of military assistance.[550]

This begs the question, "Why would a country, often vocal in the area of human rights, and often amongst the first to promote human rights as a global issue in the past refuse to sign, and deliberately undermine an international law and institution designed to protect human rights?"

+++

### THE "GOOD" EVIL OF PUNISHMENT
Wendy C. Hamblet, Ph.D., SAC (Dip)

"While society in the United States gives the example of the most extended liberty, the prisons of the same country offer the spectacle of the most complete despotism."
—G. Beaumont, A. de Tocqueville, 1833, 47

Crime is bad. What makes crime bad is the fact that it effects harm upon a member or members of the social group. In harming individuals, crime also harms the whole society, undermining the sense of security that enriches people's lives and renders them happy. Punishment is a retributive act undertaken by state authorities to balance the social offense, dish out just dessert to the offender, and serve as a deterrent to other potential social offenders.

Punishment, because it composes a feature of justice that is understood to heal the wounds of crime, is considered a social "good." Thomas Aquinas defines punishment as a form of vengeance consisting in "the infliction of a penal evil on one who has sinned." A secularization of Thomas's definition identifies punishment as "an act of justice which consists in a harm inflicted upon a social offender by a legitimate authority." The particular harm or evil of punishment, no matter how harsh or painful, is considered a "good" in the society where it is practiced.

How is punishment understood as a social "good"? Plato features

---

548  Ibid.
549  Ibid.
550  Ibid.

Socrates and Glaucon speaking of three forms of "good" in the opening of the second Book of the Republic, his dialogue that meditates explicitly upon justice. Glaucon offers a first and superior kind of good: "There is a kind of good which we could choose to possess, not from desire for its after-effects, but welcoming it for its own sake . . . for example, joy and such pleasures as are harmless" (2.357b). Then there is a second kind of good "that we love both for its own sake and for its consequences, such as understanding, sight, and health" (2.357c). A third kind of good "under which falls exercise and being healed when sick and the art of healing and the making of money generally . . .of them we would say that they are laborious and painful yet beneficial, and for their own sake we would not accept them, but only for the rewards and other benefits that accrue from them" (2.357cd). Punishment, because it composes a feature of justice that is understood to heal the wounds of crime, is considered a social "good." Thomas Aquinas defines punishment as a form of vengeance consisting in "the infliction of a penal evil on one who has sinned." A secularization of Thomas's definition identifies punishment as "an act of justice which consists in a harm inflicted upon a social offender by a legitimate authority." The particular harm or evil of punishment, no matter how harsh or painful, is considered a "good" in the society where it is practiced.

Punishment of social offenders is surely not a "good" of the first kind, since it is not akin to joy and harmless pleasures, but admits itself as harm-doing. Thus, it is not of the second kind either, since the second kind must necessarily include the first. Therefore, punishment of social offenders must comprise a "good" of the third kind—one that is valued solely for its beneficial effects. This conclusion begs the question: What are the beneficial effects that society expects to receive from the practice of punishment? In modern Western states, punishment of social offenders has been reduced to three primary forms—fines, communal service, imprisonment, and death. Let us consider the benefits derived from each of these punitive forms.

The only punishments that seem to offer undeniable and direct benefits for the society in which they are practiced are fines and communal service. These practices add to the communal purse in fiscal and practical ways. Furthermore, because these responses to crime are lenient and non-exclusionary, they avoid the negative counter-effects that often result from harsher punishments.

Incarceration is by far the most common state response to crime in modern states. At the end of 2006, more than 2.25 million prisoners were being held in federal or state prisons or local jails in the United States and as many as 13 million pass in and out of prisons over the course of a year. African-American males (aged 25 to 29) represent 45.7 per cent of the male prison population (compared to 1% whites and 3%

Latinos), almost four times their representation in American society.[551] These figures beg the question about the relationship between socioeconomic conditions and crime.[552]

A prison sentence removes the social offender for a prescribed amount of time from the social body, but ultimately the benefit sought in incarceration is the reinstatement of the offender into society with a renewed commitment to the social good. The enlightened welfare state, assuming the perfectibility of human beings under the right educative conditions, offers medical treatment to the addict, job training to the petty thief, and expert counseling to the criminal body in general. However, in the past thirty years, across the globe and particularly in the USA, prison reform has moved away from expert intervention and in the direction of simple social control which issues from a much darker vision of human nature as incapable of reform.[553] As a result, US prisons are among the worst in the world.[554] Ironically, the educability of prison populations is definitively proven in the very prisons that refuse the possibility of reform. US prisons are currently serving as excellent training grounds for the production of criminal skills.[555]

The death penalty has the most permanent effects, because it enduringly disables the social offender. In some cases, a further benefit is reported, as the families of the victims of the offender occasionally find closure to their painful ordeal when the murderer is executed. The benefit of the death penalty, its permanence, also composes its greatest drawback: one never can be quite certain that new evidence will not emerge to prove the innocence of the convicted. Since 1973, 129 people across 26 states have been released from death row when new evidence proved their innocence.[556] So the first benefit of the death penalty seems to be doubtful enough to raise questions about its validity. Indeed, if innocent persons are executed, use of the death penalty undermines the justice of the system.

---

551  Bureau of Justice Statistics, US Department of Justice, posted at http://www. ojp. usdoj. gov/bjs/prisons. htm
552  See foe example the excellent study, David Putwain and Aidan Sammons, *Psychology and Crime* (East Essex: Routledge, 2002), 16 ff.
553  See especially David Garland, *The Culture of Control* (Chicago: University of Chicago Press, 2001) for a current study of the American and British psychology of crime.
554  According to Human Rights Watch Report (HRW Index No. : 1-56432-046-4), the United States imprisons a larger number of its citizens than any other country. After visits to more than twenty institutions in the U.S. and Puerto Rico, including state, INS, and federal prisons and jails, Human Rights Watch concludes that the human rights situation in U.S. prisons (which it labels "Marionization") follows the example of the maximum-security federal prison in Marion, Illinois, super maximum-security institutions where inmates suffer extremely harsh conditions, which lack independent supervision. They report numerous human rights abuses and frequent violations of the U.N. Standard Minimum Rules for the Treatment of Prisoners. Human Rights Watch. (1991). *Prison Conditions in the United States: A Human Rights Watch Report.*
555  Graham Sykes, *The Society of Captives* (Princeton: Princeton University Press, 1971).
556  Five prisoners were executed since 1973 despite doubts about their guilt (five of these in Texas).

The second benefit too proves far from universal. *Dead Man Walking*, Sister Helen Prejean's autobiographical account of her work with death row convicts in the Louisiana Prison system's Death Row, reports mixed responses in victim-families to witnessing executions.[557] Some family members reported that the execution actually intensified their frustration and exacerbated rather than soothed the pain of their loss. One witness asserted that such a fierce desire for revenge was enflamed by the execution that he was left with the distinct longing to see the offender executed again and again. Once was simply not enough!

The questionable domestic benefits of the death penalty must be combined with the moral disadvantage that accrues for the executing state, by placing it in the company of the most radically oppressive states in the world. Most developed countries of the world have long ago abolished the death penalty. The United States is the only modern industrialized state still practicing the punitive relic, with Texas holding the dubious distinction as the state with the highest record for killing its social offenders. According to Amnesty International, during 2007, 1,252 executions were carried out in twenty-four countries; the leading four (88% of executions worldwide) are China, Iran, Pakistan, Saudi Arabia, and the United States.[558]

Punishments are designed for the express purpose of persuading against violence in the social body. This means that the distinction between acts of justice revered in the state *as a social good* and criminal acts in the population condemned *as social evils* amounts to a difference in who is committing the violence — the social actors, not differences in the nature or quality of the acts. Both acts are deeds of violence. The violences of illegitimate agents, agents not legally sanctioned to violate, are punished by the violences of the system, through actors and agencies sanctioned with the authority to violate its members.

Philosophers have struggled with the problem of "just punishment" as long as they have struggled with the concept of "just war." Is punishment always justifiable when administered by the "legitimate authorities" of the state? Or is punishment simply the right of the powerful to abuse their social lessers? Is punishment an act of mercy that purifies the soul of the offender, balancing the scales of justice so that the criminal, freed from the stain of misdeed, may make peace with his gods and his fellows? One thing seems perfectly clear. In modern societies that strive to rehabilitate offenders, punishment is designed to serve the offender and serves to protect the society by returning a healthier social actor to the streets. But in nations that practice harsher penal policies, the only service that seems to be accomplished is a potent affirmation of the status quo of power relations.

---

557 Helen Prejean, *Dead Man Walking* (Grand Rapids: Zondervan, 1996), 67.

558 Nearly 3,350 people were sentenced to death in 51 countries last year, with over 20,000 prisoners on death row across the world at the present time. (Amnesty International Report, May 2008)

Many people believe crime to be a phenomenon spread by a base criminal element that rots at the socio-economic base of the society, their abjection seeping out the decaying base of the system to be collected neatly into jail cells. The demographics of inmate populations confirm the existence of this popular myth. They also confirm the hierarchical structure of the society and the socio-economic inequities that characterize the system. The inexplicable demographics of prison populations and the rabid fervor with which petty thieves and drug addicts are tossed into prisons (alongside the conspicuous absence of corporate criminals) confirm the popular myth upon which the judicial system so often rests: the myth that those who excel in our societies do so because of their greater merit, their greater effort, and their greater commitment to the social good, while those who populate the prisons are abject by reason of their lesser intellectual merit, their weaker work ethic, and their utter disregard for the good of society.

One suspects, with Michel Foucault, that crime exists at every social level in forms peculiar to the values of each level. Present practices of punishment that focus upon the bicycle thief and the drug addict and ignore the corporate criminal or presidential abuses of power largely serve to confirm society's racial and ethnic prejudices and to reconfirm the *status quo* of social and power relations, by providing a public display of the power of the dominant authority and the powerlessness of those who oppose the system.[559] It does not seem to occur to the voter on the street of their modern democratic societies that their societies may suffer from a new type of classism that preserves the bathwater of aristocratic elitism but jettisons the babies of merit, social responsibility, and patronage of the poor, once expected of the noble class.

To draw attention to the new irresponsible elitism that exists in modern democratic states, Robert W. Fuller, has developed a new social theory that he labels "rankism." That theory calls for moral, as well as behavioral, accountability from those people in our society who believe that they are superior to others. Fuller urges, in *Somebodies and Nobodies*, that we take notice of those who set themselves apart as special "somebodies"—moral elites of their society—while excluding themselves from the moral requirements that (in theory) govern their societies.[560] Fuller cites the obvious culprits—mean bosses, derisive doctors, condescending politicians, stage mothers, belittling coaches, and arrogant professors—who abuse the persons they ought to be serving. Fuller calls for a popular movement to demand moral accountability from the people we place in charge of our governments, companies, patients, employees, and students. Prison officials and judicial personnel at every level would be well added to this list.

However veiled the ideology may be, our democratic societies

---

559   Michel Foucault, *Discipline and Punish* (New York: Vintage Books, 1995), 25.
560   Robert W. Fuller, *Somebodies and Nobodies* (Gabriola Island, BC, Canada: New Society Publishers, 2004), 13.

are racist and classist. Rituals of inclusion and exclusion maintain the levels of social power into distinct levels of power and powerlessness. Punishment practices in the modern state serve the continuing purpose of keeping intact the traditional power relations, by keeping the have-nots in their place. The power of divine kings and popes no longer finds expression in public shamings and bloody spectacles of public tortures, but instead contempt for the socio-economically challenged has crept into a realm of more elaborate, more subtle, less visible tortures, exacted behind the very thick walls of penal institutions where they now restructure the criminal soul rather than scar the criminal body.[561] But the new forms to which the criminal soul is being trained in prisons ought to give us pause for the society's future.

Marking off the good from the evil can grant a comforting sense of stability to a community in the midst of a chaotic and confusing world. When we moralize, criminalize, isolate, and murder deviance, we re-enact an ancient custom deeply embedded in the processes of civilization itself. However, it is crucial to appreciate that cruel punishments do not banish the criminal from our midst. The death penalty, like wars against external enemies, simply produces hysterias for social purity that stimulate violent behavior against those who are visibly different. The hysteria begins in social numbering systems—in demands for forms in triplicate, licenses, passports, and visas for movement. It grows more frantic in demeaning airport friskings, tighter border controls, harsher immigration laws, and electronic surveillances of citizen activities. It proliferates into rituals that affirm inclusion and exclusion—identity cards and citizen profiling—but in good time, it fulfills itself in overt public displays of radical violence—racism, sexism, religious persecution, ethnic tribalism, and ultimately genocide.

The more seriously we take our systems and the ordering mechanisms that secure them against change, the more we give rise to the "evil" that we are attempting to purge from our midst. The more we demonize the alien other, the more we guarantee the production of an army of thieves and murderers to further plague social peace and justice. The best advice that can be offered to those who throw their trust in harsher penal policies, to keep those troublesome black men off the streets and rich white males in power, is to grant social offenders the tools and opportunities to succeed in their societies.

## REFERENCES

1. Gustave Beaumont, Alexis de Tocqueville, On the Penitentiary System in the United States and its Applications in France (Philadelphia: Carey, Lee and Blanchard, 1833)

2. Michel Foucault, Discipline and Punish (New York: Vintage Books, 1995)

---

561  Michel Foucault, *Discipline and Punish* (New York: Vintage Books, 1995), 29.

3. Robert W. Fuller, Somebodies and Nobodies, (Gabriola Island, BC, Canada: New Society Publishers, 2004).

4. David Garland, The Culture of Control (Chicago: University of Chicago Press, 2001)

5. Robert Martinson, Rehabilitation, Recidivism and Research (National Council on Crime & Delinquency, 1976)

6. James McGuire, What Works: Reducing Reoffending (John Wiley & Sons, 1999)

7. Martha Minow, Between Vengeance and Forgiveness (Boston: Beacon Press, 1978)

8. Graham Sykes, The Society of Captives (Princeton: Princeton University Press, 1971)

Wendy C. Hamblet, Ph.D., SAC (Dip)
Assistant Professor, Department of Liberal Studies, Division of University Studies
North Carolina A&T State University

Wendy C. Hamblet is a Canadian philosopher, alumna of Brock University, Canada, and Penn State University, USA. The compelling question that drives my research is the persistent problem of violence in human communities. My philosophical interest especially challenges the phenomenon of legitimate violence, where harming others comes to be understood as a social good. In my first book, *The Sacred Monstrous*, I investigate violence as embedded in human rituals of identity construction. In my second monograph, *Savage Constructions: The Myth of African Savagery*, I explore violence as a phenomenon of "rebounding" oppression in postcolonial societies. In *The Lesser Good*, I consider the gap between state institutions of justice and the philosophical ideal of ethics. I serve as a faculty member of the Zoryan Institute's *Genocide and Human Rights University Program*, an international graduate seminar held at the University of Toronto each summer. I am an alumna of UNC Asheville's "Institute for NonProliferation" and a dual alumna of the United States Holocaust Memorial Museum's "Center for Advanced Holocaust Studies." As testimony to my conviction of the link between suffering and the perpetration of violence, I serve in private practice as a professional counselor, mediator, and Organizational Ethics educator to individuals, corporate workplaces, and government agencies, including the military. My interest in punishment issues from a *National*

*Endowment for the Humanities* Summer Seminar in "Punishment, Politics, and Culture," with Austin Sarat of Amherst College, Mass.

+++

CONTROVERSY: DOING BUSINESS WITH DISEASE

*The Perfect Crime: Pharmaceutical corporations accused of Genocide before ICC in The Hague*

In January, 2003, criminal charges were brought before the International Criminal Court against American Pharmaceutical corporations and individual executives including ex president George W. Bush. The charges, which also involved accusations of war crimes against U.S. President George W. Bush, U.K. Prime Minister Tony Blair and other top political figures, are contained in a detailed complaint filed with the ICC by one Dr. Mathias Rath[562]. Dr. Rath has accused pharmaceutical companies including Pfizer, Merck, GlaxoSmithKline, Novartis, Amgen and Astra Zeneca of deliberately preventing life-saving natural alternatives to drug based treatments from being applied in prevention and cure, and of deliberately undertaking a worldwide disinformation campaign which, he says has caused the death of millions of people. This complaint brings before the International Court of Justice (ICC) what could potentially be the greatest crimes ever committed in the course of human history. Those accused are being charged with causing injury to and the death of millions of people through the "business with disease", war crimes and other crimes against humanity. As such, these crimes fall under the jurisdiction of the International Criminal Court.[563]

Before we proceed we must make something very clear—whether or not the case is brought to trial and whether or not culpability is established is not our concern in this forum. Our concern is with the degree of criminality necessary to execute crimes of this magnitude. More importantly, if these acts are true then our traditional concepts of crime and criminality will have to be reevaluated.

According to Dr. Rath, these charges are the basis for the U.S.' attempt to discredit the ICC, and put itself above international law, and

---

562   www. 4. dr-rath-foundation. org/pdf-files/hague_complaint.pdf. Complaint against genocide and other crimes against humanity committed in connection with the pharmaceutical 'business with disease' and the recent war against Iraq. ; DR. Rath Charges Pharma-Cartel and political leaders with genocide before International Criminal Court at The Hague. June 14, 2003 http://www. prolife. org. ph/forum/anti-life-collections/dr-rath-charges-pharma-cartel-and-political-leaders-with-genocide-before-icc/

563   Ibid.

continue their crimes to the detriment of all mankind. The charges presented in the official complaint relate to two main areas of crime:

1. Genocide and other crimes against humanity committed in connection with the pharmaceutical business with disease.
2. Crimes of war and aggression and other crimes against humanity committed in connection with the recent war against Iraq and the international escalation towards a world war.

Rath further claims that the pharmaceutical industry is an Organized Fraud Business committed only to the "Business with Disease". He goes on to describe the human body as the market place of the pharmaceutical industry and explains that a return on investment depends on the continuation and expansion of diseases. Since profits, he says depend on the patentability of drugs rendering this industry the most profitable industry on the planet then the prevention and eradication of any disease significantly reduces or totally eliminates the markets for pharmaceutical drugs. He accuses the pharmaceutical corporations of systematically obstructing the prevention and the eradication of diseases making them responsible for the deaths of hundreds of millions of people who continue to die from cardiovascular disease, cancer and other diseases that could have been prevented and largely eliminated long ago.

He also points out that the pharmaceutical corporations by necessity must use a maze of executors and accomplices in science, medicine, and the mass media and in politics and that the governments of entire nations are manipulated or even run by lobbyists and former executives of the pharmaceutical industry.

In addition, he says, these natural therapies can effectively help prevent and eliminate diseases. This is why, he say, the systematic elimination of natural health therapies and the takeover of the healthcare systems in most countries of the world was a necessary strategy of the pharmaceutical industry which according to Rath, has brought millions of people and almost all nations into dependency upon what is no longer the business of health but is really the business of investment. Rath says that the pharmaceutical industry offers "health" to millions of patients—but does not deliver the goods. Instead it delivers products that merely alleviate symptoms while promoting the underlying disease as a precondition for its future business.

To cover the fraud, this industry spends twice the amount of money in covering it up than it spends on research on future therapies. In his court filings Rath targets the two largest export nations of pharmaceutical products, the United States of America and Great Britain. This may sound more like an Episode of the Sopranos or The Wire, but it is the recounting of real and recent events in World History.

Whether or not Rath is a mad scientist or a rational observer, whether or not his accusations are taken seriously or he is laughed out of the courtroom, we owe it to ourselves to ask the question, "What if? What if his accusations are well founded? Then who are the real criminals and what impact does race and ethnicity really have on the determination of criminality?

## CONCLUSION

Is crime really an issue of race and ethnicity or is it an issue of context? Yes, minorities disproportionately reside in higher crime areas and high crime areas are more likely to be characterized by poverty, family disruption, poor schools etc. So, given, all these issues with high crime areas the important question is, "Why do minorities disproportionately reside in high crime areas?" Is it because of residential segregation, social disorganization or lack of residential mobility? Moreover, would it be fair to say that the racial differences in offending and victimization can be largely explained by contextual differences based on where different racial and ethnic groups tend to reside? More importantly, we must ask ourselves if minorities do, indeed, commit more crimes than non-minorities and if so, why? Yes, homicide is now one of the leading causes of death for African-American men, and, the data on homicide also indicate that, more often than not, the perpetrator in these homicides is usually another African-American man.[564]

On the other hand, research also indicates that White-Americans are also more likely to be serial murderers, child molesters, and school shooters.[565] Furthermore, there is also research that suggests that child molesters, who are primarily White-American men, serve shorter average sentences than crack offenders, who are primarily African-

---

564  Deirdre Conner. Study: "Homicide leading cause of death among young black males." The Florida Times Union. Retrieved from http://jacksonville. com/news/crime/2010-05-05/story/study-homicide-leading-cause-death-among-young-black-males ; Morley D. Glicken. 2005. "Clinical work with African American men." Chapter 13. In *Working with troubled men: a contemporary practitioner's guide*. New Jersey: Lawrence Erlbaum Associates, Inc. ; Hattery 3/20/2007. Chapter 9. "African American males and the incarceration problem: Not just confined to prison" pp. 233-284. http://www. sagepub. com/upm-data/14873_Chapter9. pdf

565  CBC news. "Why serial killers target prostitutes." December 16, 2006. http://www. cbc. ca/news/background/crime/targeting-prostitutes. html ; Hattery 3/20/2007. Chapter 9. "African American males and the incarceration problem: Not just confined to prison," pp. 233-284. http://www. sagepub. com/upm-data/14873_Chapter9. pdf ; Maaren Alia Choski. January 27, 2006. "Sex Offender re-entry: A summary and policy recommendation on the current state of the law in California and how to "safely" re-introduce sex offenders into our communities." California Prison Reform. California Sentencing and Corrections Policy Series Stanford Criminal Justice Center Working Papers.

---

American men.[566] Therefore, the racial gap in incarceration rates cannot be explained entirely by racial differences in the rate of committing crime. Part of the incarceration rate seems to be driven by differences in sentencing that keep certain people in prison for longer periods of time than others.

This brings us to the question of the social construction of crime. According to Berger and Luckman, the determination of what is a crime and who is a criminal is the determination of construction, that is, the image created by those in society who have the power to create the image—which, by necessity means that the image of the crime and the criminal will not be reflective of the one creating the image in the first place.[567] The process of interpreting an event or a phenomenon as a crime and assigning the title of "criminal" to the perpetrator is determined by the knowledge and perception of the act. As we saw in Chapter 3, people's knowledge or perception of crime is acquired through the legal official action toward crime, as well as through the mass media.

Therefore, how the law and the media portray or treat an act and the actor will determine how threatened members of society should feel by the act and person. It should be no surprise therefore, that most of our attention is focused on conventional crimes—particularly violent crimes—and rarely on white-collar crimes. This process of assimilating knowledge and perception of the reality of crime is known sociologically as social construction. As a result of this assimilation, we accept the given definition of crime as a social reality as well as a visible reality.

Moreover, the manner in which the punishment for each category of crime is administered also raises questions. The purpose for regulating corporate crimes appears to be improvement or indemnity, while the purpose for regulating conventional crime, seems to have moved away from rehabilitation to retribution. This is evidenced by the severity or lack thereof, of legal sanctions given to corporate criminals i.e., civil and administrative sanctions with criminal sanctions considered as an insignificant by product. It is interesting to also note that the institutions which carry out these Corporation Acts are administrative institutions e.g., the FDA, SEC and the orientation of these types of institutions is totally different from that of law enforcement agencies.

---

566   Hattery 3/20/2007. Chapter 9. "African American males and the incarceration problem: Not just confined to prison" pp. 233-284. http://www. sagepub. com/upm-data/14873_ Chapter9. pdf ;

567   Berger, Peter, L. & Luckman, Thomas (1967). *The social construction of reality: a treatise in the sociology of knowledge.* Harmondsworth: Penguin Books

Notwithstanding the various types of crime—crime defined by law or crime defined by morality, whether one take people's lives or one takes people's money, whether white collar or street crime, violent or non-violent, a crime is still a crime and it is driven by a darker vice—greed, anger, a need for power and control or simply a human failing. The history books clearly show that throughout our history crimes have been committed by and to every, race, most notably:

1. 1637: Pequot War–conflicts between the Massachusetts militia and eastern Native Americans resulted in the attack on the stockade Mystic village, burning it to the ground and killing escapees.
2. Boston Massacre
3. Revolutionary War
4. 1836: Battle of the Alamo
5. 1846: U.S. Invasion of Mexico
6. Confederate Henry Wirz
7. Confederate Nathan Bedford
8. 1864: Sand Creek Massacre
9. 1868: Custer's Washita raid
10. Battle at Little Bighorn

Indeed, one could argue that since criminality and crime are nothing more than social constructions then guilt or innocence are merely consequences of the society in which you happen to live. In other words the rules can change depending on who you are. The degree of criminality with which an incident is viewed arguably depends on who's committing the crime and who's doing the evaluation of how serious the crime is. How the action is punished or rewarded is determined by how the actions and the actors are perceived. Perhaps the crimes committed by individuals who are not in financial need are an indication of a greater degree of sociopathy.

If criminality is determined by race then how do we account for the White-Americans who were involved in and directly responsible for the almost 5000 lynchings of African-Americans during slavery and the civil rights era[568] or the 50 White-American Mormons who, in 1857 cold bloodedly murdered 120 White–American men, women and children in a wagon train under the orders of their religious leaders.[569] If race is an indication of criminality then how do we categorize the Germans who murdered over 6 million Jews during the Nazi

---

568 Charles J. Ogletree, Jr. Black Man's Burden: Race and the Death Penalty in America. http://www. criminology. fsu. edu/penology/news/Ogletree%20Article%20(Race%20and%20 DP). pdf

569 Tim Egan (2007). "Memories of a Massacre: A point of view." BBC News 31 August 2007.

reign and the Japanese who murdered some 30 million Chinese civilians during World War II? [570] How different are these, White-American, Japanese and German criminals from the Hutu tribesmen in Africa who murdered hundreds of thousands of their fellow Tutsi tribesmen in Rwanda and Burundi [571] or Sudanese Military and the Janjaweed militia, Sudan Liberation Movement and the Justice and Equality Movement, whose ongoing warfare have killed almost 500, 000 and displaced some 2.5 million innocent Sudanese since it began in 2003[572] In each of these cases either race or ethnicity was the driving force behind the senseless blood bath i.e.—one socially defined group attempting to eliminate another socially defined group based on physical characteristics and/or perceived genealogical differences. The one thing that all these groups (White-Americans, Germans, Japanese and Africans) have in common, however, was the propensity to kill, needlessly, and in large numbers. In the final analysis, every race and every ethnicity, over time has shown traits of criminality. Indeed, since the beginning of time the Human Race has been guilty of genocide, ethnic cleansing and mass murders. Despite the focus today on specific races, and specific ethnicities as being more prone to criminality and being the predominant perpetrators of crime, based on the evidence presented in the foregoing chapters, you should be left with the burning question, "Is crime really an issue of race, ethnicity and social forces or is criminality simply a human failing—a natural trait of the Human Race?

## CRITICAL THINKING QUESTIONS

1. Suppose an effort to reach a peace accord is riding on the cooperation or persons likely to be indicted by an international criminal court. Should the court grant immunity from prosecution or engage in plea bargaining?
2. In whose custody should convicted war criminals be kept?
3. Should the definitions of genocide and ethnic cleansing be reviewed to allow for greater inclusiveness of those actions described as crimes against humanity?
4. Under what basic circumstances should the United Nations intervene in a situation of ethnic cleansing or genocide?
5. Will the International Criminal Court be an effective remedy to the continuing problem of genocide and ethnic cleansing?

570   Denny Neave, and Craig Smith. (2009)*Aussie soldier: prisoners of war*. Australia: Big Sky Publishing Pty Ltd.

571   Burundi: Revolt of the Hutu. May 22, 1972. Time Magazine, http://www. time. com/time/magazine/article/0,9171,879084,00. html

572   Savo Heleta. The Darfur conflict from the perspective of the rebel justice and equality movement. January 2009.

CHAPTER RESOURCES

Key Terms
Crimes against Humanity
Ethnic Cleansing
Genocide
International Criminal Court
War Crimes
White Collar Crime
Ready for Review
Objectives
Case Study
War Crimes
Introduction
- What is Crime? Who is the Criminal?
- The Crime of Genocide and Ethnic Cleansing
  - Cambodia
  - Bosnia & Coatia
  - Sudan
  - Chad
In the News
- Body Parts for Sale: He's a Doctor. He can't be a criminal!
Race, Ethnicity and Policy
- International Criminal Court

REFERENCES

1. The "Good" Evil of Punishment Controversy
2. Business with Disease: The Perfect Crime: Pharmaceutical corpora-tions accused of Genocide before ICC in The Hague

# Bibliography

14th Amendment of the U.S. Constitution. (n.d.). In *U.S. Constitution online* Retrieved from http://www.usconstitution.net/xconst_Am14.html

A Good Year for Those Who Fight to Save the Innocent from Death. (1999). *Criminal Justice Weekly*, pp. 24-25.

AAPA Statement on Biological aspects of Race. (1996). American Journal of Physical Anthropology, 101, 569-570.

Abizadeh, A. (2001). Ethnicity, Race and a possible humanity. *World Order*, 33 (1), 23-34.

Ackman, D. (2002, August 07). Where are the indictments? *Forbes Magazine* .

ACLU. (n.d.). ACLU Death Penalty Campaign - Reason #3 to Support a National Moratorium on Executions. Retrieved from http://www.prison-policy.org/scans/aclu_dp_factsheet3.pdf

Adalian, R. (1997). The American Genocide. In S. Totten, W. S. Parsons, & I. W. Charny (Eds.), *Century of Genocide: Eyewitness Accounts and Critical Views* (pp. 41-77). New York and London: Garland Publishing Inc.

Africa, I. (2007, October 26). CHAD: French NGO accused of trafficking children. In *IRIN: humanitarian news and analysis*. Retrieved from http://www.irinnews.org/report.aspx?ReportId=75019

African Tourism and Development Organization. (2006, September 27). Seminar on Human Trafficking & Illegal Migration as a development issue in Sub-Saharan Africa.

Ah Sin v Whittman, 198 U.S.500 (1905).

Akers, R. (1996). Is Different Association/Social Learning Cultural Deviance Theory? *Criminology*, 34 (2), 229-247.

Albanese, J. S. (2001). *Criminal Justice*. Boston: Allyn and Bacon.

Albonetti, C. (1991). An Integration of theories to explain judicial discretion. *Social Problems*, 38 (2), 247-266.

Albonetti, C. A. (1989). Bail and Judicial Discretion in the District of Columbia. *Sociology and Social Research*, 74 (1), 40-45.

Albonetti, C. A., Hauser, R. M., Hagan, J., & Nagel, I. H. (1989). Criminal Justice Decision Making as a Stratification Process: The role of Race and
Stratification resources in Pretrial Release. *Journal of Quantitative Criminology*, 5, 57-82.

Alpert, G., & Dunham, R. (1988). *Multi-ethnic neighborhoods*. New York:
Greenwood Press.

American Anthropological Association (1998). American Anthropological
Association Statement on "Race". Retrieved from http://www.aaanet.
org/stmts/racepp.htm

American Bar Association (1991). Resolution 107, ABA House of Delegates.
Chicago: American Bar Association.

American Bar Association (2003). American Bar Association Standing Committee on Legal Aid and Indigent Defendants Special Committee on
Death Penalty Representation. Retrieved from http://www.abanet.org/
leadership/recommendations03/107.pdf

American Bar Association (1989). 1989 Recommendations-ABA Section of
Individual Rights and Responsibilities. Retrieved from http://www.
abanet.org/irr/feb89a.html

American Society of Criminology (n.d.). The Use of the Death Penalty? Retrieved from http://www.asc41.com/polcypaper2.html

Amnesty International. (1999). United States of America, Killing with Prejudice: Race and the Death Penalty in the USA. Retrieved from http://asia-
pacific.amnesty.org/library/Index

Amnesty International. (2003). United States of America: Death by Discrimination - The continuing role of race in capital cases. Retrieved from
http://www.amnesty.org/en/library/info/AMR51/046/2003/en

Amnesty International. (2008, May). Amnesty International Report.

Analysis: Defining Genocide. (2010, February 03). In BBC News. Retrieved
from http://news.bbc.co.uk/2/hi/3853157.stm

Annan, K. (1999, December 08). Press Release on the occasion of the fiftieth
Anniversary of the 1948 Convention on the Prevention and Punishment
of the Crime of Genocide SG/SM/6822.

Aquinas, T. (n.d.). Summa Theologica.

Armstrong, R.-M. (2003, July 12). Turning to Islam - African-American Conversion Stories. *The Christian Century*, pp. 19-23.

Baldus, D. C., Woodworth, G., & Pulaski Jr., C. A. (1990). *Equal Justice and the
Death Penalty: A legal and empirical analysis*. Boston: Northeastern University Press.

Baldus, D. C., Woodworth, G., Zuckerman, D., Weiner, N. A., & Broffitt, B.
(1998). Racial discrimination and the death penalty in the post-Furman
era: An empirical and legal overview, with recent findings from Philadelphia. *Cornell Law Review*, 83, 1638-1770.

Baldus, D., Pulaski, C., & Woodworth, G. (1986). Arbitrariness and Discrimination in the Administration of the Death Penalty: A Challenge to State
Supreme Court. *Stetson Law Review*, 15, 133-231.

Batson v Kentucky, 476 US 79, 89, 106 S.Ct. 1712, 1719, 90 L.Ed2d 69 (1986).

Ba-yunus, I. (2000). Unifying Muslim North America. Islamic Horizons, 20,
p. 1421-2000.

Becker, K. (n.d.). Genocide and Ethnic Cleansing. In *Model United Nations
Far West*. Retrieved from http://www.munfw.org/archive/50th/4thl.htm

Becker, M. (1992). Biological and the New Racism. In D. T. Goldberg (Ed.), *Anatomy of Racism* (pp. 18-37). Minneapolis: University of Minnesota Press.

Beckett, K., & Theodore, S. (2004). *The Politics of Injustice: Crime and Punishment in America.* Thousand Oaks, California: Sage Publications.

Bedau, H. A., & Cassess, P. G. (2005). *Debating the death penalty: Should America Have Capital Punishment? The experts on both sides make their case.* United Kingdom: Oxford University Press.

Benjamin, D., & Simon, S. (2002). *The Age of Sacred Terror.* New York: Random House.

Bennet, L. D. (2006). Media put accuser on trial in Duke Rape. In *National Organization for Woman.* Retrieved from http://www.now.org/issues/media/061506duke.html

Berger v United States, 295 U.S. 78, 88, 55 S.Ct. 629, 79 L. Ed. 1314 (1935).

Berger, P., & Luckmann, T. (1967). *The Social Construction of Reality: A Treatise in the Sociology of Knowledge.* Harmondsworth: Penguin Books.

Birzer, M. L., & Birzer, H. (2000). Race Matters: A critical profiling, it's a matter for the courts. *Journal of Criminal Justice,* 34 (6), 643-651.

Black, H. C. (2004). Black's Law Dictionary (8th edition ed.). St. Paul, Minnesota: West Publishing Company.

Black, P. (1990). Forced labor in Concentration Camps. In M. Berebaum (Ed.), *A Mosaic of victims: Non-Jews persecuted and murdered by Nazis* (pp. 46-63). New York: New York University Press.

Blume, J., Eisenberg, T., & Wells, M. T. (2004). Explaining Death Row's Population and Racial Composition. *Journal of Empirical Legal Studies,* 1 (1), 165-207.

Blumstein, A. (1993). Racial Disproportionality of U. S. Prison revisited. *University of Colorado Law Review,* 64, 743-760.

Boutin, C. (n.d.). Organized Crime - Drug and Human Trafficking in Europe (France) 141 CCDG 03 E. In Nato Parliamentary Assembly. Retrieved from: http://www.nato-pa.int/Default.asp?SHORTCUT=368

Brazil, J., & Berry, S. (1999, August 23). Color of Driver is key to stop in I-95 Videos. *Orlando Sentinel,* p. A1.

Bridges, G. S., & Steen, S. (1998). Racial disparities in official assessment of juvenile offenders: Attributional stereotypes as mediating mechanisms. *American Sociological Review,* 63 (4), 554-571.

Bright, S. (n.d.). Council for the Poor: The Death Sentence not for the worst crime but for the worst Lawyer. Retrieved from http://www.schr.org/files/resources/counsel3.pdf

Brown, R. G., & Brown, B. B. (2000). The crime control industry and the management of the surplus population. *Critical Criminology,* 9 (1-2), 39-62.

Brown, S., & Coon, C. (2003). Trojan Horse. *Z Magazine Online* V16 N 6. Retrieved from frontpagemagazine.com

Burg, S. L. (1997). Genocide in Bosnia-Herzegovina? In S. Totten, W. S. Parsons, & I. W. Charny (Eds.), *Century of Genocide: Eyewitness Accounts and Critical Views* (pp. 424-433). New York and London: Garland Publishing Inc.

Burtman, B. (2002, October 16). Criminal Injustice: Criminal Justice Independent Weekly. *In Death Penalty Information Center.* Retrieved from http://www.deathpenaltyinfo.org/node/533

Burundi: Revolt of the Hutu. (1972, May 22). *Time Magazine*. Retrieved from http://www.time.com/time/magazine/article/0,9171,879084,00.html

Bushman, B. J., & Andrew, C. A. (2001). Media Violence and the American Public: Scientific facts versus media misinformation. *American Psychologist*, 56 (6-7), 477-489.

Butler v Cooper, No 75-49-N, 8 (E.D. Va August 13, 1975).

Butterfield, F. (1990). Dispute emerges in Boston Murder. *The New York Times*. Retrieved from http://query.nytimes.com.

Caldwell, G., Galster, S., & Steinzor, N. (1997). Crime and Servitude: An Expose of the Traffic in Women for Prostitution from the Newly Independent States. Collaboration between Global Survival network and International League for Human Rights.

Campbell, R., Martin, C. R., & Fabos, B. (2005). *Media and Culture: An introduction to Mass Communication*. Boston: Bedford/St. Martin's.

Canada, A. I. (n.d.). Extreme Prejudice - Racism and the Death Penalty. In *Amnesty International*. Retrieved from http://www.amnesty.ca/usa/racismphp

Cannon, L. (2000, October 1). One Bad Cop. *The New York Times Magazine*.

Canon, L. (1999). *Official Negligence: How Rodney King and the Riots change Los Angeles and the LAPD*. Boulder Colorado: Westview Press.

Capital Punishment in Context. (n.d.) Race and the Death Penalty. Retrieved from http://www.capitalpunishmentincontext.org/issue/race

Capital Punishment-World body life history person human. (n.d.). Retrieved from http://www.deathreference.com

Center for problem oriented policing. (n.d.) Responses to the problem of street prostitution. Retrieved from http://www. popcenter. org/problems /street_prostitution/3/

Centre for Prosecution Ethics: Quotes about prosecutors and the prosecution function. (n.d.). In *National District Attorneys Association Education Division: National College of District Attorneys*. Retrieved from http://www.ethicsforprosecutors.com/quotes.html

Chad 'kidnapping' angers Sarkozy. (2007, October 29). In *BBC News*. Retrieved from: http://news.bbc.co.uk/2/hi/africa/7066770.stm

Chad—Genocide Watch. Genocide Warning: The International Campaign to end Genocide. (n.d.). Retrieved from http://www.genocidewatch. org/chad/html

Chambliss, W., & Seidman, R. (1971). *Law Order and Power*. Reading MA: Addison-Wesley.

Champion, D. J. (1989). *The U.S. Sentencing Guidelines: Implications for Criminal Justice*. New York: Praeger.

Chawaki, J. M., & Wahab, M. D. (2005). Technology is a double-edged sword: Illegal human trafficking in the information age. Computer Crime Research Center.

Chiricos, T. (2004). The Media, Moral Panic and the Politics of Crime Control. In G. F. Cole, M. C. Gertz, & A. Bunger (Eds.), *In the Criminal Justice System: Politics and Politics*. Elmont, California: Wadsworth.

Chiricos, T., & Bales, W. (1991). Unemployment and Punishment: An Empirical Assessment. *Criminology*, 29 (4), 718, 701-724.

Choski, M. A. (2006, January 27). Sex Offender re-entry: A summary and policy recommendation on the current state of the law in California and how to "safely" reintroduce sex offenders into our communities. California Prison Reform: California Sentencing and Corrections Policy Series. [Stanford Criminal Justice Center Working Papers.]

Christie, N. (2000). *Crime control as industry: Towards GULAGS, Western Style.* London: Routledge.

Civilian Complaint Review Board (CCRB), N. Y. (2004). Status Report: January-December 2003. Retrieved from http://www.nyc.gov/html/ccrb/pdf/ccrbann2003.pdf

Clark County Prosecuting Attorney's Office (n.d.). The Death Penalty. US executions since 1976. Retrieved from http://www.clarkprosecutor.org/html/death/usexecute.htm

Clarke, S. H., & Koch, G. G. (1976). The Influence of income and other factors on whether criminal defendants go to prison. *Law and Society Review, 11,* 57-92.

Clausewitz, C. V. (1942). Principles of War. (H. W. Gatzke, Trans.) The Military Service Publishing Company.

Colbert, D. (n.d.). Professional Responsibility in Crisis. In Digital Commons-Law. Retrieved from http://www.digitalcommons.law.umaryland.edu

Cole, D. (1999). *No Equal Justice: Race and class in the American Criminal Justice System.* New York: New York Press.

Committee on The Judiciary Of The. U.S. House Of Representatives (2008). Testimony - Hearing on the Impact of Federal Habeas Corpus Limitations on the Death Penalty Appeals. Retrieved from http://www.judiciary.house.gov/hearings/pdf/Hanlon091208.pdf

Committee, C. J. (1997). Racial and Ethnic Bias in the Courts. In Final Report of the California Judicial Advisory Committee. Retrieved from http://www.courtinfo.ca.gov/reference/documents/rebias.pdf

Conner, D. (2010, May 05). Study: Homicide leading cause of death among young black males. In *The Florida Times Union.* Retrieved from http://jacksonville.com/news

Consumer Federation of America. (2003, May). Promoting the public interest through Media Ownership Limits September 2002.

Cooper, M. (2003). Promoting the Public Interest through Media Ownership Limits: A Critique of the FCC's Draft Order. Consumer Federation of America.

Cordes, C. (1984, June). Media found able to "prime" votes. *APA Monitor,* p. 31.

Crank, J., & Gregor, P. (2005). *Counterterrorism after 9/11.* Cincinnati: Lexis Nexis Anderson.

Darley, W. (2005, Summer). War Policy support and the Media. In *Parameters.* Retrieved from https://www.carlisle.army.mil/USAWC/Parameters/05summer/darley.pdf

Davenport, C. B. (1910). *Eugenics: The Science of Human Improvement by better Breeding.* New York: Henry Holt and Company.

David, F. (1952). Crime News in Colorado Newspapers. American Journal of Sociology, 57, 325-330.

Davis, A. (1998). Masked Racism: Reflections of the Prison Industrial Complex. Retrieved from Corp Watch: www.corpwatch.org/article.php/id=849

Davis, M. (2006). Car Bombs with Wings-History of the Car Bomb (part 2). In *Tom Dispatch*. Retrieved from http://www.tomdispatch.com

Dearnley, R., & Chalke, S. (2005). Prevention, Prosecution and Protection - Human Trafficking. *UN Chronicle*

Death Penalty in Tennessee: A View from the Federal Bench. (n.d.). Retrieved from http://www.hawaii.edu/hivaids/ The_Death_Penalty_in_Tenn_View_from_the_Fedpdf

Death Penalty Information Center. (2002). The Death Penalty in 2001 year end report. Retrieved from http://www.deathpenaltyinfo.org/YearEndReport2001.pdf

Death Penalty Information Center. (n.d.) The Future of the Death Penalty in the US: A Texas Sized Crisis. Retrieved from http://www.deathpenaltyinfo

Death Penalty Information Organization (2010). Arbitrariness. Retrieved from http://www.deathpenaltyinfo.org/arbitrariness

Death Penalty Information Organization (n.d.). Racial Disparities in Federal Death Penalty Prosecutions 1988-1994. Retrieved from http://www.deathpenaltyinfo.org

Death Penalty Information Organization (n.d.). Understanding Capital Punishment: A guide through the death penalty debate. Retrieved from http://www.heathpenaltyinfo.org

**Defending Justice,** an Activist Resource Kit. How the System itself is Violent. (n.d.) In *Defending Justice* Retrieved from http://www.defendingjustice.org

Democracy Now. (n.d.) Retrieved from http://www.democracynow.org/1997/12/3/fbi_crime_lab.

Department of Justice (2000). Sourcebook of Criminology. In Justice Statistics Online 2005. Retrieved from http://www.albany.edu/sourcebook/pd/t612005.pdf

Dept. of Homeland Security (2003). *Operation Predator*. [Fact Sheet] Retrieved from http://www.dhs.gov/xnews/releases/press_release_0210.shtm

Dershowitz, A. (1997). *Reasonable Doubts: The Criminal Justice System and O.J. Simpson case.* New York: Touchstone.

Dershowitz, A. M. (1969b). The psychiatrist's power in civil commitments: A knife that cuts both ways. *Psychology Today, 2,* 43-47.

Dershowitz, A. M. (1994). *The Abuse Excuse and other Copouts, Sob Stories and Evasion of Responsibility.* Boston: Little Brown and Company.

Dershowitz, A. M. (1997). *Reasonable Doubts: The Criminal Justice System and O.J. Simpson case.* New York: Touchstone.

DiJoseph, S. (2006, April 08). Illegal Harvesting and Sale of Body Parts, Tissue and Organs: Dr. Frankenstein would have been proud. In *Newsinferno.com: News that matters.* Retrieved from http://www.newsinferno.com/archives/1064

Ditton, J., & Chadee, D. (2006). People's Perceptions of their likely future risk of Criminal Victimization. *British Journal of Criminology, 46,* 505-518.

Dixon, T. L. (2006a). Psychological reactions to crime news portrayals of black criminals: understanding the moderating roles of prior news viewing and stereotype endorsement. *Communication Monographs, 73* (2), 162-187.

Dixon, T. l. (2006b). "Race coding" and white opposition to welfare. *American Political Science Review*, 90 (3), 593-604.

Dixon, T. L. (2007). Black criminal and White officers: The effects of racially misrepresenting law breakers and law defenders on television news. *Media Psychology*, 10, 270-291.

Dixon, T. L., & Linz, D. G. (2000b). Race and misrepresentation of victimization on local television news. *Communication Research*, 27 (5), 547-573.

Dixon, T. L., & Linz, D. G. (2002). Television News, Pretrial Publicity and the Depiction of Race. *Journal of Broadcasting and Electronic Media*, 46 (1), 112-136.

Dixon, T. L., & Linz, D. G. (2006a). Overrepresentation and underrepresentation of African Americans and Latinos as lawbreakers on television news. *Journal of Communication*, 50 (2), 131-154.

Dixon, T. L., & Maddox, K. B. (2005). Skin Tone, Crime News and Social Reality Judgments: Priming the Stereotype of the Dark and Dangerous Black Criminal. *Journal of Applied Psychology*, 38 (8), 1555-1570.

Dixon, T. L., Azocar, C., & Casas, M. (2003). The Portrayal of Race and Crime on Television Network News. *Journal of Broadcasting and Electronic Media*, 47 (4), 498-423.

DOJ Office of Justice Programs (n. d.) Homicide trends in the U.S. Retrieved from http://www.ojp.usdoj.gov/bjs/homicide/tables/totalstab.htm.

DOJ Office of Justice Programs (2000). Special Report: Defense Counsel in Criminal Cases NCJ 179023.

DOJ Office of Justice Programs (2003). Prison Statistics: Summary Findings. In Bureau of Justice Statistics: Retrieved from http://www.ojp.usdoj.gov/bjs/prisons.htm

Dominick, J. R. (1994). Crime and Law Enforcement on Primetime Television. *Public Opinion Quarterly*, 37, 241-250.

Don, T. (1995, August 28). Philadelphia Shaken by Criminal Police Officers. In *The New York Times*. Retrieved from http://www.nytimes.com/1995/08/28/us/philadelphia-shaken-by-criminal-police-officers.html

Donna M. Hughes, P. (2007, January 17). Reducing Demand for Victims of Sex Trafficking in the U.S. Women in Federal Law Enforcement. Retrieved from http://www.uri.edu/artsci/wms/hughes/256,1

Donohue, B., & Barrett, K. (2000, June 8). Motorist City disagree over Civil Rights Lawsuit. *La Cruces Sun-News*, p. 1.

Dorfman, L., & Schiraldi, V. (2001). *Off balance: Youth, race and crime in the news*. Washington DC: Justice Policy Institute.

Dowler, K. (2002). Media influence on attitudes of guns and gun control. *American Journal of Criminal Justice*, 26 (2), 235-247.

Dray, P. (2002). *At the hands of persons unknown: The lynching of Black Americans*. New York: Random House.

Driving while Black on I-95. (1996, November 16). *Washington Post*.

Durkheim, E. (1995). The rules of the sociological method. (W. D. Halls Trans.) New York: The Free Press. (Original work published 1982)

Economic and Social Commission for Asia and the Pacific. Gender and Development [Discussion Paper

Effective Assistance of Counsel in Capital Cases. (n.d.). Retrieved from http://www.press.umich.edu/pdf/0472099116-ch2.pdf

Economic and Social Commission for Asia and the Pacific. Gender and Development Discussion Paper. Violence against and Trafficking in Women as Symptoms of Discrimination: The Potential of CEDAW as an Antidote. [Series No. 17] Retrieved from http://www. Unescap. org/esid/ gad/Publication/DiscussionPapers/17/CEDAW%20discussion%20 paper%20no. %2017%20-%20revised%2023%20March%202006. pdf

Egan, T. (2007, August 31). Memories of a Massacre: A point of view. BBC News.

Eggen, D. (2007, August 10). Study: Almost Half of Murder Victims Black. *Washington Post.* Retrieved from http://www.washingtonpost.com

Ellis, C. (2000). How Islam is winning Black America.) Christianity Today, 3.

Entman, R. M. (1990). Modern racism and the images of Blacks in local television news. *Critical Studies in Media Communication*, 7 (4), 332-345.

Entman, R. M. (1992). Blacks in the news: Television, modern racism and cultural change. *Journalism Quarterly*, 69 (2), 341-361.

Entman, R. M. (1994). Representation and Reality in the Portrayal of Blacks on Network News. *Journalism Quarterly*, 71 (3), 509-520.

Entman, R. M., & Rojecki, A. (2001). *The Black Image in the White Mind: Media and Race America.* Chicago, Illinois: University of Chicago Press.

Equal Justice USA. How Racism Riddles the US Death Penalty. (n.d.)Retrieved from http://www.ejusa.org/moratorium_now/broch_race.html

Erickson, K. (1962). Notes on the Sociology of Deviance. *Social Problems*, 9, 397-414.

Etzioni, & Marsh, J. (2003). Rights vs. Public Safety after 9/11. Lanham, MD: Rowman & Littlefield.

Facts about Human Trafficking. US Dept. of State (n.d) In Democracy and Global Affairs: Retrieved from http://www.salvationarmyusa.org/usn/ www_usn_2.nsf/0/56E8CA3E6B2D13E88525765D0

Farnsworth, M., & Horan, P. (1980). Separate Justice: An analysis of race differences in Court Processes. *Social Sciences Research*, 9 (4), 381-399.

Farrel, R. A., & Swigert, V. L. (1978). Prior offense record as a self-fulfilling prophecy. *Law and Society Review*, 12, 437-453.

Fatal Flaws: Innocence and the Death Penalty in the USA (1998). In *Amnesty International*. Retrieved from http://www.amnesty.org

Feagin, J. R., & Sikes, M. P. (1994). *Living with Racism: The black middle-class experience*. Boston: Beacon Press.

Federal Bureau of Investigation (FBI) Uniform Crime Reporting (2003). Uniform Crime Reports: Crime in the United States. Washington DC: U.S. Government Printing Office.

Federal Bureau of Investigation (FBI) Uniform Crime Reporting (2003). Crime in the United States - 2002. Washington DC: Government Printing Office.

Federal Communications Commission. (2003). Consumer Survey on Media Usage. Nielsen Media Research

Feinberg, S. L. (2002). Media Effects: The influence of local newspaper coverage on Municipal Police size. *American Journal of Criminal Justice*, 26 (2), 249-268.

Fields, B. J. (1990). Slavery, Race and Ideology in the United States of America. *New Left Review*, 181, 94-118.

Fight the Death Penalty in the USA (n.d.). Ineffective Defense Counsel. Retrieved from http://www.fdp.dk/uk/couns-uk.htm

Finckenauer, J. O., Gavin, P., Hovland, A., & Storvoll, E. (1999). *Scared straight: The panacea phenomenon revisited*. Prospect Heights, Illinois: Waveland Press.

Fishman, M. (1976). Crime Waves as Ideology. *Social Problems*, 25, 531-543.

Flanagan, T. J., & Vaughn, M. S. (1996). Public Opinion about Police Abuse of Force. In W. Geller, & H. Toch (Eds.), *Police Violence* (pp. 113-128). New Haven, Connecticut: Yale University Press.

Florida State College Of Criminology & Criminal Justice. (n.d.). Black Man's Burden: Race and the Death Penalty in America. Retrieved from http://www.criminology.fsu.edu/penology/news/Ogletree

Foucault, M. (1995). *Discipline and Punishment*. New York: Vintage Books.

Fox, R., & Van Sickel, R. W. (2007). *Tabloid Justice: Criminal Justice in an age of media frenzy*. Boulder, USA: Lynne Reinner Publishers.

Frazier, C. E., Bock, E. W., & Herretta, J. C. (1980). Pretrial Release and Bail Decision. *Criminology*, 18 (2), 162-181.

Freeman, J. L. (2007). Television violence and aggression: Setting the record straight. *Policy Review*.

Fuller, R. W. (2004). *Somebodies and Nobodies*. Gabriola Island, BC, Canada: New Society Publishers.

Garland, D. (2001). *The Culture of Control*. Chicago: University of Chicago Press.

Gerbner, G., Mowlana, H., & Schiller, H. I. (1996). *Invisible crises: What conglomerate control of media means for America and the World: Critical Studies in Communication and in the Cultural Industries*. Colorado: Westview press.

Gersman, B. (2010). Bad Faith Exception to Prosecutorial Immunity for Brady Violations. Retrieved from http://digitalcommons.pace.edu/cgi/viewcontent.cgi?article=1635&context=lawfaculty

Gideon v Wainwright, 372 U.S. 335 U. S. Supreme Court (1963)

Gilbert, D. (2001). Capitalism and Crisis: Creating a Jailhouse Nation. *Monthly Review*, 52 (10).

Gilens, M. (1996a). Race and Poverty in America: Public misperceptions and the American news Media. *Public Opinion Quarterly*, 60, 515-541.

Gilens, M. (1999). *Why Americans have welfare: Race, media and the politics of antipoverty policy*. Chicago: University of Chicago Press.

Gilliam, F. D., Iyengar, S., Simon, A., & Wright, O. (1996). Crime in the Black and White: The violent, scary world of Local News. *Harvard International Journal of Press/Politics*, 1 (3), 6-23.

Gilly, T. A., Gilinskiy, Y., & Sergevnin, V. (2009). The ethics of terrorism: innovative approaches from an international perspective (17 lectures). Springfield, Illinois: Charles C. Thomas Publisher Ltd.

Gitlin, T. (1979). Prime Time Ideology: The Hegemonic Process in Television Entertainment. *Social Problems*, 26, 251-266.

Glicken, M. D. (2005). *Clinical work with African American men. In Working with troubled men: A Contemporary practitioner's guide*. New Jersey: Lawrence Erlbaum Associates Inc.

Goldkamp, J. S., & Gottfredson, M. (1979). Bail decison making and Pretrial Detention surfacing Judicial Policy. *Law and Human Behavior*, 3 (4), 227-249.

Graber, D. A. (1980). Crime, Crime News and Crime Views. *Public Opinion Quarterly*, 45, 492-506.

Greer, C., & Jewkes, Y. (2005). Extremes of otherness: Media images of social exclusion. *Social Justice*, 32 (1), 20-31.

Gross, K., & Aday, S. (2003). The scary word in your living room and neighborhood: using local broadcast news, neighbor crime rates and personal experience to test agenda setting and cultivation. *Journal of Communication*, 53, 411-426.

Gross, S. R., & Barnes, Y. (2002). Read Work: Racial Profiling and Drug Interdiction on the Highway. *Michigan Law Review*, 101 (3), 651-754.

GSN. (1998). Trafficking of NIS women abroad: Moscow Conference Report. Washington DC: GSN.

Hacker, A. (1997). Are the Media really "White". In E. E. Dennis, & E. C. Pease (Eds.), *The media in black and white* (pp. 71-76). New Brunswick: Transaction.

Hacker. (2008). *In Merriam-Webster Online Dictionary*. Retrieved April 7, 2008. http://www.merriam-webster.com/dictionary/hacker

Halliday, S. (2000). Institutional Racism in Bureaucratic Decision Making: A Case Study in the Administration of Homelessness Law. *Journal of Law and Society*, 27 (3), 449-471.

Hallin, D. C. (1984). The Media, the War in Vietnam and Politics Support: A Critique of the Thesis of an Oppositional Media. *Journal of Politics*, 46, 2-24.

Hallin, D. C. (1986). *The Uncensored War*. New York: Oxford University Press.

Hann, M. S. (1997). *Apocalypse in Oklahoma: Waco and Rubyridge revenged*. Boston: Northeastern University Press.

Hansen, B. (2003, September 19). *Combating Plagiarism*. The QC Researcher, pp. 773-796.

Harrell, E. (2007). *Black victims of violent crime*. Washington DC: Office of Justice Program, U.S. Department of Justice.

Harris, D. (1999). The Stories, the statistics and the law: Why "driving while black" matters. Minnesota *Law Review*, 84 (2), 265-326.

Harris, D. (1999, June 07). Driving While Black: Racial Profiling on our Nation's Highways. Retrieved from http://www.aclu.org/racialjustice/racialprofiling/15912pub19990607.html

Harris, D. (2002). *Profiles in Injustice: Why racial profiling cannot work*. New York: The New Press.

Harris, P. (1997). *Black Rage confronts the Law*. New York: New York University Press.

Harris, S. (2006). *Terrorist Profiling, Version 2.0*. National Journal: National Journal Group Inc .

Hattery. (2007, March 20). African American males and the incarceration problem: Not just confined to prison. Retrieved from http://www.sagepub.com/upm-data/14873_Chapter9.pdf

Heleta, S. (2009). *The Darfur Conflict from the perspective of the Rebel Justice and Equality Movement*. MPhil Thesis .Nelson Mandela Metropolitan University: Port Elizabeth, South Africa

Hernandez, C. A., Haug, M. J., & Wagner, N. N. (1976). *Chicanos: Social and Psychological Perspectives*. St. Louis: C. V. Mosby.

Hippel, W. V., Sekaquaptewa, D., & Vargas, P. (1995). On the role of encoding processes in stereotype maintenance. *Advances in Social Psychology*, 177-254.

Holmes, S. (2008, February 15). Trafficking: A very modern slavery. Retrieved from BBC News: http://www.news.bbc.co.uk

Icard, L. D. (1998). Racial Minority status and distress among children and adolescents. *Journal of Social Service Research*, 25 (1/2).

International Criminal Court. (2003, June 14). Dr. Rath charges Pharma-Cartel and political leaders with genocide before International Criminal Court at the Hague. Retrieved from http://www.profile.org.ph/forum/anti-life-collections/dr-rath-charges-pharma-cartel-and-political-leaders-with-genocide-before-icc/

Is Prosecutorial Misconduct a widespread problem in capital cases? (n.d.). Retrieved from http://deathpenalty.procon.org/view.answers.php?questionID=0000993

Johnson, C. (n.d.). Trafficking in Russian Women: Sexual Exploitation as a Growing form of International Trade. TED case studies. Retrieved from http://american.edu/ted/traffic.htm

Johnson, D. (2008). Racial Prejudice, Perceived Injustice and the Black-White gap in punitive attitudes. *Journal of Criminal Justice*, 36 (2), 198-206.

Johnson, E. H. (1957). Selective factors in Capital Punishment. *Social Forces*, 58, 168-169.

Johnson, J. G., Cohen, P., Smailes, E. M., & Kasen, B. J. (2002). Television viewing and aggressive behavior during adolescence and adulthood. *Science Magazine* 29, 295 (5564), 2468-2471.

Johnson, K. A. (1987b). *Media images of Boston's Black community*. Boston: William Monroe Trotter Institute.

Johnson, S. L. (1998). Responsibility, Race Neutrality and Truth Reviewed work(s): Race, Crime and the Law by Randall Kennedy. *The Yale Law Journal*, 107 (8), 2619-2659.

Johnston, D. (2002, January 16). Enron's collapse: the investigation. Justice Department's inquiry into Enron is beginning to take shape, without big names. *New York Times*.

Jones, D.E. et al (2002). *Religious Congregations and Membership in the United States 2000: An Enumeration by Region, State and Country based on data reported by 149 Religious Bodies*. Nashville, TN: Glenmary Research Center.

Juergensmeyer, M. (2003). The Religious Roots of Contemporary Terrorism. In W. Kegley (Ed.), *The New Global Terrorisms: Characteristics, Causes and Controls* (pp. 185-193). Upper Saddle River, NJ: Prentice Hall.

Justice, U. D. (2003). Crime in the U. S. 2002. Federal Bureau of Investigation. Washington DC: Government Printing Office.

Justice, U. D. (2004). Crime in the U. S. 2003. Federal Bureau of Investigation. Washington DC: Government Printing Office.

Kappeler, V. E. (2004). Inventing criminal justice with social construction. In P. Kraska (Ed.), *Theorizing Criminal Justice: Eight essential orientations*. Long Grove, Illinois: Waveland Press.

Keil, T. J., & Vito, G. F. (1995). Race and the death penalty in Kentucky murder trials: 1976-1991. *American Journal of Criminal Justice*, 20 (1), 17-36.

Keil, T. J., & Vito, G. F. (2006). Capriciousness or Fairness? Race and Prosecutorial decisions to seek the death penalty in Kentucky. *Journal of Ethnicity and Criminal Justice*, 4 (3), 27-49.

Kennedy, S. (1997, January 29). Making Traffic Stops based on Race. *Indianapolis Star*.

Kennickell, A. (2003). A Rolling Tide: Changes in the Distribution of Wealth in the U.S. 1989-2001 - Working Paper No. 393. Levy Economics Institute of Bard College.

Kentucky Government Information. Crime Control and the Death Penalty. (1997, November). Retrieved from www.e-archives.ky.gov/pubs/Pub_Adv/Nov97/crime_control.htm

Klein, S., Petersilia, J., & Turner, S. (1990). Race and Imprisonment Decision in California. *Science*, 247, 812-816.

Koch, K. (1998, December 25). Journalism under Fire. The QC Researcher, p. 1121-1144.

Korematsu v. United States, No. 22, 323 U.S. 214, 65 S.Ct. 193, 89 LEd. 194 Supreme Court (1944).

Kramer, J. H., & Ulmer, J. T. (1996). Sentencing disparity and departure from guidelines. *Justice Quarterly*, 13, 401-425.

Kramer, J., & Ulmer, J. T. (2000). Report prepared for the Pennsylvania Supreme Court Committee on Race and Gender Bias. Appendix Volume I.

Kristof, N. D. (2008, February 28). Southern Sudan: A Genocide Foretold. *The New York Times*.

Lafree, G. (1995). Race and crime trends in the United States 1946-1990. In D. F. Hawkins, *Ethnicity, race and crime: perspectives across time and place* (pp. 169-193). New York: Albany State University of New York Press.

LaFree, G. D. (1980). The Effect of Sexual Stratification by Race on Official Reactions to Rape. *American Sociological Review*, 45, 842-854.

Lemert, E. M., & Rosberg, J. (1948). The Administration of Justice to Minority Groups in L.A. County. *Culture and Society*, 1-27.

Leonnig, C., & Frankel, G. (2005). U.S. to send 5 detainees home from Guantanamo. In *Washington Post* Retrieved from http://www.washingtonpost.com

Lesley, M. (1988). *Subway Vigilante: A Juror's Account of the Bernhard Goetz Trial*. Latham: New York: British American Publishing.

Liebman, J., Fagan, J., & West, V. (n.d.). *A Broken System: Error in Rates in Capital Cases 1973-1995*. Retrieved from http://papers.ssrn.com

Lienert, A. (2008, June 19). *Toyota looking into allegations of Human Trafficking and Sweatshop abuses*. Retrieved from http://www.insideline.com/toyota/toyota-looking-into-allegations-of-human-trafficking-and-sweatshop-abuses.html

Linder, D. (2003). *The McMartin Preschool Abuse Trial: A Commentary*. Retrieved from http:www.law.umkc.edu/faculty/projects/ftrials/mcmartin/mcmartinaccount.html

Lyon, A. (n.d.). *Defending the Life or Death Case*. Retrieved from works.bepress.com/cgi/viewcontext.cgi?article=1000&context=andrea_lyon

Magazine, T. F. (2001, August). *Behind Bars: Native incarceration rates increase.* Retrieved from http://www.towardfreedom.com/2001/aug01/native-prison.htm

Mahta, S. (2002, December 25). Anaheim to settle profiling lawsuit. In *Los Angeles Times.* Retrieved from http://www.latimes.com/news/local/la-me-profile25dec25.story

Mann, C. R. (1993). *Unequal Justice: A question of color.* Bloomington: Indiana University Press.

Marcus, R. (1994). Racism in our Courts: The Underfunding of public defenders and its disproportionate impact upon racial minorities. *Hastings Constitutional Law Review, 22,*219-268.

Markon, J. (2007, September 23, 24). Human Trafficking Evokes Outrage, Little Evidence: US Estimates Thousands of Victims, Efforts to find them fall short. *Washington Post*

Markon, J. (2007, September 30). *Human Trafficking - really such a big issue?* Retrieved from http://articles.sfgate.com/2007-09-30/news/17262541_1_human-trafficking-task-forces-victims

Marks, J. (2003). *What it means to be 95% Chimpanzee.* Los Angeles: University of California Press.

Marsh, J. (1991). A Comparative Analysis of crime coverage in newspapers in the United States and other Countries from 1960 to 1989: A Review of the literature. *Journal of Criminal Justice, 19,* 67-79.

Martin, S. T. (2002, January 14). Are prisons a breeding ground for terrorists? *St. Petersburg Times .*

Matusow, B. (1988, January). If it Bleeds, it Leads. *Washingtonian,* p. 102.

Mauer, M., & Huling, T. (1995). Young Black Americans and the Criminal Justice System: Five Years Later. In *The Sentencing Project.* Retrieved from http://www.sentencingproject.org

McClesky v. Kemp, 481 U.S. 279 (1987).

McCord, D., & Latzer, B. (2010). *Death Penalty Cases: Leading U.S. Supreme Court Cases on Capital Punishment* (3rd edition ed.). Burlington, MA: Butterworth-Heinemann.

Media Spinning the Iraq War. (n.d.). Retrieved from http://www.discover-thenetworks.org

Media, T. S. (2004). *An Annual Report on American Journalism.* Retrieved from http://www.stateofthemedia.org/2004/narrative_radio_ownership.asp?cat=5&media=8

Merton, R. (1968). *Social Theory and Social Structure.* New York: The Free Press.

Michigan Supreme Court (1997). *Report of Michigan Supreme Court Task Force on Racial/Ethnic issues in the Courts.* Retrieved from http://www.courts.michigan.gov/mji/webcast/alimony/execsummary.pdf

Miko, F. T., & Park, G. J.-H. (2002). *Trafficking in women and children: The U.S. and International response.* Congressional Research Service, Washington DC: The Library of Congress.

Milbank, D. (2004, July 17). Bush Speech on Human Trafficking targets Castro. The *Washington Post* Retrieved from http://www.washingtonpost.com

Miles, J. (1991). Imagining Mayhem: Fictional Violence vs. 'True Crime'. *North American Review,* 57-64.

Monahan, J. (1981). *Predicting Violent Behaviour: An Assessment of Clinical Techniques*. Beverly Hills: Sage Publications Inc.

Moore, C., & Miethe, T. (1986). Regulated and non-regulated sentencing practices under Minnesota felony sentencing guidelines. *Law and Society Review*, 20, 253-265.

Mueller, Robert S. III Director, Federal Bureau of Investigation. Testimony before the Senate Committee on Intelligence of the United States Senate. (2005, February 16).

Museum, U. S. (n.d.). Rwanda: The First Conviction for Genocide. In *United States Holocaust Memorial Museum*. Retrieved from http://www.ushmm.org/wlc/article.php?lang=en&ModuledId=10007157

Mustard, D. (2001). Racial Ethnic and Gender Disparities in Sentencing: Evidence from the U.S. Federal Courts. *Journal of Law and Economics*, 44, 285-314.

NAACP. (2009). NAACP Legal Defense and Educational Fund Inc. New York: NAACP Legal Defense and Educational Fund Inc.

NAACP. *Death Row USA*. (2004). Retrieved from: www.naacpldf.org/content/pdf/drusa/DRUSA_Spring_2004.pdf

Nagel, I. H. (1983). The Legal/Extra-Legal Controversy: Judicial decision in Pretrial Release. *Law and Society Review*, 17, 481-515.

Neave, D., & Smith, C. (2009). *Aussie Soldier: Prisoners of War*. Australia: Big Sky Publishing Pty Ltd.

New Jersey Supreme Court (1992). New Jersey Supreme Court Task on Minority Concerns Final Report. Retrieved from http://www.judiciary.state.nj.us/reports2002/minconpart1.pdf

Newman, G. R. (1990). Popular culture and Criminal Justice: A preliminary analysis. *Journal of Criminal Justice*, 18 (3), 261-274.

Newport, F. (1999). *Racial Profiling is seen as widespread particularly among young black men*. Princeton New Jersey: Gallop News Service.

North Carolina Court System. (n.d.) *Indigent Defense Services*. Retrieved from www.aoc.state.nc.us.www/ids/

O'Boye, S. (2000, December 14). Death row prisoner cleared by DNA test 11 months after he dies of cancer. *Sun Sentinel*.

Office of Inspector General U.S. Agency for International Development. (2009, December 10). Audit of US/AID/Cambodia's Counter Trafficking in person's project. Audit report No. 9-000-10-002-P.

Office of the United Nations High Commission for Human Rights. (2000, November 15). Protocol to Prevent, Suppress and Punish Trafficking in Persons Especially Women and Children, supplementing the United Nations Convention against Transnational Organized Crime. Retrieved from http://www2.ohchr.org/english/law/protocoltraffic.htm

Oliver, M. B. (1994). Portrayals of Crime, Race and Aggression in "Reality-Based" Police Shows: A content analysis. *Journal of Broadcasting and Electronic Media*, 38 (2), 179-192.

O'Shea, K. (1999). *Women and the Death Penalty in the United States 1900-1998*. Connecticut: Praeger Publishers.

Ostrom, E., & Whitaker, G. (1974). Community control and Governmental responsiveness: The case in black neighborhoods. In D. Rogers, & W. Hawley (Eds.), *Improving the Quality of the Urban Environment* (pp. 303-334). California: Sage Publications Inc.

Paris, M. H. (2001, June 24). The Skin Trade. *Time Magazine* in partnership with CNN.

Paternoster, R. (1991). *Capital Punishment in America*. New York: Lexington Books.

Paternoster, R. (1991). Prosecutorial discretion and capital sentencing in North and South Carolina. In R. M. Bohm (Ed.), *The death penalty in America: Current Research* (pp. 39-52). Cincinnati, Ohio: Anderson.

Patterson, B. E., & Lynch, M. J. (1991). Biases in formalized bail procedure. In M. J. Lynch, M. J. Lynch, & B. E. Patterson (Eds.), *Race and Criminal Justice* (pp. 36-53). Albany, New York: Harrow and Heston.

Pattillo, M., Weinman, D., & Western, B. (2006). *Imprisoning America: The Social Effects of Mass Incarceration*. New York: Russell Sage Foundation.

Pearson, E. (n.d.). The Mekong Challenge Human Trafficking: Redefining Demand. *Destination factors in the trafficking of children and young women in the Mekong Sub region*. International Programme on the Elimination of child labor. Bangkok: International Labor Office Bangkok.

Peelo, M., Francis, B., Soothill, K., Person, J., & Ackerley, E. (2004). Newspaper Reporting and the Public Construction of Homicide. *British Journal of Criminology*, 256-275.

Pelaez, V. (2008). The Prison Industry in the United States: Big Business or New form of slavery? In Global Research. Retrieved from http://www. globalresearch.ca/index.php?context=va&aid=8289

Petersilia, J. (1983). *Racial Disparities in the Criminal Justice System*. Santa Monica, California: Rand Corporation.

Phillips, S. (2009). Legal Disparities in the Case of Capital Punishment. *Journal of Criminal Law and Criminology*.

Phillips, S. (2010). Death more likely if victim is high-status. *Law and Society Review*, 807-837.

Pineiro, N. (2004, January 06). Is trafficking in Human Beings demand driven? International Organization for Migration. Geneva-Migration Research Series. [Press Briefing Notes] Retrieved from http://www. america.gov/st/washfile-english/2004/January/20040106152916retro pc0.8637964.html

Pokorak, J. (1998). Probing the capital prosecutor's perspective: Race and gender of the discretionary actors. *Cornell Law Review*, 83 (6).

Police Prosecution and Judicial Misconduct. (n.d.). Retrieved from http:// truthinjustice.org/index.htm

Political Research Associates (2005, May). How is the Criminal Justice System Racist. In Defending Justice: An Activist Resource Guide. [Factsheet]Retrieved from http://www.defendingjustice.org/pdfs/ factsheets/10-Fact%20Sheet%20-20System%20as%20Racist.pdf

Porter, G. (1997, November). *Crime control and the death penalty*. The Advocate, 19 (6).

Prejean, H. (1996). *Dead Man Walking*. Grand Rapids: Zondervan.

Prevention vs. Control. (n.d.). Retrieved from http://www.justiceblind.com/ death/dpfouranew1

Prison Activist Resource Center (n.d.) Latinos and the Criminal Injustice System. [Factsheet] Retrieved from http://www.prisonactivist.org/ar- chive/factsheets/racism.pdf

Putwain, D., & Sammons, A. (2002). *Psychology and Crime*. East Essex: Routledge.

Quinney, R. (1970). *The Social Reality of Crime*. Boston: Little Brown.

Race and Crime Data Source and Meaning. (n.d.). Retrieved from http://www.law.jrank.org

Race and Sentencing: A Meta-Analysis of Conflicting Empirical Research Results. (n.d.). Retrieved from http://www.sciencedirect.com

Race and the Death Penalty Part I: Who gets the Death Penalty in America. (n.d.). Retrieved from http://www.racismreview.com

Radelet, M. (1981). Racial Characteristics and the Imposition of the Death Penalty. *American Sociological Review*, 46, 918-927.

Ramirez, D. M., & Fellel, A. (2000). *A Resource Guide on Racial Profiling Data Collection System: Promising Practices and Lessons Learned*. Washington DC: U.S. Department of Justice.

Raymond, J., & Hughes, D. (2001, March). Sex Trafficking and Women in the United States: International and Domestic Trends. *In Coalition against trafficking in women*. Retrieved from http://www.uri.edu/artsci/wms/hughes/sex_traff_us.pdf

Reiman, J. (2007). *The Rich get Richer and the Poor get Prison: Ideology, Class and Criminal Justice*. Boston: Allyn and Bacon.

Reports and Curricula: Justice on Trial Racial Disparities in the American Criminal Justice System. Leadership Conference on Civil and Human Rights. (n.d.). Retrieved from http://www.civilrights.org/publications/justice-ontrial

Reports and Curricular-Justice on Trial: race and prosecution discretion. Leadership Conference on Civil and Human Rights. (n.d.). Retrieved from http://www.civilrights.org/publications/justice-on-trial/prosecutorial.html

Riley, K. J., Rodriguez, N., Ridgeway, G., Barnes-Proby, D., Fain, T., Forge, N. G., et al. (2005). *Just Cause or Just Because*. Santa Monica, California: Rand Corporation.

Rodin, D. (2004). Terrorism Without Intention. Ethics, 114 (4), 752-771.

Romer, D., Jamieson, K. H., & De Coteau, N. J. (1998). The treatment of persons of color in television news: ethnic blame discourse or realistic group conflict. *Communication Research*, 25, 268-305.

Roshier, B. (1973). The Selection of Crime News by the Press. In S. Cohen, & J. Young (Eds.), *The Manufacture of News* (pp. 28-39). Beverly Hills: Sage Publication.

Schlosser, E. (1998, December). *The Prison Industry Complex*. Atlantic Monthly, 51-77.

Schmitt, C. (1991, December 8). Plea Bargaining Favours Whites, as Blacks and Hispanics pay Price. *The San Jose Mercury News*.

Schwartz, R. S. (2001). Racial Profiling in Medical Research. The New England Journal of Medicine, 344 (18).

Scott, D. (1981). Citizen Attitudes towards the Police: A view of past findings and suggestions for future policy. *Journal of Police Science and Administration*, 9, 80-87.

Seigel, L. (2010). *Introduction to Criminal Justice*. California: Wadsworth.

Sellin, T. (1935). Race Prejudice in the Administration of Justice. *American Journal of Sociology*, 212-217.

Shah, A. (2005, September 25). United States and the International Criminal Court. In *Global Issues*. Retrieved from http://globalissues.org/Geopolitics/icc/us.asp

Shanyang, Z. (2006). Humanoid social robots as a medium of communication. *New Media and Society*, 8 (3), 401-419.

Short, J., & Nye, I. (1958). Extend undetected delinquency: Tentative conclusions. *Journal of Criminology and Police Science*, 49, 296-302.

Simons, M. (1993, April 9). The Sex Market: Scourge on the World's Children. *New York Times*.

Smith, B. L., Damphouse, K. R., Jackson, F., & Sellers, A. (2002). The Prosecution and Punishment of International Terrorists in Federal Courts: 1980-1998. *Criminology & Public Policy*, 1, 311-338.

Smith, D., Graham, N., & Adams, B. (1991). Minorities and the Police: Attitudinal and Behavioral Questions. *In Race, Crime and Punishment in America* (pp. 22-25). New York: Oxford University Press.

Smith, T., & Kennedy, K. (2007, September 12). Against their will - The realities of human trafficking: In the end, it's the customers who keep teen sex rings a viable source of profit. *CBS The Early Show*.

Sorenson, S. B., Manz, J. G., & Berk, R. A. (1998). News Media Coverage and Epidemiology of Homicide. *American Journal of Public Health*, 88 (10), 1510-1514.

Spohn, C., Gruhl, J., & Welch, S. (1981-1982). The effects of race on sentencing: A re-examination of an unsettled question. *Law and Society*, 16, 71-88.

Spohn, C., Gruhl, J., & Welsh, S. (1987). The Impact of the Ethnicity and Gender of Defendants on the decision to reject or dismiss felony charges. *Criminology*, 25, 175-191.

Spreading the Word of the Cambodian Genocide. (n.d.). In *The Dith Pran Holocaust Awareness Project Inc*. Retrieved from http://www.dithpran.org/

State of New York v. Goetz, 68 N.Y.2d 96 N.Y. (1986).

State v Thacker, 301 N.C. 348, 351-352, 271 S.E.2d 252,255 (1980).

State v. Pedro Soto, 734 A.2d 350 352-353 (NJ. Super. Ct. Law Div.) ((NJ. Super. Ct. Law Div.) (1996).

Steffensmeier, D., Ulmer, J. T., & Kramer, J. (1998). The interaction of race, gender and age in sentencing: The punishment cost of being young, black and male. *Criminology*, 36 (4), 763-798.

Stewart convicted on all charges. In *CNN News*. Retrieved from http://www.CNNmoney.com

Stewart sentenced to five months in prison. Reuters. (2004, July 17). *The Sydney Morning Herald*.

Stienman, R. (2002). *Inside Television's first War*. Columbia, Missouri: University of Missouri Press.

Stix, N. (2005). Howard Beach II: More White Male Monsters. *Men's News Daily*.

Stoecker, D. S. (2000). The Rise in Human Trafficking and the Role of Organized Crime. Third International Parliamentary Roundtable on "Contemporary legal Policy in countering Transnational Organized Crime and Corruption". Irkutsk, Russia: The Transnational Crime and Corruption Center, American University.

Stoll, D. (1999). *Rigoberta Menchu and the story of all poor Guatemalans.* Boulder, Colorado: Westview Press.

Stone, C. L. (1991). Estimate of Muslims Living in America. In Y. Y. Haddad (Ed.), *The Muslims of America* (p. 25). New York: Oxford University Press.

Strickland v Washington, 466 U.S. 668 Volume 466 Supreme Court (1984).

Superseding Indictment returned in UCLA body parts case. (2008, May 16). Retrieved from http://da.lacounty.gov/mr/archive/2008/052608a.htm

Surrette, R. (1998). *Media, Crime and Criminal Justice: Images and Realities* (2nd edition ed.)Belmont, California: Wadsworth Publishing Co.

Sutherland, E. (1940). White Collar Criminality. *American Sociological Review,* 5 (1), 1-12.

Sutherland, E. H. (1939). *Principles of Criminology* (Revised edition ed.). New York: J. P. Lippincott Co.

Sutherland, E. H. (1949). *White Collar Crime.* New York: Dryden Press.

Sutherland, E. H. (1949). *White Collar Crime.* New York: Holt, Rinehart and Winston.

Swarns, C. (2004). The Uneven Scales of Capital Justice: How Race and Class affect who ends up on death row. In from The American Prospect: Liberal Intelligence. Retrieved from http://www.prospect.org/cs/articles?articleId=7882

Sykes, G. (1971). *The Society of Captives.* Princeton: Princeton University Press.

Syuker, N. R., & Hagan, J. (1983). Methodology Issues and Court Research: Pretrial Release decision for Federal Defendants. *Sociological Methods and Research,* 11, 469-500.

Teece, M., & Makkai, T. (2000). Print Media Reporting on drugs and crime 1995-1998. *In Trends and Issues in Crime and Criminal Justice No. 158.* Canberra: Australian Institute of Criminology.

The Constitutional Failure of Strickland Standard in Capital Cases under the Eighth Amendment. (2000). Retrieved from http://www.law.duke.edu

The Constitutional Project. (n.d.). Mandatory Justice: Eighteen reforms to the Death Penalty. Retrieved from http://www.constitutionproject.org/pdf/MandatoryJustice.pdf

The Death Penalty in Black and White: Who lives, Who dies, Who decides. (n.d.) Retrieved from http://www.deathpenaltyinfo.org/article.php?did=539

The Effects of Social Class on the Adjudication of Criminal Cases: Class Linked Behavior Tendencies, Common Sense and the Interpretive Procedures of Court Appointed Defense Attorneys. (1994). Retrieved from http://www.caliber.ucpress.net/doi/abs/10.1525/si.1994.17.1.1?journalCode=si

The Future of Capital Punishment in the State of New York. (n.d.). Retrieved from http:// www.nyclu.org

The Immigration Act of 1924. (n.d.). Retrieved from http://www.history.state.gov/milestones/1921-1936/ImmigrationAct

The Justice Project: Statement by the Justice Project on the 100th Death Row Exoneration. (n.d.). Retrieved from http://www.thejusticeproject.org

The Legal System - The Price of Defending the Criminal Poor. (n.d.). Retrieved from http://www.social.jrank.org

The People History. (2001). In *News and Events from October 26^th^*. Retrieved from http://www.thepeoplehistory.com/october26th.html#2001

The Sentencing Project (2008). Facts about prison and prisoners. (B. o. Statistics, Editor) Retrieved from http://www.sentencingproject.org/publicationDetails.aspx?publicationID=425

The Story of Race. (2007). In *American Anthropological Association*. Retrieved from http://www.understandingrace.org/history/history_trans.html

Thorming-Gale, S., & Caywood, K. (1999, August). Shareef Cousin: Will Justice be done? Justice Denied: In *The Magazine for the wrongly convicted*. Retrieved from http://www.justicedenied.org/v1issue2.htm#Shareef Cousin

Titillating Channels: TV is going tabloid as shows seek sleaze and find profits too. (1988, May 18). *The Wall Street Journal, 15*.

Title, C. (1988). Two Imperial Regularities (maybe) in search of an explanation: Commentary on the age/crime debate. *Criminology, 26*, 75-85.

Trafficking in Persons Report 2009. US Dept. of State (2009). Retrieved from http://www.state.gov/documents/organization/123357.pdf

Tyner, J. (2002, February 16). The Struggle against War, Racism and Repression. In *People's Weekly World Newspaper*. Retrieved from http://www.pww.org/article/view/635/1/57/

U.N. General Assembly (1948, December 09). Convention on the Prevention and Punishment of the Crime of Genocide. Adopted by Resolution 260 (III) A.

Union, A. C. (2004, December). The Forgotten Population: A Look at Death Row in the United States through the experiences of Women. In *American Civil Liberties Union*. Retrieved from http://www.aclu.org/files/FilesPDFs/womendeathrow.pdf

United Nations (n.d.). *International Criminal Court* [Factsheet]Retrieved from http://www.un.org/News/facts/iccfact.htm

United Nations Economic and Social Commission for Asia and the Pacific. Gender and Human trafficking. (n.d.). Retrieved from http://www.unescap.org

United States v. Armstrong, No. 95-157, 517 U.S. 456, 116 S. Ct. 1480, 134 L. Ed. 2d 687 Supreme Court (1996).

United States v. Brignoni-Ponce, No. 95-157, 517U.S. 456, 116 S. Ct. 1480, 134 LEd. 2d 607 Supreme Court (1975).

United States v. Clary, 846 F.Supp. 768, 786 n62(E.D.Mo) rev'd, 34 F.3d 709 (8th Cir. 1994) (Circuit Court 1994).

United States v. Martinez-Fuertes et al, No. 74-1560, 428 U.S. 543, 96 S.Ct.2574, 45 LEd. 2d 1116 Supreme Court (1976).

University, Y. (n.d.). Cambodian Genocide Program. Retrieved from http://www.yale.edu/cgp/cgpintro.html

Unnever, J. D. (1994). Direct and Organizational Discrimination in the Sentencing of Drugs Offenders. *Social Problems*, 212-225.

U.S. Bureau of Statistics (1987b). *Jail Inmates 1986*. Washington DC: U.S. Government Printing Office.

U.S. Census Bureau (2002). Percent of People below poverty level in the past 12 months (State Level). 2002. In *American Community Survey*. Retrieved from http://www.census.gov/acs/www/Products/Ranking/2002/R01T040.htm

U.S. Census Bureau (2005). Annual Social and Economic Supplement. In U.S. Census Bureau Current Population Survey. Retrieved from http://www.census.gov/hhes/www/cpstc/cps_table_creator.html

U.S. Census Bureau (2006). Statistical Abstract of the United States 2003-2005: The National Data Book. Washington DC: Government Printing Office.

U.S. Census Bureau (2008). Retrieved from http://www.census.gov/hhes/www/poverty/poverty08/pov08hi.html

U.S. Census Bureau (2009). Current Population Survey, Annual Social and Economic Supplement. Retrieved from U.S. Census Bureau: www.census.gov

U.S. Census Bureau (2010). Percent of People 25 years and over who have completed High School (State level). In *American Community Survey.* Retrieved from http://www.census.gov/acs/www/Products/Ranking/2002/R01T040.htm

U.S. Census Bureau, P. D. (n.d.). U.S. and World Population Clocks. Retrieved from http://www.census.gov/main/www/popclock.html

U.S. Constitution Amend V; N.C. Constitution Art. 1 22, N.C. GEN. STAT. 15-144 (1983).

U.S. Department of Labor, Bureau of Labor Statistics (2003). Regional and State Employment and Unemployment: December 2002. Retrieved from http://www.bls.gov/news.release/archives/laus_01282003.pdf

U.S. Department of State (2008). Stopping Human Trafficking, Sexual Exploitation, and Abuse by International Peacekeepers.

U.S. Dept. of Labor, Bureau of Statistics (1992). Capital Punishment 1991. Washington DC: Government Printing Office.

U.S. Dept. of Labor, Bureau of Statistics (1998). Compendium of Federal Justice Statistics, 1998, Bureau of Justice Statistics Report NCJ 180258: Table 5.1. Retrieved from http:www.findalawyerfast.com/lawyer-articles/defense-counsel-in-criminal-cases.

U.S. Dept. of Labor, Bureau of Statistics (1999). Criminal Offenders' Statistics. Washington DC: U. S. Department of Justice.

U.S. Dept. of Labor, Bureau of Statistics (2001). Uniform crime report of Federal Bureau of Investigation, indigent defense statistics 1999. Washington DC: U.S. Department of Justice, Office of Justice Programs.

U.S. Dept. of Labor, Bureau of Statistics (2002). Retrieved from http://www.bls.gov/news.release/empsit.t02.htm

U.S. Dept. of Labor, Bureau of Statistics (2005). Sourcebook Criminal Justice Statistics. In Bureau of Justice Statistics. Retrieved from http://www.albany.edu/sourcebook

U.S. Dept. of Labor, Bureau of Statistics (2006). Office of Justice Programs. In *Characteristics of Drivers stopped by police* 2006 Retrieved from http://www.ojp.usdoj.gov/bjs/abstract/cdsp02.htm

U.S. Dept. of Labor, Bureau of Statistics (2007). Homicide Report of Federal Bureau of Investigation, National Crime Victimization Survey.

U.S. Dept. of Labor, Bureau of Statistics (n.d.). Retrieved from U.S. Department of Justice: Retrieved from http://www.ojp.usdoj.gov/bjs/prisons.htm

U.S. Dept. of Labor, Bureau of Statistics (n.d.). State and Local Defender Offices. Retrieved from http://www.bjs.ojp.usdoj.gov

U.S. Dept. of State (2005). Country Reports on Terrorism 2004. Washington DC: Office of the Coordinator for Counterterrorism.

U.S. Government Accountability Office (GAO). (1990). Death Penalty Sentencing: Research indicates pattern of racial disparities. Washington DC: GAO.

U.S. State Department (2007, June). Human Trafficking and Modern Slavery. Trafficking in Persons Report. Retrieved from http://www.gvnet.com/humantrafficking/USA.htm

U.S. Supreme Court (n.d.). U.S. Supreme Court cases from Justia and Oyez. Retrieved from http://supreme.justia.com/construction/amendment-08/06-capital-punishment.html

USA, A. I. (2009). Amnesty International Death Penalty Statistics 2009. In *Amnesty International.* Retrieved from http://www.amnestyusa.org

USA, A. I. (n.d.). The Death Penalty Claims Innocent Lives. In Amnesty International Retrieved from http://www.amnestyusa.org/abolish/innocence.html

Vago, S. (2006). Law and Society. New Jersey: Pearson Prentice Hall.

Valentino, N. (1999). Crime news and the priming of racial attitudes during evaluations of the President. *Public Opinion Quarterly*, 63, 293-320.

Verkaik, R. (2007, June 09). UK Provided Base for Rendition Flights, says European Inquiry. In *Belfast Telegraph – Ireland*. Retrieved from http://www.mindfully.org/Reform/2007/CIA-Secret-Prison9jun07.htm

Voices: Ending Racial Injustice and Prosecutorial Misconduct. (2009). Retrieved from http://www.southerstudies.org/2009/07/post-44.html

Voigt, L., Thorthon Jr., W. E., Barrile, L., & Seamon, J. M. (1994). *Criminology and Justice*. New York: Mc Graw Hill Inc.

Waller, M. J. (2003). Testimony before the United States Senate Committee on the Judiciary on Terrorist Recruitment and Infiltration in the United States: Prisons and Military as an Operational Base. Retrieved from http://judiciary.senate.gov/testimony.cfm?id=960&wit_id=2719

Wang, V. O., & Sue, S. (2005). In the eye of the storm: race and genomics in research and practice. *American Psychologist*, 60 (1), 37-45.

Wang, X., Mears, D. P., Spohn, C., & Dario, L. (2009). Assessing the differential effects of Race and Ethnicity on Sentence Outcomes under different sentencing systems. Crime and Delinquency .

Ward, M. R. (2009). Video Games, Crime and Violence. Net Institute [Working Paper No. 07-18.]

Ward, N. (2001). The Fire Last Time - The 1920 Wall Street Bombing. American Heritage. Retrieved from http://www.freerepublic.com/focus/f-news/577915/posts

Watch, D. P. (n.d.). *Capital Punishment Statistics from ACLU*. Retrieved from http://www.exchanges.outness.net/

Watch, H. R. (1991). Prison Conditions in the United States: A Human Rights Watch Report. Human Rights Watch.

Watch, H. R. (2001, March 20). Letter to U.S. Attorney General Ashcroft on Human Rights Agenda. In *Human Rights Watch*. Retrieved from http://www.hrw.org

Watch, H. R. (2002, November). Opportunism in the face of tragedy: Repression in the name of anti-terrorism. In Human Rights Watch. Retrieved from http://www.hrw.org/campaigns/september_11/opportun-ismwatch.htm

Weitzer, R. (1996). Racial discrimination in the Criminal Justice System: Findings and problems in the literature. *Journal of Criminal Justice*, 24 (4), 309-322.

Welch, M. (2002). *Detained: Immigration Laws and the Expanding I.N.S. Jail Complex*. Philadelphia: Temple University Press.

Welch, M. (2003, January 21). It takes a Nation of Detention Centers to hold Us Back. (S. J. Talvi, Interviewer) *LiP Magazine*.

Welch, R., & Angulo, C. (2000). Justice on Trial: Racial Disparities in the American Criminal Justice System. Washington DC: Leadership Conference on Civil Rights.

West, H. C., & Sabol, W. J. (2008). Prisoners in 2007. In Bureau of Justice Statistics Bulletin: Retrieved from http://www.ojp.usdoj.gov/bjs/pub/pdf/p07.pdf

White, R. S. (1975). Racism, Black Crime and American Justice. *Phylon*, 36, 14-22.

Whitlock, C., Priest, D., & Magnuson, W. (2005, December 05). CIA ruse on missing cleric misled Italians. *Washington Post*.

Why Serial Killers target Prostitutes. (2006, December 16). Retrieved from CBC news: http://www.cbc.ca/news/background/crime/targeting-prostitutes.html

Wilbanks, W. (1993). *The Myth of a Racial Criminal Justice System*. California: Brooks and Cole.

William, P., & Dickinson, J. (1993). Fear of crime: Read all about it. The relationship between Newspaper Crime Reporting and Fear of Crime. *British Journal of Criminology*, 33, 33-56.

Wilson, B. J., Kunkel, D., Linz, D., Potter, J., Donnerstein, E., Smith, S. L., et al. (1998). Violence in television overall: University of California Study. In M. Seawall (Ed.), *National television violence study II* (pp. 3-204). Thousand Oaks, California: Sage Publications.

Wilson, J. W., & Herrnstein, R. (1985). *Crime and Human Nature*. New York: Simon and Shuster.

Wilson, W. J. (1987). *The truly disadvantaged*. Chicago, Illinois: University of Chicago Press.

Wimmer, R. D., & Dominick, J. R. (2005). *Mass Media Research: An Introduction*. Belmont, California: Wadsworth.

With Justice for Few: The Growing Crisis in Death Penalty Representation. (n.d.). In Death Penalty Info. Retrieved from http://www.deathpenalty-info.org/node/742

Worden, A. P. (1993). Counsel for the poor: An evaluation of contracting for indigent Criminal Defense. *Justice Quarterly*, 10 (4), 613-637.

Wright, J. P., Cullen, F. T., & Blankenship, M. B. (1995). The social construction of corporate violence: Media coverage of the Imperial Food Products Fire. *Crime and Delinquency*, 4 (1), 20-36.

Wrongful Convictions Resources. (n.d.). Retrieved from http://lawinfo.com/en/Articles/Post-Sentencing-Criminal-Defense/Federal/wrongful-conviction.html

Wyatt, C. R. (1986). At the Connon's Mouth: The American press and the Vietnam War. *Journalism History*, 104-113.

Wyatt, C. R. (1995). *Paper Soldiers: The American Press and the Vietnam War.* Chicago: University of Chicago Press.

Wyer, R. S., & Srull, T. (1989). *Memory and cognition in its social context.* Hillsdale, NJ: Erlbaum.

Yamada, K. (n.d.). *Desert reclaims Japanese-American Camp.* Retrieved from http://www.asu.edu/studentaffairs/studentmedia/archives/bulldog/971212/japan.html

Zatz, M. S. (1984). Race, Ethnicity and Determinate Sentences: A new dimension to an old controversy. *Criminology, 22,* 147-171.

# INDEX